Essentials of

PSYCHOLOGICAL ASSESSMENT
Series

Essentials of Psychological Assessment Series
Series Editors, Alan S. Kaufman and Nadeen L. Kaufman

Essentials of CAS Assessment
by Jack A. Naglieri

Essentials of Millon Inventories Assessment
by Stephen N. Strack

Essentials of NEPSY Assessment
by Sally Kemp, Ursula Kirk, and Marit Korkman

Essentials of Forensic Assessment
by Marc J. Ackerman

Essentials of Bayley Scales of Infant Development II Assessment
by Maureen M. Black and Kathleen Matula

Essentials of MMPI-2 Assessment
by David S. Nichol

Essentials

of WAIS-III Assessment

Alan S. Kaufman and

Elizabeth O. Lichtenberger

John Wiley & Sons, Inc.

NEW YORK • CHICHESTER • WEINHEIM • BRISBANE • SINGAPORE • TORONTO

Library of Congress Cataloging-in-Publication Data:
Kaufman, Alan S.
    Essentials of WAIS-III assessment / Alan S. Kaufman and Elizabeth O.
Lichtenberger.
        p.   cm.
    Includes bibliographical references (p.   ).
    ISBN 0-471-28295-2 (alk. paper)
    1. Wechsler Adult Intelligence Scale.   2. Intelligence tests.
I. Lichtenberger, Elizabeth. O.   II. Title.
BF432.5.W4K385   1999
153.9'323—dc21   98-30739
                                                                    CIP

Printed in the United States of America.
11 12 13 14 15 16 17 18 19 20

CONTENTS

SERIES PREFACE

I n the *Essentials of Psychological Assessment* series, we have attempted to provide the reader with books that will deliver key practical information in the most efficient and accessible style. The series features instruments in a variety of domains, such as cognition, personality, education, and neuropsychology. For the experienced clinician, books in the series will offer a concise yet thorough way to master utilization of the continuously evolving supply of new and revised instruments, as well as a convenient method for keeping up to date on the tried-and-true measures. The novice will find here a prioritized assembly of all the information and techniques that must be at one's fingertips to begin the complicated process of individual psychological diagnosis.

Wherever feasible, visual shortcuts to highlight key points are utilized alongside systematic, step-by-step guidelines. Chapters are focused and succinct. Topics are targeted for an easy understanding of the essentials of administration, scoring, interpretation, and clinical application. Theory and research are continually woven into the fabric of each book, but always to enhance clinical inference, never to sidetrack or overwhelm. We have long been advocates of "intelligent" testing—the notion that a profile of test scores is meaningless unless it is brought to life by the clinical observations and astute detective work of knowledgeable examiners. Test profiles must be used to make a difference in the child's or adult's life, or why bother to test? We want this series to help our readers become the best intelligent testers they can be.

In *Essentials of WAIS-III Assessment,* the authors have attempted to ease the transition of examiners who have been longtime WAIS-R users, and to provide a solid foundation for new examiners who are learning their first or second Wechsler test. The WAIS-III reflects the blend of its rich 50-year tradition with innovations that include brand-new subtests and Factor Indexes. So, too, this book integrates the research and clinical history of the test's direct ancestors (Wechsler-Bellevue, WAIS, and WAIS-R) with sets of guidelines that enable the examiner to give, and then systematically interpret and apply, this thoroughly revised and restandardized instrument.

Alan S. Kaufman, Ph.D., and Nadeen L. Kaufman, Ed.D., Series Editors
Yale University School of Medicine

Essentials
of WAIS-III Assessment

One

The field of assessment, particularly intellectual assessment, has grown tremendously over the past couple decades. New tests of cognitive abilities are rapidly being developed, and older tests of intelligence are being revised to meet the needs of the professionals utilizing them. There are many good sources for reviewing major measures of cognitive ability (Flanagan, Genshaft, & Harrison, 1997; Kaufman, in press; Kaufman & Lichtenberger, 1998; Sattler, 1988, 1992). However, the new and revised measures multiply rapidly, and it is often difficult to keep track of new instruments, let alone know how to administer, score, and interpret them. One of the goals of this book is to provide an easy reference source for those who wish to learn the essentials of the Wechsler Adult Intelligence Scale—Third Edition (WAIS-III) in a direct, no-nonsense, systematic manner.

Essentials of WAIS-III Assessment was developed with an easy-to-read format in mind. The topics covered in the book emphasize administration, scoring, interpretation, and application of the WAIS-III. Chapters include "Rapid Reference," "Caution," and "Don't Forget" boxes, which highlight important points for easy reference. At the end of each chapter, questions are provided to help you solidify what you have read. The information provided in this book will help you to understand, in depth, the latest of the measures in the Wechsler family and will help you become a competent WAIS-III examiner and clinician.

For all cases presented in this book, the names and other pertinent identifying information have been changed to protect confidentiality of clients.

HISTORY AND DEVELOPMENT

The first assessment instrument developed by David Wechsler came on the scene in 1939. However, the history of intelligence testing began several decades before that, in the late 19th century, when Sir Francis Galton (1869, 1883) developed the first comprehensive test of intelligence (Kaufman, 1983). Galton's interest was in studying gifted people, and his theory was that since people take information in through their senses, the most intelligent people must have the best developed senses. As Galton was a strict scientist, he developed tasks that he could measure with accuracy. However, his sensory and motor tasks, though highly reliable, proved ultimately to have limited validity as measures of the complex construct of intelligence.

At the turn of the 20th century, Alfred Binet and his colleagues developed tasks to measure the intelligence of children within the Paris public schools (Binet & Simon, 1905). Binet had concluded that simple tasks like Galton's did not discriminate between adults and children and were not sufficiently complex to measure human intellect. Binet's tasks, primarily language oriented instead of nonverbal, like Galton's sensory-motor tasks, emphasized judgment, memory comprehension, and reasoning. In 1908 Binet revised his scale and included age levels ranging from 3 to 13 years; in its next revision in 1911, the Binet-Simon scale was extended to age 15 and included five ungraded adult tests (Kaufman, 1990).

Lewis Terman (1916) adapted and translated the Binet-Simon scale for use in the United States. Other Americans adapted Binet's test (e.g., Goddard, Kuhlmann, Wallin, and Yerkes), but only Terman had the foresight to adapt the French test to American culture (instead of virtual word-for-word translations) along with the insight and patience to obtain a careful standardization sample composed of American children and adolescents (Kaufman, in press). For more than 4 decades, Terman's Stanford-Binet and its revisions (Terman & Merrill, 1937, 1960) reigned as the most popular IQ test in the United States.

The assessment of children expanded rapidly to the assessment of adults when the United States entered World War I in 1917 (Anastasi & Urbina, 1997). There was a strong need for a method to select officers and place recruits. To meet the practical needs of the military, Arthur Otis (one of Terman's graduate students) helped to develop a group-administered IQ test, called the Army Alpha, which had verbal content quite similar to Stanford-Binet tasks. To assess immigrants who spoke little English, the group-administered Army Beta was developed, which consisted of nonverbal items. Ultimately, the individually administered Army Performance Scale Examination was developed by army psychologists to assess those who simply could not be tested validly on the group-administered Alpha or Beta tests (or who were suspected of malingering). The nonverbal tasks included in the Beta and the individual examination had names (e.g., Picture Completion, Picture Arrangement, Digit Symbol, Mazes) that would become familiar to future generations of psychologists.

In the mid-1930s David Wechsler became a prominent player in the field of assessment by blending his strong clinical skills and statistical training (he studied under Charles Spearman and Karl Pearson in England) with his extensive experience in testing, which he gained as a World War I examiner. Wechsler's approach gave equal weight to the Stanford-Binet/Army Alpha system (Verbal Scale) and to the Performance Scale Examination/Army Beta system (Performance Scale). Wechsler created his battery with the idea that these tasks could be used to obtain dynamic clinical information extending well beyond their previous use as psychometric tests. The first in the Wechsler series of tests was the Wechsler-Bellevue Intelligence Scale (Wechsler, 1939), so named because Wechsler was the chief psychologist at Bellevue Hospital in New York City (a position he held from 1932 to 1967). That first test, followed in 1946 by Form II of the Wechsler-Bellevue, had as a key innovation the use of deviation IQs (standard scores), which were psychometrically superior to the MA/CA (mental age divided by chronological age) formula that Terman had used to compute IQ. The WAIS-III is the great-grandchild of the original 1939 Wechsler-Bellevue Form I; it is also a cousin of the WISC-III, which traces its lineage to Form II of the Wechsler-Bellevue.

The development of Wechsler's tests was not based on theory (except perhaps on Spearman's [1927] g, or general intelligence theory) but instead on practical and clinical perspectives. (The origin of each of the WAIS-III subtests is shown in Rapid Reference 1.1.) Wechsler's view of IQ tests was that they were a way to peer into an individual's personality. Years after the development of the Wechsler scales, extensive theoretical speculations have been made about the nature and meaning of these tests and their scores, but originally the tests were developed without regard to theory.

When put in historical perspective, Wechsler made some mighty contributions. His insistence that every person be assessed on both Verbal and Performance Scales went against the conventional wisdom of his time. Why, examiners asked, should we administer nonverbal tests to a person who speaks English well? Why spend 3 minutes administering a single Object Assembly

DON'T FORGET

History of Wechsler Intelligence Scales

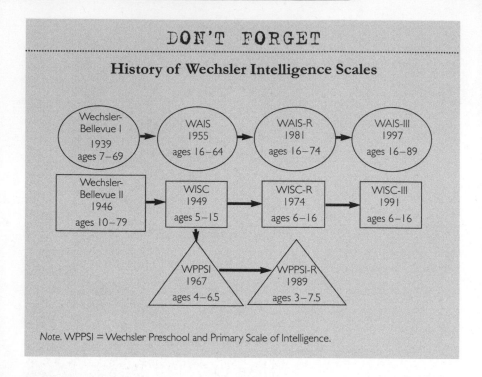

Note. WPPSI = Wechsler Preschool and Primary Scale of Intelligence.

puzzle when you can give maybe 15 or 20 Information items in the same time frame? Yet discrepancies between Verbal and Performance IQs would prove to have critical value for understanding brain functioning and theoretical distinctions between fluid and crystallized intelligence. Furthermore, Wechsler's stress on the clinical value of intelligence tests would alter the face of intellectual assessment forever, replacing the psychometric, statistical emphasis that accompanied the use and interpretation of the Stanford-Binet. Finally, Wechsler's inclusion of a multiscore subtest profile (as well as three IQs instead of one) met the needs of the emerging field of learning disabilities assessment in the 1960s to such an extent that Wechsler's scales replaced the Stanford-Binet as the king of IQ during that decade. It has maintained that niche ever since.

The popularity of the revised WAIS (WAIS-R) is undisputed. Kaufman (1990) reported data from a survey of 402 clinical psychologists that showed 97% of these professionals utilized the WAIS or WAIS-R when administering an adult measure of intelligence. In a survey of graduate-level instructors, Oakland and Zimmerman (1986) found that the Wechsler instruments were those emphasized most heavily in instruction of assessment measures. Al-

≡ *Rapid Reference*

1.1 Origin of WAIS-III Subtests

Verbal Subtest	Source of Subtest
Vocabulary	Stanford-Binet
Similarities	Stanford-Binet
Arithmetic	Stanford-Binet/Army Alpha
Digit Span	Stanford-Binet
Information	Army Alpha
Comprehension	Stanford-Binet/Army Alpha
Letter-Number Sequencing	Gold, Carpenter, Randolph, Goldberg, & Weinberger (1997)

Performance Subtest	Source of Subtest
Picture Completion	Army Beta/Army Performance Scale Examination
Digit Symbol-Coding	Army Beta/Army Performance Scale Examination
Block Design	Kohs (1923)
Matrix Reasoning	Raven (1938)
Picture Arrangement	Army Performance Scale Examination
Symbol Search	Shiffrin & Schneider (1977) and S. Sternberg (1966)
Object Assembly	Army Performance Scale Examination

though many new instruments for measuring intellectual functioning have been developed in the past decade, the Wechsler scales are the most frequently used (Daniel, 1997). In light of clinicians' familiarity with and level of comfort with the WAIS-R, it is axiomatic that the new WAIS-III will be just as popular.

PURPOSES OF ASSESSING ADULTS AND ADOLESCENTS

As mentioned earlier in this chapter, historically adults were assessed because of a need to place men into the appropriate level of the military service or to determine how mentally deficient a person was. Today reasons for assessing adolescents and adults commonly include measuring cognitive potential or neurological dysfunction, obtaining clinical information, making educational or vocational placement decisions, and developing interventions for educational or vocational settings. Harrison, Kaufman, Hickman, and Kaufman (1988) found that practitioners who assess adults most often report using intelligence tests to measure cognitive potential and to obtain clinically relevant information. About 77% of practitioners reported using intelligence tests for obtaining information about neurological functioning, and under 50% reported using intelligence tests for making educational or vocational placements or interventions (Harrison et al., 1988).

FOUNDATIONS OF THE WAIS-III: THEORY AND RESEARCH

Wechsler (1944) defined intelligence as "the capacity to act purposefully, to think rationally, and to deal effectively with his [or her] environment" (p. 3). His concept of intelligence was that of a global entity, which could also be categorized by the sum of many specific abilities. All of Wechsler's adult tests from the Wechsler-Bellevue (1939) to the WAIS (1955) to the WAIS-R (1981) take the same basic form, with several subtests each composing the Verbal and Performance Scales, and the global entity of intelligence characterized by the Full Scale IQ. The WAIS-III continues in the same Wechsler tradition but includes some improvements on the basic structure, which are described in the following pages.

Description of WAIS-III

Several issues prompted the revision of the WAIS-R, and the manual clearly details these and the changes that were made (Wechsler, 1997, pp. 8–14). Rapid Reference 1.2 lists key features that were adapted for the third edition.

In the WAIS-III, many of the core Wechsler subtests will be recognized by WAIS-R examiners, but there have also been several notable changes with the addition of new subtests and modifications to the overall structure. There are three new subtests.

- Matrix Reasoning (added to the Performance Scale to replace Object Assembly)

≡ Rapid Reference

1.2 WAIS-III Key Revisions

- updating of norms
- extension of the age range to 89 years (WAIS-R upper limit was 74 years)
- modification of items
- updating artwork on Picture Completion, Picture Arrangement, and Object Assembly
- extension of floor
- decreased reliance on timed performance for computing Performance IQ (by replacing Object Assembly with Matrix Reasoning and by decreasing the number of items with time-bonus points)
- enhancement of fluid reasoning measurement by adding Matrix Reasoning subtest
- strengthening the framework based on factor analysis
- statistical linkage to other measures of cognitive functioning and achievement
- extensive testing of reliability and validity

- Symbol Search (added to the Performance Scale as a supplementary subtest)
- Letter-Number Sequencing (added to the Verbal Scale as a supplementary subtest)

In addition to these three new subtests (see Rapid Reference 1.3 for a description), optional procedures have been added to the Digit Symbol-Coding subtest (previously named Digit Symbol), which were developed to help examiners assess what skills (or lack thereof) may be impacting examinees' performance on the subtest. These optional procedures involve recalling shapes from memory (Pairing and Free Recall) and perceptual and graphomotor speed (Digit Symbol-Copy).

The major structural change in the WAIS-III is the addition of index scores. The WAIS-III comprises four factor indexes, similar to its child counterpart, the Wechsler Intelligence Scale for Children—Third Edition (WISC-III), although there are notable differences between WISC-III and WAIS-III factors. Most factor-analytic studies of the WAIS-R had shown a model with

≡ *Rapid Reference*

1.3 New WAIS-III Subtests

New Subtest	Description	Measures
Matrix Reasoning	26 items containing incomplete gridded patterns that the examinee completes by choosing from five possible choices	Visual information processing, abstract reasoning skills, fluid reasoning, and simultaneous processing
Symbol Search	60 items consisting of paired groups of symbols; the examinee indicates whether the target symbol appears in the search group of symbols	Visual processing speed, planning, and perceptual organization
Letter-Number Sequencing	21 trials requiring the examinee to order sequentially a series of letters and numbers orally presented in a mixed-up order	Working memory, attention, and sequencing ability

three factors (Leckliter, Matarazzo, & Silverstein, 1986), whereas the WISC-III displayed a four-factor structure (Kaufman, 1994; Wechsler, 1991). A goal for the WAIS-III was to have subtests that would relate to four hypothesized factors: Verbal Comprehension, Perceptual Organization, Working Memory, and Processing Speed. The results of factor analyses from the WAIS-III standardization data did, in fact, support this four-factor model of the test. The addition of the four factor indexes to the psychometric profile is a plus when it comes to understanding how to interpret individual profiles.

As was true for the WISC-III, the framework of the WAIS-III was expanded to encompass one more tier of scores with the inclusion of the factor indexes (Figure 1.1). Eleven of the 14 WAIS-III subtests are used to create the four factor indexes. Comprehension, Picture Arrangement, and Object Assembly are not included in calculation of any of the index scores. Like the IQs, the indexes have a mean of 100 and a standard deviation of 15. The *WAIS-III and WMS-III Technical Manual* (The Psychological Corporation,

1997) has reported the details of several exploratory and confirmatory factor analysis studies that support the underlying four-factor structure of the WAIS-III. For most ages there is strong support for the four-factor structure, but for ages 75 to 89 the Perceptual Organization factor was not strongly supported. Most of the Performance subtests joined the Processing Speed Index, and only Matrix Reasoning had a loading above .40.

> # DON'T FORGET
> ### New WAIS-III Four-Factor Structure
> **Verbal**
> 1. Verbal Comprehension
> 3. Working Memory
>
> **Performance**
> 2. Perceptual Organization
> 4. Processing Speed

The relationship between the WAIS-III and its predecessor, the WAIS-R, was examined in a sample of 192 adults aged 16 to 71 (Wechsler, 1997). Each test was administered in a counterbalanced order with a 2- to 12-week interval between testings. The overall correlation coefficients showed that the Ver-

Figure 1.1 WAIS-III Structure: Four-Tier Hierarchy

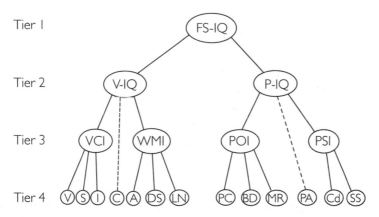

Note. FS-IQ = Full Scale IQ; V-IQ = Verbal IQ; P-IQ = Performance IQ; VCI = Verbal Comprehension Index; WMI = Working Memory Index; POI = Perceptual Organization Index; PSI = Processing Speed Index; V = Vocabulary; S = Similarities; I = Information; C = Comprehension; A = Arithmetic; DS = Digit Span; LN = Letter-Number Sequencing; PC = Picture Completion; BD = Block Design; MR = Matrix Reasoning; PA = Picture Arrangement; Cd = Digit Symbol-Coding; SS = Symbol Search. Object Assembly can substitute for a Performance subtest for ages 16 to 74.

Table 1.1   Changes in Scores From the WAIS-R to the WAIS-III

Scale	WAIS-R M^a	SD	WAIS-III M^a	SD	WAIS-R Minus WAIS-III IQ	WAIS-R to WAIS-III Correlation[b]
Verbal IQ	103.4	14.5	102.2	15.1	+1.2	.94
Performance IQ	108.3	14.4	103.5	15.4	+4.8	.86
Full Scale IQ	105.8	14.3	102.9	15.2	+2.9	.93

Note. N = 192. Correlations were computed separately for each order of administration in a counterbalanced design and corrected for the variability of the WAIS-III standardization sample (Guilford & Fruchter, 1978).

[a] The values in the mean columns are the average of the means of the two administration orders.

[b] The weighted average was obtained with Fisher's z transformation.

bal IQs for the WAIS-III and WAIS-R were the most highly related ($r = .94$) of the global scales, followed by the Full Scale IQ ($r = .93$) and the Performance IQ ($r = .86$). As shown in Table 1.1, the average WAIS-III Full Scale IQ is 2.9 points lower than the WAIS-R Full Scale IQ. The difference between the two instruments on the Verbal IQ is small (1.2 points) and is lower on the WAIS-III. On the Performance Scale, the average WAIS-III IQs were 4.8 points less than on the WAIS-R. These differences are similar to what has been found in comparisons of other tests with their revised versions (Flynn, 1987) and indicate that when an examinee's performance is referenced to outdated norms (WAIS-R) rather than to current ones (WAIS-III), the IQ score may be inflated.

Standardization and Psychometric Properties of the WAIS-III

The standardization sample for the WAIS-III (N = 2,450) was selected according to 1995 U.S. census data, and was stratified according to age, sex, race/ethnicity, geographic region, and education level. Thirteen age groups were created from a large sample of adolescents and adults, with 100 to 200 subjects in each group between the ages of 16 to 17 and 85 to 89. The average split-half reliability for the IQs across the 13 age groups was strong, ranging from .94 to .98 (see Rapid Reference 1.4 for split-half and test-retest reliability for all scales and subtests). The factor indexes had average reliability coefficients ranging from .88 for Processing Speed to .96 for Verbal Comprehension. Individual subtest reliabilities ranged from an average of .93 on Vocabulary to .70 on Object Assembly; median values were .88 for the seven Verbal subtests and .83 for the seven Performance subtests. A subset of the standardization sample (394 adults) provided test-retest data, with an average of 5 weeks between testings. The results of the test-retest study showed that for the four subsamples (19–29, 30–54, 55–74, and 75–89 years), reliability coefficients ranged from .94 to .97 for Verbal IQ, .88 to .92 for Performance IQ, and .95 to .97 for Full Scale IQ (see Rapid Reference 1.4).

One of the criticisms of the WAIS-R was that the norms for ages 16 to 19 were suspect (Kaufman, 1983, 1990). The two age groups (16–17 and 18–19) earned nearly identical scores on the WAIS-R, although the 18- to 19-year-olds have more formal education than the 16- to 17-year-olds, and IQ is substantially related to educational attainment. Further questions were drawn about the WAIS-R norms for individuals under age 20 because these young adults scored strikingly lower than did the individuals who were aged 20 to 24. Kaufman (1990) hypothesized that the problem with the WAIS-R norms for ages 16 to 19 was likely due to some sort of unknown sampling bias.

Kaufman (1999b) examined the WAIS-III standardization data to determine whether the norms seemed valid for the 16- to 19-year-olds. He used a procedure that involved the special reference group of 20- to 34-year-olds, thereby permitting comparisons across age groups. He observed expected increases in test scores from ages 16 to 17 to ages 18 to 19. However, from ages 18 to 19 to ages 20 to 24 there was no increase at all. Many more individuals in the 20 to 24 age range have attended college than among those in the 18 to 19 age range, which makes the lack of difference between the groups on WAIS-III tasks (especially on the Verbal Scale) surprising. Although questions are again raised about the norms for the youngest age groups in the standardization sample, our conclusion is that the norms for 16- to 19-year-olds are probably valid, especially for ages 16 to 17 years.

....

≡ Rapid Reference

1.4 Average WAIS-III Reliability

WAIS-III Scale, Index, or Subtest	Split-Half Reliability	Test-Retest Reliability
Verbal IQ	.97	.96
Performance IQ	.94	.91
Full Scale IQ	.98	.96
Verbal Comprehension Index	.96	.95
Perceptual Organization Index	.93	.88
Working Memory Index	.94	.89
Processing Speed Index[a]	.88	.89
Vocabulary	.93	.91
Similarities	.86	.83
Arithmetic	.88	.86
Digit Span	.90	.83
Information	.91	.94
Comprehension	.84	.81
Letter-Number Sequencing	.82	.75
Picture Completion	.83	.79
Digit Symbol-Coding[a]	—	.86
Block Design	.86	.82
Matrix Reasoning	.90	.77
Picture Arrangement	.74	.69
Symbol Search[a]	—	.79
Object Assembly	.70	.76

[a]For Digit Symbol-Coding and Symbol Search and the composite of these two (Processing Speed), only test-retest coefficients are reported because of the timed nature of the subtests.

≡ Rapid Reference

1.5 Wechsler Adult Intelligence Scale—Third Edition

Author: David Wechsler

Publication date: 1997

What the test measures: Verbal, nonverbal, and general intelligence

Age range: 16–89 years

Administration time: 11 subtests to obtain IQs = 60–90 minutes, 13 subtests to obtain both IQs and Index scores = 65–95 minutes (Object Assembly adds an additional 10–15 minutes)

Qualification of examiners: Graduate- or professional-level training in psychological assessment

Publisher: The Psychological Corporation
555 Academic Court
San Antonio, TX 78204-2498
Ordering phone number: 800-211-8378
http://www.PsychCorp.com
WAIS-III Complete kit test price = $595 (as of April 1998)

COMPREHENSIVE REFERENCES ON TEST

The *WAIS-III Administration and Scoring Manual* (Wechsler, 1997) and the *WAIS-III and WMS-III Technical Manual* (The Psychological Corporation, 1997) currently provide the most detailed information about the WAIS-III. These manuals review the development of the test; descriptions of each of the subtests and scales; and their standardization, reliability, and validity. *Assessing Adolescent and Adult Intelligence* (Kaufman, 1990) provides an excellent review of the research on the WAIS-R, much of which is still pertinent for the WAIS-III. Rapid Reference 1.5 provides basic information on the WAIS-III and its publisher.

TEST YOURSELF

1. **Many of the tasks that David Wechsler used in his WAIS, WAIS-R, and WAIS-III were adapted from what sources?**

2. **The WAIS-III is based on what theory?**
   (a) Horn's fluid-crystallized theory
   (b) the verbal-nonverbal theory
   (c) Galton's sensory-motor theory
   (d) none of the above, as Wechsler used a practical clinical approach rather than theoretical

3. **What was the major structural change implemented from the WAIS-R to the WAIS-III?**

4. **Which three subtests are not included in any of the four WAIS-III factors?**
   (a) Block Design, Object Assembly, Comprehension
   (b) Picture Arrangement, Comprehension, Object Assembly
   (c) Digit Symbol-Coding, Picture Arrangement, Digit Span
   (d) Object Assembly, Matrix Reasoning, Comprehension

5. **Which subtest is not new to the WAIS-III?**
   (a) Letter-Number Sequencing
   (b) Object Assembly
   (c) Matrix Reasoning
   (d) Symbol Search

6. **Which subtest has added two new optional procedures?**
   (a) Digit Span
   (b) Object Assembly
   (c) Digit Symbol-Coding
   (d) Picture Arrangement

7. **For which age group was the Perceptual Organization factor not strongly supported?**
   (a) 16–19
   (b) 20–34
   (c) 35–54
   (d) 55–74
   (e) 75–89

Answers: 1. Army Alpha, Army Beta, Army Performance Scale Examination, and Stanford-Binet; 2. d; 3. Addition of four factor indexes; 4. b; 5. b; 6. c; 7. e

Two

HOW TO ADMINISTER THE WAIS-III

O
ne of the strengths of a standardized test such as the WAIS-III is that it is able to provide scores that represent an individual's performance compared with other individuals of about the same age. However, to obtain results that are comparable to the national norms, one must be careful to adhere to the same administration and scoring procedures that were used during the standardization of the test. At the same time, examiners must not be rigid and unnatural in their manner of presentation. Thus a delicate balance must take place to ensure the best possible administration.

APPROPRIATE TESTING CONDITIONS

Testing Environment

The physical surroundings in which the testing takes place may vary. Some examiners may test in a school, office, clinic, nursing home, or hospital, whereas others may find it necessary to test in a home. The most important features of the testing environment are that it is quiet, free of distractions and interruption, and comfortable for the examinee. The ideal situation would provide a room for only the examiner and the examinee, as the presence of a third person can be disruptive.

A table is a necessity for testing. Because writing and drawing will be done, a smooth tabletop is ideal; however, a clipboard may provide a smooth writing surface if the table is rough. It is recommended that you sit opposite the examinee. This arrangement allows easy observation of test-taking behaviors as well as easy manipulation of all test materials by the examiner.

Testing Materials

During the testing, only the materials necessary for the task at hand should be on the table. Visible presence of other testing materials, such as the Block Design blocks or Object Assembly puzzles may be distracting or cause anxiety. Many examiners find it useful to place unused test materials on a chair close to them but out of the examinee's view.

The *WAIS-III Administration and Scoring Manual* (Wechsler, 1997) should be positioned so that it provides a shield behind which the record form can be placed. This setup allows the examiner to have easy access to all the directions and also makes the record of the examinee's scores less visible. However, the examiner should avoid being secretive.

Almost everything needed to perform the assessment is included in the WAIS-III kit. However, necessary testing materials that do not come with the WAIS-III kit include a stopwatch, clipboard, two No. 2 graphite pencils without erasers, and extra paper for taking notes.

RAPPORT WITH EXAMINEE

Providing a comfortable interpersonal situation for the examinee is key to obtaining the best possible administration. Throughout the assessment session, it is important to facilitate a positive rapport. The tone of conversation should be natural, pleasant, and professional. To provide this natural and smooth interpersonal interaction, it is important to be completely familiar with all of the administration and scoring procedures of the test. If the examiner is uncertain of how a task is to be administered or is fumbling with the testing materials, this indecision will likely cause awkward pauses and distract the adult or adolescent who is being tested. Although it is not necessary to memorize the test manual, it will be extremely advantageous to be completely familiar with the details of the manual, such as wording of the directions and when particular test materials should be used. Also, know exactly where to locate the needed information regarding start, stop, and timing rules.

Establishing Rapport

To facilitate building rapport at the beginning of the testing session, it is a good idea to provide a general introduction to the test, as was done during the collection of the standardization sample. Questions or concerns that the examinee may have should be addressed at this time too. As stated in the standard WAIS-III instructions, spend some time explaining to the examinee that most test takers find some questions easy and some questions quite difficult. This helps to reassure them that it is okay if they don't know every answer. Elderly individuals may voice concern about their memory or ability to maneuver objects quickly. They should be reassured that they just need to do the best they can. They also may be told that the scores they earn are always based on the test performance of other adults about their age.

Maintaining Rapport

Once the testing has begun, care should be taken to adhere to the standardized language given in the administration manual. However, small talk and reassuring statements are also needed throughout the testing to promote a comfortable testing environment. The examiner must be vigilant in watching the examinee's level of fatigue, anxiety, and cooperation. Speeded tests or tests requiring fine motor coordination may be more taxing for older adults; thus, signs of fatigue should be especially considered if testing an older person. If anything appears to be impinging on the examinee's performance, such as loss of motivation, tiredness, or nervousness, try to insert more casual conversation between the subtests or provide more supportive statements. When providing supportive or encouraging statements, be careful not to give clues regarding the correctness of an examinee's answer. Indeed, it is important *not* to give encouraging comments and feedback *only* when an examinee is doing

DON'T FORGET

Keys to Positive Examiner-Examinee Rapport During Assessment

- Effectively introduce examinee to the testing activities by using the standardized introduction on page 63 of the *WAIS-III Administration and Scoring Manual;* begin establishing rapport.
- Interact comfortably with examinee. Don't be stilted.
- Give eye contact. Don't bury your head in the manual.
- Make smooth transitions *between* subtests. Use some small talk.
- Avoid small talk *during* a subtest.
- Familiarize yourself ahead of time with test directions and test materials.
- Use precise wording of questions and directions. Only the mildest of paraphrasing is acceptable occasionally.
- Be subtle, not distracting, when using a stopwatch.
- Use abbreviations when writing down examinees' responses.

poorly or to praise only when correct. This type of selective feedback may inadvertently give cues to individuals that they are responding correctly or incorrectly to items, based on the examiner's verbalizations. Examinees should be praised for their level of effort ("You are really working hard") or recognized for attempting items that were notably difficult ("Those were tough ones, but you're trying hard; let's try another one").

Breaks during testing are allowed but should only be taken between two subtests, not during the middle of a subtest. If an adult's level of motivation has been clearly lowered during a very difficult subtest, some encouraging comments plus a brief break may be warranted. If, during a challenging subtest, an examinee indicates that he or she will not go on, you may need to provide encouragement such as "Just try your best" or "Give it your best shot." During administration of timed subtests, examiners will find it useful to allow examinees to have a few extra seconds past the time limit to work if they are actively involved in the task. These little tips in administration may lessen potential discouragement and will extend rapport throughout the session.

TESTING INDIVIDUALS WITH SPECIAL NEEDS

Adults or adolescents with special needs for testing may include those who have hearing impairment, visual problems, motor difficulties, or those who are not fluent in English. When testing such individuals, special consideration needs to be taken to accommodate the particular examinee while maintaining standardized procedures to

the degree possible. It is important to obtain as much information as possible about the adolescent's or adult's impairment prior to the assessment session with the individual. Ask a caretaker about the examinee's vision, hearing, physical condition, or any other limitations. With this information you will be able to determine how the test procedures need to be modified. Testing should be done in such a manner that the examinee is not penalized because of sensory or motor deficits. If major modifications in the standardized procedure are made, these changes may impact test scores or invalidate the use of the norms. Clinical judgment must be used to determine whether the examinee's impairment prohibits obtaining valid scores on part or all of the test.

Modifications to the test administration for accommodating an examinee's special needs may include some of the following: administering the test in American Sign Language to a deaf individual (if you are specially trained), adding printed words to facilitate understanding of directions to hard-of-hearing individuals, administering only the Verbal Scale subtests to a blind individual, eliminating time limits for adolescents or adults with motor difficulties, or extending the testing over more than one session for any adult with special needs. When any modification is used, such as translation into another language, problems in interpreting the scores may arise. Careful consideration must be used to determine whether using such modifications are best or whether choosing another instrument or supplemental instruments may provide the most useful information.

CAUTION

Appropriate Feedback and Encouragement

- Praise and encourage the examinee's level of effort.
- Be careful *not* to give feedback on whether a particular response is right or wrong.
- Give encouragement throughout items, not just when examinee is struggling.

CAUTION

Modifying Standardized Procedure

- Modifications to the standardized procedure to accommodate examinees' limitations may invalidate the scores on the test.

- Clinical judgment is key in determining what quantitative and qualitative data are interpretable from the test administration.

- If adaptations are made in the time limits allowed on speeded subtests, this will invalidate the use of the norms.

- Translating the test into another language may also cause problems in interpreting the scores.

ADMINISTRATION CONSIDERATIONS

Special Considerations for 16-year-olds: WAIS-III versus WISC-III

For adolescents age 16 years, 0 months to age 16 years, 11 months, there are two Wechsler instruments that may be administered, the WAIS-III and the WISC-III. Examiners must decide whether the WAIS-III or the WISC-III is most appropriate for the particular client to be assessed. Taking into account the reliability of each subtest, the floor of each subtest, the ceiling of each subtest, and the recency of the test's norms, we make the recommendations outlined in Table 2.1 when assessing adolescents in this overlapping age range:

Table 2.1 Deciding on the WISC-III Versus WAIS-III

Estimated ability level of adolescent	Wechsler test to administer
Below Average	WISC-III
Average	WAIS-III
Above Average	WAIS-III

The WISC-III will allow adolescents with Below Average cognitive ability to better demonstrate what they are capable of answering. On the WAIS-III, on the other hand, there is a risk of a floor effect for individuals who are functioning at a low level. The opposite is true for a 16-year-old functioning in the Above Average range. Such an Above Average adolescent may not be able to achieve a ceiling on the WISC-III, but will be able to be properly assessed with the WAIS-III's more difficult items. For those adolescents who are estimated to be functioning in the Average range of intelligence, the WAIS-III is preferable because its norms are more recent. Because of the Flynn effect (Flynn, 1987), which has demonstrated that norms in the United States become outdated at the rate of 3 points per decade, newer norms are generally preferable to older norms. We make the exception, however, for Below Average 16-year-olds. The better "floor" on the WISC-III than WAIS-III outweighs the WAIS-III's advantage of having more recent norms than the WISC-III (which was standardized in 1990, about six years earlier than the WAIS-III standardization).

There is a benefit to the overlap in ages between the WAIS-III and WISC-III. If an adolescent who has recently been tested on the WAIS-III needs to be reassessed, then the adolescent may be retested using the WISC-III, as long as he or she has not yet had his or her seventeenth birthday. The same benefit is true for assessing an adolescent who has recently been tested on the WISC-III and needs retesting. The WAIS-III may be administered rather than reusing the WISC-III and increasing the risk of practice effects.

Starting and Discontinuing Subtests

The administration rules have been simplified from the WAIS-R to the WAIS-III. Important rules such as when to begin and end each subtest are listed both in the administration manual and on the record form itself. The general overall rules are described here.

Many of the subtests on the WAIS-III start at items other than the first one. This procedure allows examiners to curtail testing time for most adults, and it also enables them to administer earlier, simpler items to adults who cannot correctly answer items at the designated starting point. Most often examinees who are functioning at a low intellectual level will need to go back to these easier items. The rule that is employed to enable examiners to go back to easier items if the first set of items are causing difficulty is called the reverse rule. Reverse rules require administration of earlier subtest items in reverse order if a perfect score is not obtained on either one or the other of the first two items administered. Until the examinee obtains perfect scores on two consecutive items, this reversal procedure continues. Sample items are

≡ Rapid Reference

2.1 Summary of Subtests With and Without Reverse Rules

Subtests With Reverse Rules	Subtests Without Reverse Rules
Verbal	**Verbal**
Vocabulary	Digit Span
Similarities	Letter-Number Sequencing
Arithmetic	
Information	**Performance**
Comprehension	Digit Symbol-Coding
Performance	Picture Arrangement
Picture Completion	Symbol Search
Block Design	Object Assembly
Matrix Reasoning	

not part of the reverse-sequence procedure. Figures 3.2, 3.3, and 3.4 in the *WAIS-III Administration and Scoring Manual* (Wechsler, 1997) show examples of how the reverse rules are applied. The following Verbal subtests use a reverse rule: Vocabulary, Similarities, Arithmetic, Information, and Comprehension. The Performance subtests with a reverse rule are Picture Completion, Block Design, and Matrix Reasoning.

In contrast, the Verbal subtests that do not use a reverse rule include Digit Span and Letter-Number Sequencing. The Performance subtests that do not use a reverse rule are the following: Digit Symbol-Coding, Picture Arrangement, Symbol Search, and Object Assembly. Subtests without a reverse criterion begin either with Item 1 or with a sample item. These subtests end either when a specified time has elapsed (Digit Symbol-Coding and Symbol Search) or when the discontinue rule has been met. Object Assembly is the only subtest that requires all items to be administered. Rapid Reference 2.1 reviews subtests with and without reverse rules. A summary of starting points, reverse, and discontinue rules for each subtest can be found in the Subtest-by-Subtest Rules of Administration section on pages 27–53.

Sometimes during administration of a subtest, it may be unclear how to score a response and, therefore, whether the subtest should be discontinued.

This situation occurs most frequently during the Vocabulary,
Similarities, and Comprehension
subtests that have some subjectivity in their scoring. If it is not possible to determine quickly whether
a response is correct, it is best to
continue administering further
items until you are certain that the
discontinue rule has been met.
This procedure is safest because
the scores can always be reviewed
later and items that are passed after the discontinue criterion has
been met can be (indeed, must be)
excluded from the adult's raw score
on the subtest (although such successes on hard items may provide

> # CAUTION
> ## Common General Errors in Administration
>
> - forgetting that if examinee gets the second item administered *partially* correct you may have to apply the reverse rule (even though the examinee got the first item administered correct)
> - forgetting that when applying the reverse rule you administer until *two* consecutive perfect scores are obtained, *including* previously administered items
> - forgetting to administer enough items to meet the discontinue rule

the examiner with valuable *clinical* information). However, if upon review of
the scores it is noted that items should have administered beyond where the
subtest was ended, it will be too late, and the test may be unscorable.

Recording Responses

While administering the WAIS-III, it is crucial to write down responses for all
items administered or attempted. This recording is especially important for Verbal subtests such as Vocabulary, Similarities, Information, and Comprehension.
However, even brief verbal responses produced in Arithmetic, Digit Span,
Letter-Number Sequencing, and Picture Completion are important to record.
Some examiners are tempted to write down only a score for a subject's response
to an item, but this practice is discouraged. Irretrievable information may be
lost if only a 0 or 1 is recorded. Useful clinical information and patterns in responding may be apparent when all responses are written down. When recording what an examinee says, you should try to capture most of what is said
verbatim. Using abbreviations frequently helps balance the maintenance of rapport with the recording of essential information (see Rapid Reference 2.2 for

≡ Rapid Reference

2.2 Abbreviations for Recording Responses

@	at	PC	points correctly
B	both	PPL	people
DK	don't know	PX	points incorrectly
EO	everyone	Q	question or query
F	fail (examinee responded incorrectly)	R	are
		Shd	should
INC	incomplete (response wasn't completed within the time limit)	SO	someone
		ST	something
LL	looks like	↓	decrease
NR	no response	↑	increase
OT	overtime	U	you
P	pass (examinee responded correctly)	w/	with
		w/o	without
Prmt	prompt	Wld	would

commonly used abbreviations). At times it will be necessary to record your own statements. For example, if you probed to clarify an answer by saying "Tell me more about that," you should always record the letter Q in parentheses on the record form directly after the response that you queried to indicate that you had to prompt the adult. When interpreting the recorded information clinically, you may then want to note whether many responses were elicited by querying, or whether the examinee produced them spontaneously. It is also of clinical value to note the adolescent's or adult's response to queries: Did they usually improve the quality of their answers? Did they tend not to add anything to their first responses, saying simply "Don't know"? Did they talk and talk after a query yet fail to improve their item scores?

Timing

Six of the seven Performance subtests require a stopwatch for exact timing, as does Arithmetic. Careful planning is necessary when administering these seven subtests so that your timing is not distracting to the examinee. The watch should be unobtrusive, but if the examinee asks whether he or she is being timed you may want to say something like "Yes, but you don't need to worry about that." When giving directions to these subtests you must have your stopwatch ready to go because properly starting the timing exactly when the examinee is told to begin is critical. Impulsive individuals, for example, may start even sooner than you would anticipate, and you must be ready to time them immediately.

> ## DON'T FORGET
> ### When to Use a Stopwatch
> A stopwatch is needed for:
> - Picture Completion
> - Digit Symbol-Coding
> - Block Design
> - Arithmetic
> - Picture Arrangement
> - Symbol Search
> - Object Assembly

Once the timing for an item has begun, it is important to remember that even if the examinee asks for clarification or repetition of the instructions, the timing must continue. On some of the performance subtests, such as Picture Arrangement and Object Assembly, the examinee may not tell you when he or she is finished (although you requested them to do so in the directions). Closely observe the examinee. If it appears that he or she has completed an item, ask "Are you done?" and immediately record the time. Similarly, if you had stopped the time because you thought the examinee was done, and then the examinee continues working, be sure to restart the stopwatch and to count the entire time during which the examinee was working. (You are required to estimate the number of seconds that the stopwatch was off.)

Querying

At times, an examinee's response may be too vague or ambiguous to score. When such answers are given you need to ask the examinee to clarify his or her response. The administration manual lists responses to Vocabulary, Similarities, and Comprehension items that should be queried, but these responses are only illustrative. Examiner judgment is necessary to query similar responses to ones listed in the administration manual's scoring system. The key is incompleteness or ambiguity. Even responses that are not queried in the manual may be queried by the examiner if the adult's voice or face suggests confusion or uncertainty. The manner in which you ask for clarification is crucial. Questioning or querying should be done with neutral statements. For example, say "Tell me more about that" or "Explain what you mean." Be careful not to provide any hints or clues to the answer when you are querying, except when following the administration manual's specific queries (e.g., "Tell me another reason why *restate the question.*"). If a completely incorrect answer is spontaneously produced by the examinee, you do not want to query. As mentioned earlier, when discussing recording responses, queried responses should be indicated on the record form with the letter Q in parentheses. As a rule, it is best to query with a gentle command ("Tell me more") than with a question. The easiest response to "Can you tell me more about it?" is "No."

Repeating Items

The general rule for repeating questions or instructions is that you may do so if the examinee requests it or if the examinee does not seem to understand the task at hand. However, for Digit Span, a number sequence may not be repeated, and in Arithmetic, a question may be repeated only one time. When questions are repeated, the entire verbal question, not just a portion of it, should be repeated.

Occasionally, you may find that an adult is able to provide answers to more difficult items on a subtest when he or she responded "I don't know" to earlier, easier items. When this situation occurs, the earlier items can be readministered if you believe that the examinee knows the answers to the items. Anxiety or insecurity may have been originally interfering with the subject's responses on the easier items, or the person's behaviors may have been responsible for a few quick "Don't knows" before being able to take a risk. However, you may not readminister timed items or items on the Digit Span subtest.

Teaching the Task

Sample items and the first two items administered on many of the WAIS-III subtests are included to ensure that examinees understand what they are supposed to do to respond to the items on the subtest. These items afford the opportunity to give extra instruction if the examinee fails one of the first items in

DON'T FORGET

When to Teach the Task

- Teaching the task is only allowed when specified in the directions for:
  - Picture Completion
  - Digit Symbol-Coding
  - Block Design
  - Matrix Reasoning
  - Picture Arrangement
  - Symbol Search
  - Letter-Number Sequencing
  - Object Assembly
- Usually teaching is allowed during the sample item and first two items administered.
- Providing answers beyond what is stated in the instructions will lead to an inaccurate assessment of examinee's abilities.

the subtest. This teaching after a failed item does not change an adolescent's or adult's score, but it does provide clarification of the directions. The underlying premise of teaching the task is that examinees should be given the opportunity to do as well as possible on items, and the items should be measuring their ability to do the task, not their ability to quickly grasp the instructions.

SUBTEST-BY-SUBTEST RULES OF ADMINISTRATION

Detailed rules for subtest-by-subtest administration are provided in the WAIS-III administration manual. Some important reminders for competent administration of each of the subtests are presented here. This section may be used as a guide or to refresh your memory if you have already learned the details of the test. The subtests are listed in order of administration. During administration of the WAIS-III, it is important to be an astute observer of an examinee's behavior. Such behavioral observations can give great insight into how to interpret a particular subtest, and patterns of behavior across many subtests may also be critical in the process of interpretation. After the rules of each subtest, key behaviors to watch for are suggested.

2.3 Summary of Picture Completion Rules

Starting Point
Item 6

Reverse Criterion
Score of 0 on Item 6 or 7

Discontinue Criterion
After five consecutive scores of 0

Timing
20-second exposure time limit

1. Picture Completion

Prior to starting Picture Completion, the introduction to the WAIS-III on page 63 of the *WAIS-III Administration and Scoring Manual* should be given. This subtest requires the use of the administration manual, the stimulus booklet with incomplete drawings, a stopwatch, and the record form to record responses. This subtest is generally easy to administer, and is viewed as fun and gamelike by most adolescents and adults. The most common mistakes in administering Picture Completion concern the three queries that each are allowed to be given only *once* during the entire subtest, if needed.

- "Yes, but what is missing?"
- "Something is missing in the picture. What is it that is missing?"
- "Yes, but what is the *most important* part that is missing?"

Common examiner errors are either to forget to use these queries or to use each one several times instead of the mandated once. Other types of administration errors may occur if an adult or adolescent produces a verbal response that is unclear or ambiguous. If this type of response is given, it is necessary to query for clarification of the response. Responses may be verbal or nonverbal (e.g., pointing), as both are considered acceptable. It is important to keep in mind that this test's main focus is not on verbal ability but rather on visual perception, spatial ability, and holistic processing. However, important information about verbal ability may be gleaned in this first administered test. Interestingly, although Picture Completion is intended as a nonverbal subtest, the instructions to the adult subtly encourage verbalization: "Look at each picture and tell me what is missing." The word *tell* suggests a verbal response, whereas *show* would have prompted a nonverbal response.

Rapid Reference 2.3 reviews the start, reverse, discontinue, and timing rules. Following are lists of important queries, other Picture Completion rules, and telling behaviors to watch for and note while administering this subtest.

Queries
- Give each of the three queries only *once* for entire administration of Picture Completion.

Rules
- Provide correct answer to Item 6 or 7 if the examinee doesn't give correct response.
- If verbal response is ambiguous, say "Show me where you mean."
- On Items 8, 10, and 19, get clarification about where in the picture the examinee's verbal response is referring, if necessary.
- If the examinee points to the correct place but spoils the response by giving a clearly incorrect verbal response, the item is failed.

Behaviors to Note
- The speed at which an adult or adolescent responds is noteworthy. A reflective individual may take more time in responding (but most likely can respond within the 20-second time limit), whereas an impulsive individual may respond very quickly but incorrectly.
- Note whether the examinee is persistent in stating that nothing is missing from the picture (rather than responding "I don't know"), as it may reflect oppositionality or inflexibility.
- If nonverbal responses (pointing) are consistently observed, it may be evidence of a word retrieval problem in adults. Although it is acceptable to give a nonverbal response, it is far more common to give a verbal response.
- Verbal responses that are imprecise ("the thing on the wall") or overly elaborative ("the small plastic switch that, when flipped upward, allows the electricity to flow") are also noteworthy.
- Note whether an adult gives responses that consistently indicate a focus on details ("the grain" on the wood desk, "the sugar granuals" on the muffin, or "the streaks" on the window).
- After an individual has been redirected (i.e., "Yes, but what is the *most important* part that is missing?"), it is important to note whether he or

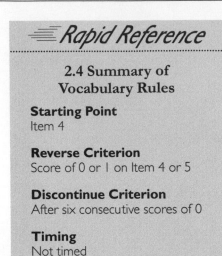

≡ *Rapid Reference*
....

2.4 Summary of Vocabulary Rules

Starting Point
Item 4

Reverse Criterion
Score of 0 or 1 on Item 4 or 5

Discontinue Criterion
After six consecutive scores of 0

Timing
Not timed

she still continues to respond with the same quality of response. This persistence in approach may be indicative of not understanding the task or inflexibility in thinking.

2. Vocabulary

This subtest requires the stimulus booklet to present a visual list of vocabulary words at the same time they are read aloud by the examiner. The manual and record form must also be used during administration. Scoring should be completed as responses are recorded to the degree possible. As mentioned previously, it is best to continue administering items if you are unsure if a difficult-to-score response will affect the discontinue rule. Because it may be necessary to review responses after the test is over, it is critical to record the exact response of the examinee as much as possible. One of the most challenging aspects of Vocabulary is querying vague responses appropriately. Be careful to use only *neutral* queries when prompting for more information. Scoring can also be difficult, as there is some subjectivity (see Chapter 3).

Rapid Reference 2.4 reviews the start, reverse, discontinue, and timing rules. Following are lists of important queries, other Vocabulary rules, and telling behaviors to watch for and note while administering this subtest.

Queries
- Use neutral questions to query vague or incomplete responses.
- Query responses that are indicated in the administration manual.
- Query responses that are similar to those in the administration manual (scoring rules are illustrative, not exhaustive).

Rules
- After administering the third item, the formal question may be omitted and the word may just be read.

- Use the general distinctions between responses scored 2, 1, or 0 (see pages 90–91 of *WAIS-III Administration and Scoring Manual*).
- Probe if the examinee responds to a word that sounds like the stimulus word, but is not the word.

Behaviors to Note

- Make note of "I don't know" responses, as such responses may be indicative of adults with word retrieval problems who struggle with this test. Word fluency can impact an individual's performance as much as his or her word knowledge.
- Hearing difficulties may be apparent on this test. The Vocabulary words are not presented in a meaningful context (although they are presented in written as well as oral form). Because the words are presented in a visual form as well as auditory, hearing problems may surface for illiterate or dyslexic adults on the WAIS-III. Note behaviors such as leaning forward during administration to hear better. Other clues to watch are indications of auditory discrimination problems ("arcade" rather than "arcane").
- Observe when an individual seems to jump ahead and proceed with the visually presented words, thereby disregarding the auditory stimulus. Such behavior may be indicative of a preference for the visual rather than auditory channel.
- Note adults who are overly verbose in their responses. They may be attempting to compensate for insecurity about their ability, or they may be obsessive or inefficient in their verbal expression.

3. Digit Symbol-Coding

Many materials are needed to administer this subtest: the administration manual, the record form, a stopwatch, and two pencils without erasers. Because there are lengthy verbal directions for this subtest, it is highly recommended to rehearse the administration multiple times. Once the examinee has gone through the sample, the test can be started. Timing should be precise—allow *exactly* 120 seconds. Some adults will quickly realize that the best strategy is to fill in one type of symbol at a time; however, skipping numbers is not allowed, and the examinee must be corrected immediately if this unacceptable

Rapid Reference

2.5 Summary of Digit Symbol-Coding Rules

Starting Point
Sample items

Reverse Criterion
No reverse

Discontinue Criterion
After 120 seconds

Timing
120 seconds[a]

[a]If Incidental Learning will be administered, the examinee should be allowed to continue working until four rows are completed, but note which item the examinee had completed after 120 seconds.

(but quite efficient) strategy is used. It is important to remember that four rows of Digit Symbol-Coding must be administered if the examiner intends to administer Incidental Learning. Thus, if four rows are not completed by the examinee within the allowed 120 seconds, have the examinee keep working until the necessary number of rows are completed. Just be sure to record the precise symbol the subject completed when the 120 seconds elapsed.

Rapid Reference 2.5 reviews start, reverse, discontinue, and timing rules. Following are lists of important Digit Symbol-Coding rules and telling behaviors to watch for and note while administering this subtest.

Rules
- Try not to paraphrase the directions, but don't lose rapport with the examinee by burying your head in the administration manual.
- While the examinee is completing the sample items, correct any errors immediately as they are made.
- If necessary, remind the examinee that he or she must start at the beginning of the row and not skip any.

Behaviors to Note
- Watching the eye movements of an adult taking the test can be very informative. Consistent glancing back and forth from the coding key to the response sheet may be indicative of a poor memory or insecurity. In contrast, someone who uses the key infrequently may have a good short-term memory and remember number-symbol pairs readily (the optional Incidental Learning procedures can help to clarify this hypothesis).

- Impulsivity in responding may be observed when an adult quickly but carelessly fills in symbols across the rows.
- Shaking hands, a tight grip on the pencil, or pressure on the paper when writing may be indicative of anxiety.
- Fatigue, boredom, or inattention may become apparent as the Digit Symbol-Coding task progresses. Noting the number of symbols copied during 30-second intervals provides helpful behavioral information.

Digit Symbol-Incidental Learning

There are two tasks to administer for Incidental Learning: Pairing and Free Recall. The Pairing procedure requires examinees to pair each number with its stimulus symbol, whereas the Free Recall procedure requires examinees to recall as many symbols as possible independently of the numbers. Both portions of the optional subtest require the response booklet, the manual, and pencils without erasers. Both the Pairing and Free Recall segments of Incidental Learning are to be administered immediately after Digit Symbol-Coding. While Pairing and Free Recall are administered, the next page of the response booklet, containing Symbol Copy, should *not* be exposed. There is no time limit for either Pairing or Free Recall. Pairing is to be administered first, then the Pairing items should be covered with a blank paper when the Free Recall task is presented. Pairing and Free Recall will be helpful in determining the effect of examinees' short-term abilities on Digit Symbol-Coding.

Rapid Reference 2.6 reviews start, reverse, discontinue, and timing rules. Following are lists of

≡ Rapid Reference

2.6 Summary of Digit Symbol-Incidental Learning Rules

Starting Point

First blank square for Pairing and empty space on bottom of page for Free Recall

Reverse Criterion

No reverse

Discontinue Criterion

Complete all possible.

Timing

Pairing and Free Recall are *not* timed.

important Digit Symbol-Coding and Incidental Learning rules and telling behaviors to watch for and note while administering this subtest.

Rules
- Pairing and Free Recall must be administered immediately after Digit Symbol-Coding.
- Do not allow the Symbol Copy page in the response booklet to be exposed during administration of Pairing and Free Recall.
- Cover the Pairing items when presenting the Free Recall task.
- Do not allow subject to skip numbers on Pairing.

Behaviors to Note
- On Pairing, observe whether the examinee seems to have more difficulty with numbers presented earlier or later in the sequence. This may suggest recency or primacy effects in memory.
- On Pairing, note whether examinees attempt to skip numbers in order to complete ones that they are most sure of or whether they write a symbol down for each number even though they are clearly guessing.
- On Free Recall, note the pattern in which subjects write the numbers down. Do they recall symbols sequentially (corresponding to 1, 2, 3, etc.)? Do they seem to randomly write symbols using no apparent strategy?
- On Free Recall, observe whether adults notice that they have not recalled all of the nine possible symbols.

Digit Symbol-Copy

This subtest is the final optional procedure in WAIS-III administration. The response booklet, the administration manual, a stopwatch, and pencils without erasers are needed. Examinees are shown a demonstration of three symbols, and they then complete four sample items before the task begins. Although the examinees are not explicitly told not to skip any symbols, credit is not given for items completed out of sequence. This copy procedure provides information about examinees' speed of motor processing with the effect of memory removed.

Rapid Reference 2.7 reviews start, reverse, discontinue, and timing rules. Following are lists of important Digit Symbol-Copy rules and telling behaviors to watch for and note while administering this subtest.

Rules
- Try not to paraphrase the directions, but don't lose rapport with the examinee by burying your head in the administration manual.
- The Incidental Learning pages of the record form should not be exposed during administration of Digit Symbol-Copy.
- While the examinee is completing the sample items, correct any errors immediately as they are made.
- Do not include sample items in the scoring of Digit Symbol-Coding.

Behaviors to Note
- As there is no pressure involved with memory on the copy task, note whether the examinee appears more relaxed in comparison to other Digit Symbol tasks.
- Because this is the last task administered to the examinee, look to see whether fatigue or boredom are interfering with performance.
- Observe whether the examinee's writing becomes more messy as the task goes on or whether he or she draws the symbols consistently throughout the copy task.
- Some adults may be more concerned with drawing the symbol perfectly than with working quickly. Observe whether signs of perfectionistic drawing are present.

> ≣ *Rapid Reference*
>
> **2.7 Summary of Digit Symbol-Copy Rules**
>
> **Starting Point**
> Sample items
>
> **Reverse Criterion**
> No reverse
>
> **Discontinue Criterion**
> 90 seconds
>
> **Timing**
> 90 seconds

4. Similarities

Like the Vocabulary subtest, Similarities is not difficult to administer. The only materials needed are the administration manual and record form. It is important to be aware of what types of answers need to be queried (those

≡ Rapid Reference

2.8 Summary of Similarities Rules

Starting Point
Item 6

Reverse Criterion
Score of 0 or 1 on Item 6 or 7

Discontinue Criterion
After four consecutive scores of 0

Timing
Not timed

that are vague and those specifically listed in the manual). When querying, the question to the examinee must be presented in a neutral fashion. This Verbal subtest also requires careful recording of verbal responses. A detailed description of how to score each subtest is presented in Chapter 3 of this book, as well as in the *WAIS-III Administration and Scoring Manual.*

To succeed in Similarities, examinees must understand that abstraction is necessary. For this reason, on Item 6 it is critical that an example of a 2-point response is given if an examinee does not spontaneously produce one. This example allows opportunity for examinees to hear that a response involving a higher degree of abstraction is more desirable than a purely concrete response.

Rapid Reference 2.8 reviews start, reverse, discontinue, and timing rules. Following are lists of important queries, other Similarities rules, and telling behaviors to watch for and note while administering this subtest.

Queries
- Use neutral questions to query vague or incomplete responses.
- Query multiple responses appropriately if wrong answers are included with correct ones or if "differences" are given.
- Don't query a string of responses; rather, score the best one if none are clearly wrong.

Rules
- Give an example of a 2-point response if examinee's response to Item 6 is not perfect.
- Use the general distinctions between responses scored 2, 1, or 0 (see pages 111–112 of *WAIS-III Administration and Scoring Manual*).

Behaviors to Note
- Observe whether the adult benefits from feedback on Item 6 (if

feedback was given). Adults who learn from the example given by the examiner may have flexibility, whereas those who cannot may be more rigid or concrete.

- Observe whether the quality of response decreases as the items become more difficult.
- Length of verbal responses give important behavioral clues. Overly elaborate responses may suggest obsessiveness.
- Quick responses or abstract responses to easy early items may indicate overlearned associations rather than high-level abstract reasoning.

5. Block Design

This Performance subtest has many details to which the examiner needs to attend. First, make sure that all of the materials—box of nine blocks, stimulus booklet with model forms, stopwatch, administration manual, and record form—are ready to be used. Correct positioning of the adult and the blocks is crucial to facilitate proper administration. The block model must be at a distance from the examinees so that they look down on the model, and then after the directions are read (Items 1 to 5), the block model is to be moved away from the edge of the table (7 inches). An important part of this Block Design task is being able to understand the relationship between two-dimensional representations and three-dimensional representations. The first five items provide a model that is three-dimensional, which is then re-created by the examinee in three-dimensional space. Items 6 to 14 require the adult to perceive and visually analyze the *two*-dimensional model and then re-create it in *three*-dimensional space. This type of problem is more complex than those that utilize three dimensions for both the model and the examinee's design. When the two-dimensional models are shown in the stimulus book, some of the visual cues are removed, such as the lines that distinguish one block from another. In general, the whole administration procedure is set up as a learning situation that graduates from simple three-dimensional designs to complex nine-block designs depicted in pictures. In fact, the final item removes the square outline of the design such that only the red portions of the design are distinguishable from the white page on which the design is presented.

Blocks must have a variety of faces showing before each administration, so as to not bias or help the examinee. Careful timing is important for scor-

Rapid Reference

2.9 Summary of Block Design Rules

Starting Point
Item 5

Reverse Criterion
Score of 0 or 1 on Item 5 or 6

Discontinue Criterion
After three consecutive scores of 0

Timing
30 seconds for Items 1–4
60 seconds for Items 5–9
120 seconds for Items 10–14

ing. At times adults may not verbalize when they have completed a design. In such instances, learn to rely on nonverbal cues to determine when to stop timing. If necessary, ask the adult if he or she is done. No credit should be awarded if it takes the examinee longer than the allowed time to complete a given Block Design item.

Rapid Reference 2.9 reviews start, reverse, discontinue, and timing rules. Following are lists of important Block Design rules and telling behaviors to watch for and note while administering this subtest.

Rules

- Begin timing after saying the last word of instructions.
- Place model approximately 7 inches from edge of table after directions are read for Items 1 to 5.
- Make sure the proper variety of faces of the blocks are showing before each item.
- Rotations of 30 degrees or more are considered failures. Rotations may be corrected only *once* during the subtest.
- Remember to give the extra five blocks for Item 10.
- Record responses by drawing the design of blocks made by examinee.

Behaviors to Note

- Observe problem-solving styles during adults' manipulation of the blocks. Some use a trial-and-error approach, whereas others systematically examine and appear to carefully plan before moving any of the blocks.
- Observe whether subjects tend to pair up blocks and then integrate the smaller segments into the whole. On the designs requiring nine

blocks, observe whether examinees work from the outside in or per-haps start in one corner and work their way around the design.
- Motor coordination and hand preference may be apparent during this task. Note whether individuals seem clumsy in their manipula-tion of the blocks, have hands that are noticeably trembling, or whether they move very quickly and steadily.
- Look to see whether examinees refer back to the model while they are working. This could be indicative of visual memory ability, cau-tiousness, or other factors.
- Examine whether adults tend to be obsessively concerned with de-tails (such as lining up the blocks perfectly). Such behaviors may negatively impact their speed.
- Observe how well examinees persist, especially when the task be-comes more difficult and they may face frustration. Note how well they tolerate frustration.
- Look to see whether examinees lose the square shape for some de-signs, even if they have managed to re-create the overall pattern. This kind of response could be indicative of figure-ground problems.
- Note whether adults are noticeably twisting their bodies to obtain a different perspective on the model, or are rotating their own designs. Such behaviors may be indicative of visual-perceptual difficulties.
- Note whether examinees fail to recognize that their designs look dif-ferent from the models.

6. Arithmetic

The materials required for this test are the administration manual, record form, nine Block Design blocks, and a stopwatch (no paper and pencil). Some examinees may exhibit frustration when they are told they may not use paper or pencil to work out the mathematical problems during this subtest. However, if they choose to write imaginary numbers in the air or on the table, this strategy is perfectly acceptable and should be noted in behavioral obser-vations. Not allowing paper and pencil on these mathematics problems re-quires examinees to utilize working memory.

Rapid Reference 2.10 reviews start, reverse, discontinue, and timing rules. Following are lists of important Arithmetic rules and telling behaviors to

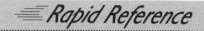
Rapid Reference

2.10 Summary of Arithmetic Rules

Starting Point
Item 5

Reverse Criterion
Score of 0 on Item 5 or 6

Discontinue Criterion
After four consecutive scores of 0

Timing
15 seconds for Items 1–6
30 seconds for Items 7–11
60 seconds for Items 12–19
120 seconds for Item 20

watch for and note while administering this subtest.

Rules
- Repeat an Arithmetic question only once per item.
- Keep the stopwatch going even if repeating a question.
- Paper and pencil are not allowed, but the examinee can use finger to "write" on table.
- Query if the examinee provides multiple responses and you are unsure which is the intended response.

Behaviors to Note
- Observe examinees for signs of anxiety. Some adults who view themselves as "poor at math" may be more anxious during this task. Be aware of statements such as "I was never taught that in school" or "I can't do math in my head."
- Watch for signs of distractibility or poor concentration, which are usually noticeable during Arithmetic.
- Note when a subject asks for repetition of a question, as it may be indicative of several things, including poor hearing, inattention, or stalling for more time.
- Take note of whether the examinee responds quickly and may be impulsive or is rather methodical and careful in his or her processing of the information.

7. Matrix Reasoning

The stimulus book, containing four types of nonverbal reasoning tasks, the record form, and the administration manual are necessary for this subtest. There are a series of sample items that begin Matrix Reasoning. The items are included to ensure that the examinee understands what is expected in the task. The standardized procedure includes teaching the task via alternative explanation if necessary. As items become progressively more difficult, some examinees may be tempted to guess for their response. If guessing occurs, such individuals should be instructed to try to reason through the solution rather than taking random guesses. It is important to note that because there is no time limit, some examinees may take a significant amount of time to solve the problems.

Rapid Reference 2.11 reviews start, reverse, discontinue, and timing rules. Following are lists of important Matrix Reasoning rules and telling behaviors to watch for and note while administering this subtest.

Rules
- Administer Samples A to C in forward order.
- Illustrate the correct response if A, B, or C is incorrect. Provide an alternative explanation to the problem if necessary.
- Regardless of performance on the sample items, proceed to Item 4.
- Point correctly to the response choices in stimulus book when indicating from which ones the examinee may choose.
- No teaching or feedback should be given on Items 1 to 26.
- The examinee should not be allowed to guess randomly.
- An adult who is color-blind will have impaired performance on this subtest. If information about such difficulties is not offered spontaneously by the examinee, be sure to inquire whether color-blindness may be affecting him or her.

Behaviors to Note
- Note whether adults "talk their way" through the problems, using verbal mediation, or whether they are more apt to simply use mental imagery to work to the solution.
- Observe whether the examinee needs to touch the stim-

Rapid Reference

2.11 Summary of Matrix Reasoning Rules

Starting Point
Sample items, then go to Item 4

Reverse Criterion
Score of 0 on Item 4 or 5

Discontinue Criterion
After four consecutive scores of 0 or four scores of 0 on any five consecutive items

Timing
None

ulus book to aid in problem solving. Touching the stimuli may help some adults visualize the solution.

- Although this test is not timed, examine whether an adult processes the information slowly, carefully, and methodically or works quickly and impulsively.
- Observe whether the examinee is distracted by unessential detail such as color if the solution to the problem only requires noting the shape and number of objects.
- Note whether the subject attends to part of the stimuli but misses other essential parts to successfully complete the matrix.
- Make note of signs of frustration or anxiety, especially when the problems become more complex.
- Note whether examinees' problem solving includes trying each of the given possible solutions one by one or first attempting to come up with a solution and then checking the row of choices to find the solution that they had created.

8. Digit Span

To administer this subtest only the record form with the number sequences and the administration manual are needed, along with a slow, steady voice. The key to administering this subtest is reading the series of digits at the proper rate: one digit per second. At times some examinees will jump in and begin to respond before all of the numbers in the sequence have been read. The examinee should be encouraged to wait until the entire sequence of numbers has been read before responding. Digits Backward provides two examples of what is required. If examinees respond correctly to the first example, then Trial 1 of Item 1 should be administered immediately; however, if they don't seem to understand the nature of the Digits Backward task, then the second example should be administered. Careful recording of the subject's individual responses on this subtest can provide useful interpretive information.

Digits Forward and Digits Backward are very distinct and measure somewhat different aspects of memory. Digits Backward requires more mental manipulation and visualization of numbers, whereas Digits Forward can be done with simple rote recall. Careful attention to processing and problem-solving style can be useful for interpretation.

Rapid Reference 2.12 reviews start, reverse, discontinue, and timing rules. Following are lists of important Digit Span rules and telling behaviors to watch for and note while administering this subtest.

Rules
- Say the numbers at a steady rate of one per second.
- Do not "chunk" the numbers into small groups.
- Drop your voice on the last digit of each series of items.
- Remember to give the second trial of each item, whether or not the first trial is passed.
- Administer Digits Backward even if subject obtains a score of 0 on Digits Forward.
- Read directions exactly; do not give extra help on Digits Backward.

Behaviors to Note
- Note whether adults are attempting to use a problem-solving strategy such as "chunking." Some examinees will use such a strategy from the beginning; others will learn a strategy as they progress through the task.
- Note whether errors are due simply to transposing numbers or completely forgetting numbers.
- Attention, hearing impairment, and anxiety can impact this test; therefore such difficulties should be noted if present.
- Watch for rapid repetition of digits or beginning to repeat the digits before the examiner has completed the series. Such behavior may be indicative of impulsivity.
- Observe whether there is a pattern of failing the first trial and then correctly responding to the second trial. Such a response pattern may be indicative of learning or may simply be a warm-up effect.

≡ *Rapid Reference*

2.12 Summary of Digit Span Rules

Starting Point
Item 1

Reverse Criterion
No reverse

Discontinue Criterion
After scores of 0 on *both trials* of any item

Timing
None

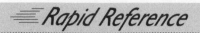

Rapid Reference

2.13 Summary of Information Rules

Starting Point
Item 5

Reverse Criterion
Score of 0 on Item 5 or 6

Discontinue Criterion
After six consecutive scores of 0

Timing
None

9. Information

The administration manual lists a series of short questions to be read orally in this subtest, and the record form is needed to record responses. The questions asked in Information were developed to tap knowledge about common events, objects, places, and people. Some examinees may ask for clarification about how to spell a word or may ask for a question to be repeated. It is acceptable to repeat a question, but the wording should not be changed whatsoever. Even if asked, the words should not be spelled or defined for the examinee because this type of help is not part of the standardized procedure. Querying an examinee's response to gain further clarification of vague or incomplete responses is perfectly acceptable but should be done with neutral prompts.

Rapid Reference 2.13 reviews start, reverse, discontinue, and timing rules. Following are lists of important Information rules and telling behaviors to watch for and note while administering this subtest.

Rules
- Administer items in reverse order if examinee scores 0 on either Item 5 or 6.
- Do not spell the words or define any words in the questions.
- If an examinee points in response to Item 6, ask him or her to verbalize what direction that is.
- Query on Item 21 regarding "what scale" examinee is referring to if he or she does not specify.

Behaviors to Note
- Note whether an examinee provides unnecessarily long responses. If such long responses filled with excessive detail are given, it may be indicative of obsessiveness.

- Make note of any observable pattern in a subject's responses. Patterns of responding that include missing earlier, easier items and having successes on harder items may suggest anxiety, poor motivation, or retrieval difficulties.
- Observe whether items on which errors are made are those that are especially related to an examinee's cultural background, such as elected U.S. officials at a certain time or famous figures in American history. Such observations should be incorporated in interpretation.

≡ *Rapid Reference*

2.14 Summary of Picture Arrangement Rules

Starting Point
Item 1

Reverse Criterion
No reverse

Discontinue Criterion
After four consecutive scores of 0 (starting with Item 2)

Timing
30 seconds for Item 1
45 seconds for Item 2
60 seconds for Items 3–4
90 seconds for Items 5–6
120 seconds for Items 7–11

10. Picture Arrangement

Multiple materials are needed to be manipulated and carefully handled by the examiner in this subtest: the administration manual, record form, 11 sets of Picture Arrangement cards, and a stopwatch. The laying out of the cards in the properly mixed-up order is critical in the presentation of this test. The cards should be laid out in numerical order starting from the subject's left. Timing in this subtest is important, as limits range from 30 to 120 seconds. Examinees may forget to say when they have completed a picture sequence, so it is important always to carefully watch to determine when the examinee is obviously finished. No credit should be awarded if it takes the examinee longer than the allowed time to complete a given Picture Arrangement item. If it is unclear whether an examinee's story begins on the left or right side, ask where the story begins. Some examinees may demonstrate a persistent pattern of starting on the right, whereas others may do this on a rare occasion.

Rapid Reference 2.14 reviews start, reverse, discontinue, and timing rules. Following are lists of important Picture Arrangement rules and telling behaviors to watch for and note while administering this subtest.

Rules

- For Item 1, lay out the cards before speaking.
- If necessary, administer the second trial of Item 1 by laying out the cards in the correct order and telling the story, before giving the second trial.
- For Items 2 to 11, lay out the cards after speaking.
- Give no demonstration of correct sequence for Items 2 to 11.
- If the examinee lays out pictures from right to left, ask where the story begins.
- Give directions with a minimum of paraphrasing, but don't lose rapport with the examinee.
- Properly give 1 point of credit on Items 5 to 9 for alternative responses.
- Don't forget that the discontinue rule does *not* include Item 1.
- *After* the *entire* subtest is completed, you may ask the examinee to tell the story of any arrangements to which they incorrectly responded in order to verify his or her logic.

Behaviors to Note

- Observation of how adults handle the cards provides insight about their problem-solving approach. Trial and error versus insightful problem solving may be noted. Adults who pair pictures seemingly at random until they make sense demonstrate one style. Another style is to select the picture that goes first in the story, then to select the second card, and so on in sequence.
- Note whether the examinee begins to move the cards before carefully examining the pictures in each. This behavior may be indicative of impulsivity. Such individuals will also be unlikely to check their work before saying that they have completed. Jumping in to start the task before the directions have been completely read may also be observed in some adults.
- Note when an adult studies the pictures for a few seconds prior to rearranging them. Such behavior may be indicative of a reflective

style. Rechecking work after completion may also be noted in individuals with a reflective style.

- Observe whether there is verbalization during problem solving. Telling the story as the cards are rearranged is a helpful strategy for some adults, whereas for others this vocalization may be disruptive.
- Note any behaviors that give clues to whether errors are made because of social or cultural misinterpretation as opposed to visual-perceptual difficulties.
- When the subtest is complete, it may be useful to return to arrangements that the examinee got wrong. Note the examinee's explanation of how his or her arrangement made sense to them, as it may provide useful clinical information. Some creative alternate arrangements may be reasonable (but not credited), whereas others may be totally nonsensical.

11. Comprehension

This subtest requires only questions written in the administration manual and the record form. Examinees may need a question repeated from time to time, and this is allowed. However, the question should be repeated in its entirety; it should not be abbreviated in any way. Five of the Comprehension questions require responses from two of the general categories. It is important to remember to query for another response if an examinee only spontaneously provides an answer from one category. When requesting a second response, be sure to restate the question in the manner indicated on page 147 of the *WAIS-III Administration and Scoring Manual.*

> *Wrong:* "Tell me another reason."
> *Right:* "Tell me another reason why you should see your dentist annually."

Whereas Items 1 to 16 require the adult to demonstrate deductive reasoning in response to socially relevant questions, note that the last two items require the adult to reason inductively in response to proverbs.

Rapid Reference 2.15 reviews start, reverse, discontinue, and timing rules. Following are lists of important Comprehension rules and telling behaviors to watch for and note while administering this subtest.

2.15 Summary of Comprehension Rules

Starting Point
Item 4

Reverse Criterion
Score of 0 or 1 on Item 4 or 5

Discontinue Criterion
After four consecutive scores of 0

Timing
None

Rules

- You may repeat a question, but it must be repeated verbatim.
- Items 5, 6, 7, 10, and 13 require two general concepts for a 2-point response; prompt for another response if only one general concept is given in the examinee's response.
- Query vague or incomplete responses.
- Do not explain the meaning of any words in the questions.

Behaviors to Note

- Observe whether unusually long verbal responses are an attempt to "cover up" for actually not knowing the correct response or because the examinee tends to be obsessive about details.
- Some of the comprehension questions have rather long verbal stimuli. Note whether inattention is affecting adults' responses to such items. For example, only part of the question may be answered.
- Note whether defensiveness is occurring in responses to some Comprehension items. For example, when asked about taxes, if the adult's response doesn't really answer the question and is something like "We shouldn't have to register our cars," this may be defensive responding.
- Note whether the adults require consistent prompting for a second response or whether they spontaneously provide enough information in their answer.
- Observe the adult's responses carefully to determine whether poor verbal ability is the cause of a low score or whether it is more the result of poor social judgment.
- Note how subjects respond to queries. Some may be threatened or frustrated with the constant interruption, and others may seem quite comfortable with the extra structure. Some people, when asked for

another reason, simply restate the first reason in different words or otherwise do not give a second "idea."

12. Symbol Search

Several materials are needed to administer this subtest: the administration manual, response booklet, stopwatch, and two pencils without erasers. The scoring template will be needed to score this subtest. The directions to Symbol Search are lengthy. It is important to read them verbatim but also to maintain rapport by not burying your head in the manual while reading the directions. Thus you should become very familiar with the directions. There are both sample and practice items, which are not timed. Sample items provide an explanation and demonstration of the task for examinees and practice items require the examinees to attempt items that are not part of the Symbol Search score. Examinees are given immediate feedback and correction on practice items. You are only to proceed with the task when the examinee clearly understands the directions and is able to successfully complete the practice items. As examinees are completing the task, you may find it necessary to remind them that they must complete the test items in order.

Rapid Reference 2.16 reviews start, reverse, discontinue, and timing rules. Following are lists of important Symbol Search rules and telling behaviors to watch for and note while administering this subtest.

Rules
- Do not proceed with the subtest unless the examinee clearly understands the task after the sample and practice items are administered.
- Read the directions verbatim (with a minimum of paraphrasing), but do not lose rapport with the examinee.
- During administration of the sample and practice items, point to the various symbols as you explain the directions (as is stated in the administration manual), which provides additional visual clarification of the task at hand.
- Consider a response incorrect if both yes and no are marked for the same item.
- A raw score is obtained by subtracting incorrect from correct responses.

2.16 Summary of Symbol Search Rules

Starting Point
Sample items

Reverse Criterion
No reverse

Discontinue Criterion
After 120 seconds

Timing
120 seconds

Behaviors to Note

- Note how the adult handles the pencil. Is there pressure? Is the pencil dropped? Does the examinee seem coordinated?
- Observe attention and concentration. Is the adult's focus consistent throughout the task, or does it wane as time goes on?
- Look to see whether adults check each row of symbols only once or if they go back and recheck the row of symbols in an item more than once. Obsessive concern with detail may be noted.
- Make note of the examinee's response style. Impulsivity and reflectivity are usually observable in this task.
- Consider whether the adult is utilizing visual memory well. Watch eye movements to determine whether the adult is moving back and forth several times between the Target and Search Groups before making a choice.
- As this subtest is one of the last administered, observe the adult for signs of fatigue or boredom.

13. Letter-Number Sequencing

The administration manual and the record form are the only materials needed to administer this subtest. Letter-Number Sequencing has five practice trials, all of which are to be administered. Even if an examinee fails all of the practice items, the subtest is to be continued. Some examinees will respond quickly and others more slowly, so you must be prepared to record quickly each response verbatim. In the directions, the examinee is asked to repeat the numbers in order first and then the letters in alphabetical order; however, the examinee will be given credit if the letters are said before the numbers, as long as they are in the correct sequence.

Rapid Reference 2.17 reviews the start, reverse, discontinue, and timing rules. Following are lists of important Letter-Number Sequencing rules and telling behaviors to watch for and note while administering this subtest.

Rules
- Administer all five practice items.
- Correct the examinee during all practice items.
- Say each combination at a rate of one number or letter per second.
- The examinee obtains credit if letters are said before numbers, as long as they are in the correct sequence.

Behaviors to Note
- Observe whether the examinee learns from errors made during the practice items. Examinees may also appear to learn from errors made within one item (i.e., miss the first trial, but get the second two correct).
- Note whether an adult responds by giving the numbers first and then the letters as requested or whether the opposite pattern is produced in responses.
- Anxiety, distractibility, and concentration may impact performance on this test. Observe any behaviors that may be indicative of such difficulties.
- Observe and note any strategies that may be used during this task. For example, a subject may keep track of numbers on one hand and letters on another. Rehearsal and "chunking" may be other strategies that are observed. An examinee who closes his or her eyes while the items are administered (and, perhaps, while responding) is probably using a visualization strategy.

≡ *Rapid Reference*

2.17 Summary of Letter-Number Sequencing Rules

Starting Point
Sample items

Reverse Criterion
No reverse

Discontinue Criterion
After scores of 0 on *all three trials* of an item

Timing
None

- Note whether there is a pattern in the errors such as missing only the letters but getting all of the numbers correct. This may be indicative of stimulus overload.
- Note errors that may be indicative of hearing difficulty, such as incorrectly repeating letters that only slightly differ from the stimuli (i.e., the letter *T* rather than *D*).

14. Object Assembly

This subtest requires the most juggling of materials. Five sets of puzzles, an Object Assembly layout shield, a stopwatch, the record form, and the administration manual are needed to administer the subtest. To facilitate administration, the directions are printed not only in the manual but also on the layout shield. Timing is critical on this subtest and begins when the last word of the directions is said. Be careful to stop timing when examinees are seemingly finished, even if they forget to say they are done. When examinees are working on the puzzles, sometimes pieces may be turned over; these should be unobtrusively turned right side up. Do not tell examinees what object they are trying to assemble, even if they ask or beg. Most often Item 5, the butterfly, elicits such questions, as its global shape tends to appear less discernible to examinees when it is in disarray. Carefully count the number of junctures completed correctly at the end of the time limit. Be sure to include in the score those segments of the object that are partially assembled but that may be separated from the figure as a whole.

Rapid Reference 2.18 reviews the start, reverse, discontine, and timing rules. Following are lists of important Object Assembly rules and telling behaviors to watch for and note while administering this subtest.

≡ Rapid Reference

2.18 Summary of Object Assembly Rules

Starting Point
Item 1

Reverse Criterion
No reverse

Discontinue Criterion
No discontinue rule

Timing
120 seconds for Items 1–2
180 seconds for Items 3–5

Rules
- Timing begins when the last word of the directions is said.
- If you allow the examinee to continue working beyond the time limit, you must note how many correct junctures were made when time expired.
- *All* Object Assembly items must be administered.
- Unobtrusively turn puzzle pieces face up if they get turned over.
- Do not name any of the puzzles for the examinee, even if requested.
- Correctly assemble the man puzzle by slowly putting the pieces together in front of the examinee if the examinee was unable to correctly assemble Item 1.

Behaviors to Note
- As on other performance subtests, observe how the adult handles the puzzle pieces. Motor coordination and hand preference may be noted on this test.
- Note the problem-solving approach (a trial-and-error method versus a systematic, planned approach), which can be discerned by observing the examinee's approach to the task.
- Note the speed at which the adult proceeds. Does the subject appear impulsive and careless, yet quick, or careful, slow, and methodical?
- Note whether the examinee appears to be rigid and inflexible in his or her consideration of what the object is. For example, someone who is convinced that the butterfly is an elephant may continue to try to turn one of the antennae into a leg or trunk.
- Note when the adult verbalizes what the object is but is unable to construct it correctly. This may be indicative of integration difficulties or problems with motor output.
- Observe and note behaviors indicative of obsessiveness with details on this test (as with Block Design). Some adults may spend unnecessary time trying to get each of the pieces perfectly aligned.

CAUTION

Common Pitfalls of Subtest Administration

1. Picture Completion
   - forgetting to provide the correct answer to Item 6 or 7 if examinee doesn't give correct response
   - giving the allowed queries too often
   - forgetting to time the Picture Completion items (20-second limit)

2. Vocabulary
   - not recording exact verbal responses
   - not querying vague responses appropriately
   - forgetting to use the stimulus booklet to allow adults to see the words they are defining

3. Digit Symbol-Coding
   - losing rapport with examinee by burying head in administration manual while reading long directions
   - forgetting to administer four rows when they are intending to administer incidental learning
   - not paying attention to examinee and allowing him or her to skip over items

   Digit Symbol Incidental Learning
   - exposing pairing items while presenting the Free Recall task
   - only administering one of the rows of Pairing items

   Digit Symbol-Copy
   - Neglecting to correct errors that are made during practice

4. Similarities
   - forgetting to give an example of a 2-point response if examinee's response to Item 6 is not perfect
   - overquerying or underquerying vague responses

5. Block Design
   - neglecting to make sure that the proper variety of block faces are showing before the item is begun
   - placing the model in an incorrect position
   - correcting block rotations more than one time during the subtest
   - remembering to use the reverse rule when adults earn 2 points on Design 5 (but score is 0 or 1 on Design 6)

6. Arithmetic
   - repeating the questions more than one time
   - stopping the stopwatch when a question is repeated
   - allowing paper and pencil to be used if asked

7. Matrix Reasoning
   - not continuing on to Item 4 if sample items are incorrect
   - giving feedback on items beyond the sample
   - allowing the examinee to guess randomly

8. Digit Span
   - reading the sequence of digits too quickly
   - inadvertently "chunking" the numbers as they are read
   - giving extra help on Digits Backward
   - forgetting to administer Digits Backward to adults who score 0 on Digits Forward

9. Information
   - defining words if asked by the examinee
   - forgetting to give required prompts (e.g., "What scale?") to an incomplete answer
   - being unaware that it is permissible to give neutral queries (e.g., "Tell me more") to Information responses that are incomplete or ambiguous (queries are not limited to responses on Similarities, Comprehension, and Vocabulary)

10. Picture Arrangement
   - placing the cards in front of the examinee in the wrong order
   - neglecting to ask where the story begins if adult lays out pictures from right to left
   - burying head in administration manual while reading directions
   - asking the adult to explain what is happening in his or her story *during* the administration of the subtest (such verbal explanations can only be requested after the entire subtest has been completed)

11. Comprehension
   - forgetting to query for a second response (Items 5, 6, 7, 10, and 13) if necessary
   - explaining the meaning of a word if asked (no explanations of definitions are allowed to be given)
   - neglecting to write down the exact verbal response

continued

12. Symbol Search

- proceeding with the task before the examinee clearly understands what is required
- burying head in manual while reading directions

13. Letter-Number Sequencing

- reading items too slowly or too quickly
- neglecting to correct examinee on any missed practice item
- counting a response as an error if the letters are read in sequence before the numbers

14. Object Assembly

- administering fewer than five Object Assembly puzzles
- neglecting to turn over puzzle pieces if they are not faceup
- forgetting to count how many junctures were correctly completed at the time limit when allowing someone to work beyond the time limit
- incorrectly counting the number of completed junctures

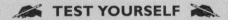

✒ TEST YOURSELF ✒

1. **What materials not included in the WAIS-III kit should the examiner be prepared to bring?**

2. **The examiner must memorize all directions to be able to appropriately administer the test.** True or False?

3. **In establishing rapport with the examinee, you may tell him or her**

   (a) "You got that answer correct, nice work."

   (b) "Most test takers find some questions easy and some questions quite difficult."

   (c) "We won't be able to complete the test unless you refrain from using the rest room during the evaluation."

   (d) "That wasn't quite right; let's do another one."

4. **If you find you need to adapt the test to accommodate an individual with special needs, it is better not to administer the test altogether.** True or False?

5. **List some modifications that may be made in the test administration procedures to accommodate individuals with special needs.**

_____

_____

6. **Which of these subtests do _not_ use a reverse rule?**

(a) Picture Completion

(b) Vocabulary

(c) Digit Symbol-Coding

(d) Similarities

(e) Block Design

(f) Arithmetic

(g) Matrix Reasoning

(h) Digit Span

(i) Information

(j) Picture Arrangement

(k) Comprehension

(l) Symbol Search

(m) Letter-Number Sequencing

(n) Object Assembly

7. **When applying the reverse rule, you must**

(a) go back to Item 1 and administer all items sequentially until you get to where you started.

(b) go back to administer items until one earlier item is correct.

(c) go back to administer items until two consecutive items are correct, not including the item with which you initially started.

(d) go back to administer items until two consecutive items are correct, including the item with which you initially started.

8. **The only subtest in which all items must be administered is**

_____

9. **If you are administering a subtest with subjective scoring and are unsure of what score an examinee's response should get, it is best to take a few minutes to carefully review that item's scoring rules and tell the examinee to wait quietly.** True or False?

10. **To preserve the balance of maintaining rapport and getting necessary clinical information, it is best to**

(a) record only the examinee's score if it can save some time and quicken the pace of the evaluation.

(b) record examinee's responses verbatim, but use abbreviations when possible.

(c) record only incorrect responses to analyze clinically.

(d) tell the examinee to wait just a few minutes while you very carefully write down every single word he or she says.

continued

11. Which subtests require the use of a stopwatch?

(a) Picture Completion

(h) Digit Span

(b) Vocabulary

(i) Information

(c) Digit Symbol-Coding

(j) Picture Arrangement

(d) Similarities

(k) Comprehension

(e) Block Design

(l) Symbol Search

(f) Arithmetic

(m) Letter-Number Sequencing

(g) Matrix Reasoning

(n) Object Assembly

12. Give examples of queries that you may use to obtain more information about a vague, ambiguous, or incomplete response.

_____

13. You may repeat questions or instructions only on Verbal subtests and never on Performance subtests. True or False?

14. What must you allow the examinee to do if you plan on administering Digit Symbol-Incidental Learning?

_____

Thought Questions

1. Why was it wise for the test developers to include sample items and allow teaching the task on the first two items?

_____

_____

2. What are some of the benefits and weaknesses of using a standardized instrument?

_____

_____

3. What may cause a disruption in the rapport between examiner and examinee, and what might you do to preserve it?

_____

_____

4. What areas of administration are likely to cause the most difficulty for novice examiners?

_____

_____

Test Yourself Answers: 1. Two No. 2 pencils without erasers, stopwatch, clipboard, extra paper, and writing utensils; 2. False; 3. b; 4. False; 5. Administering the test in American Sign Language, adding printed words, administering only one scale, eliminating time limits, extending the testing over more than one session; 6. c, h, j, l, m, n; 7. d; 8. Object Assembly; 9. False; 10. b; 11. a, c, e, f, j, l, n; 12. "Tell me more about that"; "Explain what you mean"; 13. False; 14. Complete the first four rows of items.

Thought Questions Answers:

1. Allowing examiners to teach the task ensures that the examinee understands the task; therefore allowing the examiner to determine when the examinee does not know the answer as opposed to when he or she does not understand the task.

2. Benefits of standardized instruments include being able to compare an individual to a similar group of people to gain an understanding of how he or she functions. You can obtain standardized scores, which is a common metric that is readily compared across many measures. A disadvantage of standardized instruments is that the normative sample may not always be appropriate to compare a particular individual to (i.e., if the ethnic background is very dissimilar to the normative group). Another disadvantage is that when you are testing patients with special needs, the standardized instruments do not offer flexibility in their procedures, which are often needed with these groups. Not all standardized tests offer good reliability and validity, so the values obtained from these tests may not offer totally valuable information.

3. If the examinee is terribly shy, rapport may be difficult to establish. More time may be needed prior to beginning testing to develop a relationship with the examinee. If the examinee is terribly frustrated with a particular subtest, he or she may become disinterested in the testing. The examiner may need to give the examinee extra encouragement or a break before continuing testing. If the examinee has a variable attention span, then rapport may be disrupted as well. The examiner may have to be extra vigilant in keeping the subject on track and offer more frequent breaks, or extend the testing over more than one day.

4. Novice examiners are likely to have difficulty with scoring subjective subtests, such as Vocabulary, Similarities, and Comprehension. Difficulty with utilizing multiple testing materials during the Performance subtests, while accurately recording the time with the stopwatch, is also problematic for novices. Subtests that have very lengthy directions such as Digit Symbol-Coding and Symbol Search can often cause problems to those that are new to the WAIS-III.

Three

HOW TO SCORE THE WAIS-III

TYPES OF SCORES

The WAIS-III provides three types of scores: raw scores, scaled scores, and IQs or indexes. The raw score is the first obtained and is simply the sum of points earned on a subtest. The raw score alone is meaningless, as it is not norm referenced. To interpret an examinee's performance, you must translate the raw scores into standard scores (either scaled scores or IQs/factor indexes). Rapid Reference 3.1 lists the metrics for various types of standard scores. The subtest scaled scores have a mean of 10 and a standard deviation of 3 (ranging from 1 to 19 for most subtests). The IQs and factor indexes have a mean of 100 and a standard deviation of 15 (ranging from about 45 to 155 for IQs and from about 50 to 150 for indexes).

Most individuals earn scores on the WAIS-III that are within 1 standard deviation from the mean. Specifically, about two thirds of the examinees earn IQs or indexes between 85 and 115. The number of examinees whose scores are 2 standard deviations from the mean (from 70 to 130) jumps up to about 95%. A very small number of examinees earn scores that are higher than 130 (about 2.2%) or lower than 70 (also about 2.2%). For the subtest scaled scores, corresponding values are as follows: about two thirds score between 7 and 13, and about 95% score between 4 and 16; the extreme 2.2% in each "tail" earn scaled scores of 1 to 3 (very low functioning) and 17 to 19 (very high functioning).

STEP-BY-STEP: HOW THE WAIS-III IS SCORED

Raw Scores

The first step in the process of scoring is obtaining raw scores for each of the administered subtests. Much of the scoring for this test is straight-

60

≋Rapid Reference

3.1 Metrics for Standard Scores

Type of Standard Score	Mean	Standard Deviation	Range of Values
Scaled score	10	3	1–19
IQ	100	15	45–155
Index	100	15	50–150

forward and lacking ambiguity, but there are a few subtests (mainly on the Verbal Scale) in which subjectivity presents constant thorns to the examiner during the scoring process. Later in this chapter we review some suggestions on how to properly score the more "tricky" types of responses. For the most part, all that is necessary to calculate the subtests' raw scores is careful addition.

CAUTION

Common Errors in Raw Score Calculation

- neglecting to add points earned from the first few items that weren't administered to the total raw score
- neglecting to add the points recorded on one page of the record form with the points recorded on the next (i.e., Vocabulary lists the first 7 questions on one page and the last 26 on the next, and Information lists the first 14 questions on the first page and the last 14 on the next)
- forgetting to subtract the number of incorrect responses from correct responses on Symbol search
- neglecting to multiply the number of correct junctures by the designated number on Object Assembly
- transferring total raw scores incorrectly from inside the record form to score conversion page of record form
- miscalculating the raw score sum via an addition mistake
- including points earned on items that were presented after the discontinue criterion was met

Scaled Scores

To determine an examinee's scaled scores, you will need: (a) the individual's chronological age, (b) his or her subtest raw scores from the record form, and (c) Tables A.1 and A.2 from the *WAIS-III Administration and Scoring Manual* (Wechsler, 1997). The steps to convert raw scores into scaled scores are listed in Rapid Reference 3.2.

The WAIS-R calculated IQ scores for all adults and adolescents using a "reference group" of individuals between the ages of 20 and 34. The WAIS-III now compares each individual's scores with that of an equivalent age group. However, the WAIS-III administration manual still enables examiners to compare an adolescent or adult's scores with that of the 20-to-34-year-old reference group, which may be useful if comparing old scores from a WAIS-R.

The tables used to obtain the scaled scores are user-friendly and easy to find in the tabled format of the WAIS-III administration manual. Examiners commonly make errors when rushed to look up scores or when they don't take the time to double-check their work.

≡ *Rapid Reference*

3.2 Converting Raw Scores to Scaled Scores

1. Transfer the total raw scores from the bottom right corner of each subtest on the record form to the appropriate spot on the score conversion page.

2. For each subtest find the scaled score equivalent to the obtained raw score. These scores should be obtained by looking in Table A.1 of the *WAIS-III Administration and Scoring Manual,* on the page that lists the examinee's age.

3. Record each subtest's scaled score under all of the possible columns on the record form (Verbal, Performance, Verbal Comprehension, Perceptual Organization, Working Memory, and Processing Speed).

4. *Optional Step:* If you wish to compare scores with the reference group, scores may be obtained from Table A.2 of the *WAIS-III Administration and Scoring Manual* and are recorded in the right-hand column of the score conversion page.

IQs and Factor Indexes

Once the scaled scores have been obtained you are ready to find the IQs and factor indexes. Care should be taken in the following steps to ensure that calculation errors are not made.

Converting Scaled Scores to IQ/Index

1. Calculate the sum of the appropriate subtests' scaled scores for the Verbal and Performance IQs and the four indexes (see Figure 3.7 in the *WAIS-III Administration and Scoring Manual*). Note: Symbol Search, Letter-Number Sequencing, and Object Assembly are not used in the sums of scaled scores for the Verbal IQ and Performance IQ, *unless* they are replacing another subtest.

2. Record the sums of the scaled scores on the bottom row of the respective column for each of the IQs and indexes on the score conversion page. Rapid Reference 3.3 shows which subtests comprise each IQ scale and factor index.

3. The Full Scale score is calculated by adding the sum of verbal scaled scores and sum of performance scaled scores.

4. Copy the sums of scaled scores to the profile page of the record form, where it is labeled sums of scaled scores.

5. For each scale, determine the appropriate IQ and index based on the sum of scaled scores (see Tables A.3 to A.9 of the *WAIS-III Administration and Scoring Manual*).

6. In addition, record the percentiles and confidence intervals for each of the scales, which are also found in Tables A.3 to A.9 of the *WAIS-III Administration and Scoring Manual*.

CAUTION

Common Errors in Obtaining Scaled Scores

- miscalculating a sum when adding scores to obtain the raw score or the sum of scaled scores

- writing illegibly, leading to errors

- using a score conversion table that references the wrong age group

- misreading across the rows of the score conversion tables

≋ Rapid Reference

3.3 Subtests Comprising WAIS-III IQs and Index Scores

Subtest	IQ Scale		Factor Index	
Vocabulary	V-IQ	VCI		
Similarities	V-IQ	VCI		
Information	V-IQ	VCI		
Comprehension	V-IQ			
Arithmetic	V-IQ		WMI	
Digit Span	V-IQ		WMI	
Letter-Number Sequencing[a]			WMI	
Picture Arrangement	P-IQ			
Picture Completion	P-IQ	POI		
Block Design	P-IQ	POI		
Matrix Reasoning	P-IQ	POI		
Digit Symbol-Coding	P-IQ			PSI
Symbol Search[a]				PSI
Object Assembly[a]				

Note. V-IQ = Verbal IQ; P-IQ = Performance IQ; VCI = Verbal Comprehension Index; POI = Perceptual Organization Index; WMI = Working Memory Index; PSI = Processing Speed Index.

[a] The Letter-Number Sequencing, Symbol Search, and Object Assembly subtests can substitute for other subtests under certain circumstances (see The Psychological Corporation, 1997).

Prorating and Scoring Options

Options are available for calculating the IQs if not all 14 subtests were administered or if some of the subtests were spoiled during the administration. First, some of the subtests may be replaced by others to calculate the IQs. If a score for Digit Span is not available, Letter-Number Sequencing can replace it. Likewise, a score for Symbol Search may serve as a substitute for Digit Symbol-Coding if a score for the latter is not available. Also, Object Assembly may be substituted for any of the regularly administered Performance

Scale subtests. However, for individuals aged 75 or older, Object Assembly may not be subtituted for other Performance subtests because of the low reliability at the higher age ranges.

The choice to substitute one subtest for another is not one that can be randomly made. You certainly would not want to substitute one subtest for another because a client performed better (or worse) on one or the other. The decision to substitute one subtest for another must be based on solid reasons. For example, if Digit Span were spoiled because of distracting noises that were present during the administration, then this would be a valid reason to substitute Letter-Number Sequencing. An a priori decision to substitute Symbol Search for Digit Symbol-Coding may be made if examinees' fine motor control is so poor that it would be unreasonable for them to draw small symbols, but they could write simple slashes through the Symbol Search responses. Object Assembly could be substituted for another Performance subtest, like Picture Completion, for example, if it were clear that the examinee was not able to produce verbal responses because of poor language ability. In this case, a decision may be made ahead of time to utilize Object Assembly in the Performance IQ score because it minimizes the effect of the expression of English language.

Prorating scores becomes necessary when only five Verbal subtests are available or when only four of the Performance subtests are available. In the prorating process, an estimated sum of the Verbal or Performance Scale is used to derive the IQ score. The Full Scale IQ and factor indexes should never be prorated. The Full Scale IQ, however, can be computed after the Verbal and/or Performance Scales have been prorated.

DON'T FORGET

Replacing Certain Subtests

Original Subtest	↔	Replacement Subtest
Digit Span	↔	Letter-Number Sequencing
Digit Symbol-Coding	↔	Symbol Search
Regular Performance Subtest	↔	Object Assembly (not age 75+)

CAUTION

Prorating Considerations

- The Full Scale IQ score is *never* prorated.
- Index scores should *never* be prorated because of the small number of subtests that contribute to each index.
- Verbal scale sum of 5 scaled scores is multiplied by 1.2, whereas the sum of scaled scores of 4 Performance subtests is multiplied by 1.25.

The process of prorating can be easily undertaken by utilizing Table A.10 in the *WAIS-III Administration and Scoring Manual*. Simply determine the prorated score by referencing the sum of the four or five subtests administered. If you would like to determine the prorated score manually, you may do so by using a simple formula. On the Verbal Scale, you multiply the sum of the scaled scores by 1.2 and round to the nearest whole number, which is then your prorated score. The sum of the Performance subtests is multiplied by 1.25 and rounded to the nearest whole number to get the prorated Performance score. It is important to always indicate on the record form when a score has been prorated. You may do so by using the abbreviation *PRO*.

Scoring Subtests Requiring Judgment

Four of the Verbal subtests require some level of judgment in their scoring due to the nature of examinees' highly variable verbal responses. Most often Vocabulary, Similarities, and Comprehension require such judgment, but some responses to Information questions can also require prudence in scoring. For each of these four Verbal subtests, the *WAIS-III Administration and Scoring Manual* provides sample responses in addition to scoring criteria. Because it is impossible to list every possible answer that an examinee may state, the administration manual must be used only as a guide; it is up to each examiner to interpret the scoring system for each of the unique responses.

Often Verbal responses seem to fall in a borderline area, fitting neither a 1- or 2-point response clearly. Indeed, some answers seem to be perfect 1½-point responses! Because of this commonplace occurrence of variable verbal responses, it is important to be familiar with both the specific scoring examples and the general scoring criteria given for these Verbal subtests. In general, the examinee's ability to properly express him or herself should not be included in the scoring of a response. For example, if poor grammar or improper pronunciation is used, an examinee should not be penalized. The content of what is said is what is most important. For example, if the response to a Vocabulary item such as *belittle* was "maked seemed not as important," it would earn full credit even though it contains poor grammar.

Some adults or adolescents may spontaneously give long responses that actually contain two or more responses in one. Examinees may also elaborate responses after being queried. When such elaboration occurs, a fundamental misconception about the item may be apparent in the response. This is termed a spoiled response, and the item is then scored 0 points. For example, if a response to a Similarities item ("In what way are an hour and a week alike?") is "Time," the examiner should then query the response with the letter *Q* in a parenthetical notation. If the examinee elaborates by saying "Weeks are on a calendar and hours are on my watch," the response should be considered spoiled. Although the original response, "Time," fell under the 1-point category, the examinee's elaboration clearly showed a misconception of how the two were *alike*. Therefore the entire response is scored 0 because of spoilage.

Another case of elaboration or multiple responses to a Verbal subtest item may occur when an adult gives a series of responses in which the *second* or *third* response is intended to be the actual response. If this is the case, the *final* answer should be scored. However, if multiple responses are given—some incorrect and some correct—but it is unclear which answer is the final answer, the examinee should be asked to clarify the intended final response. Then whichever answer is indicated to be the designated final answer should be the only response scored. Subtle cues in adults' responses must be used to determine which response is intended as the actual response. Usually, if a string of responses is given with the last phrase being the intended response, examinees will accentuate the last response by dropping their voice at the end of the last word or giving a nonverbal nod of the head. Other adults will give many responses, all equally accentuated and all separated by equal pauses, which tends to lead to a lack of clarity about which response was the intended final response. A helpful, but not leading, manner in which to prompt the examinee is by saying, "You said _____, _____, and _____. Which one was your answer?"

≡ Rapid Reference

3.4 Vocabulary Scoring Rules

2 Points

- shows a good understanding of the word
- expresses good synonym
- expresses major use
- expresses one or more definitive features of an object
- expresses general classification to which the word belongs
- expresses correct figurative use of the word
- indicates understanding of the word despite several less definitive but correct descriptive features
- for verbs, expresses a definitive example of action or a causal relation

1 Point

- shows poverty of content
- expresses a vague or less pertinent synonym
- expresses a minor use, not elaborated
- expresses an attribute that is correct but neither definitive nor a distinguishing feature
- expresses an example using the word itself, not elaborated
- expresses a concrete instance of the word, not elaborated
- expresses a correct definition of a related form of the word

0 Points

- expresses obviously wrong responses
- expresses verbalizations that show no real understanding even after inquiry
- offers not totally incorrect responses, but ones that even after questioning are vague or trivial or show a great poverty of content

Note. From the Administration and Scoring Manual of the Wechsler Adult Intelligence Scale: Third Edition. Copyright © 1997 The Psychological Corporation. Adapted and reproduced by permission. All rights reserved.

≡ Rapid Reference

3.5 Similarities Scoring Rules

2 Points

- expresses a general classification of the pair
- expresses a universal property of the pair
- expresses a concept pertinent to both members of the pair

I Point

- expresses a specific property common to both
- expresses a function that is common to the pair
- expresses a relative similarity between the two
- expresses less pertinent but correct general classifications

0 Points

- expresses specific properties of each member of the pair
- expresses generalizations that are incorrect
- expresses generalizations that are not pertinent
- expresses differences between members of the pair
- expresses clearly wrong responses

Note. From the Administration and Scoring Manual of the Wechsler Adult Intelligence Scale: Third Edition. Copyright © 1997 The Psychological Corporation. Adapted and reproduced by permission. All rights reserved.

On other occasions, many responses may be given that vary greatly in their quality. For example, 0-, 1-, and 2-point responses may occur in one long answer. If this case occurs, and no spoiled responses are present, then simply score the best response.

General Scoring Criteria for Verbal Subtests

Vocabulary, Similarities, and Comprehension all include a set of general scoring criteria, along with the specific examples listed in the administration manual. The fine points of each of the scoring guidelines are highlighted in Rapid References 3.5 and 3.6.

Rapid Reference

3.6 Comprehension Scoring Rules

2 Points

- expresses the 2-point general concept indicated in the administration manual
- expresses two general responses on Items 5, 6, 7, 10, and 13

1 Point

- expresses the 1-point general concept indicated in the administration manual

0 Points

- in general, expresses vague, trivial responses or does not address the question

Note. From the Administration and Scoring Manual of the Wechsler Adult Intelligence Scale: Third Edition. Copyright © 1997 The Psychological Corporation. Adapted and reproduced by permission. All rights reserved.

Subtest by Subtest Scoring Keys

Some subtests require 0- and 1-point scoring and others require 0-, 1-, and 2-point scoring. The overall scoring rules are consistent throughout the WAIS-III, but there are also subtle nuances of which the examiner should be aware. The following section includes important keys to remember for scoring each subtest.

Computer Scoring Procedures

A computerized WAIS-III "scoring assistant" for IBM and Macintosh computers is available from The Psychological Corporation. The Scoring Assistant for the Wechsler Scales for Adults (SAWS-A) creates a summary of results from the WAIS-III profile, including IQs, index scores, scaled scores, percentile ranks, and corresponding graphs. SAWS-A also calculates IQ and index differences as well as differences between the individual's mean scaled score and individual subtests. In addition, it calculates the cumulative percentage of individuals obtaining certain Digits Forward versus Digits Backward discrepancies, and the cumulative percentage of individuals scoring at certain levels on the optional Digit Symbol procedures. The benefit of using a computerized scoring program is that it reduces scoring time and examiner error, as it eliminates the need to look up scores in multiple tables. SAWS-A requires the examiner to obtain raw scores and enter those raw scores into the computer. These raw scores are then automatically converted into the appropriate scaled scores and graphs using the subject's biographical data that were entered.

DON'T FORGET

Scoring Keys

Subtest	Range of Item Scores	Scoring Pointers
1. Picture Completion	0–1	• Score 0 if examinee responds after 20 seconds.
		• If examinee points to the correct place but gives an incorrect verbal response, score 0.
		• If examinee offers correct description using a synonym or his or her own words, score 1.
		• Add 1 point to the raw score for each of the unadministered reversal items.
2. Vocabulary	0–2	• Utilize the general 0–2 point scoring criteria and specific examples.
		• Slang or regionalisms not in the dictionary are scored 0.
		• Any meaning found in a standard dictionary is scored correct.
		• Poor grammar is not penalized in scoring.
		• Add 1 point to the raw score for each of the unadministered reversal items.
3. Digit Symbol-Coding	0–133	• Use the Digit Symbol scoring template to check the examinee's responses.
		• One point is given for each correctly drawn symbol (completed within 120 seconds).
		• Spontaneous correct of an incorrect symbol is scored 1.
		• A response that is imperfect but is a clearly identifiable symbol is scored 1.

continued

Digit Symbol- Incidental Learning	0–18 (Pairing)	• Pairing items are given 1-point credit for each correctly drawn symbol.
	0–9 (Free Recall)	• Free Recall items are given 1-point credit for each correctly drawn symbol. • No bonus points are awarded for writing a symbol more than one time.
Digit Symbol- Copy	0–133	• Use the Digit Symbol scoring template to check the examinee's responses. • Sample items (7) are not included in the score. • One point is awarded for each correctly drawn symbol. • If an item is completed out of sequence, credit is *not* given for that item. • Imperfectly drawn symbols are given credit as long as they are identifiable as the target symbol. • Credit is given for spontaneous correc- tion of imperfectly drawn symbols.
4. Similarities	0–1 (Items 1–5) 0–2 (Items 6–19)	• Utilize the general 0- to 2-point scoring criteria and specific examples. • Score spontaneous improvement in responses. • Degree of abstraction is key in assigning credit to responses. • Add 1 point to the raw score for each of the unadministered reversal items.
5. Block Design	0–1 (Items 1–6) 0–7 (Items 7–14)	• For Designs 1 to 6, successful completion on the first trial earns 2 points. • For Designs 1 to 6, successful completion on the second trial earns 1 point. • If Designs 1 to 4 are not administered, then award 2 points for each of those items. • Designs completed correctly *after* the al- lowed time limit has expired are scored 0. • For Designs 7 to 14, points ranging from 4 to 7 are awarded on the basis of com- pletion time. • Partially correct responses are scored 0.

6. Arithmetic	0–1 (Items 1–18) 0–2 (Items 19–20)	• If subject gets the numeric value correct, but gives the wrong scale (e.g., dollars rather than cents), the answer is scored 0. • Problems completed correctly *after* the allowed time limit has expired are scored 0. • Add 1 point to the raw score for each of the unadministered reversal items.
7. Matrix Reasoning	0–1	• Do not add score from Sample Items A to C into calculation of the raw score. • Add 1 point to the raw score for each of the unadministered reversal items. • Examinees are not penalized due to speediness of responding. • The correct answers are displayed in **bold** font on the record form.
8. Digit Span	0–2	• Exact correct repetition is given 1 point per trial (2 points per item possible). • Self-corrections are given credit. • The raw scores from Digits Forward and Digits Backward are combined to create the Digit Span raw score.
9. Information	0–1	• The list of possible responses in the manual is not exhaustive. Give credit for any response that is of the same caliber as the samples. • Add 1 point to the raw score for each of the unadministered reversal items.
10. Picture Arrangement	0–2 (Item 1) 0 or 2 (Items 2–4) 0–2 (Items 5–8) 0 or 2 (Items 9–10)	• Designs completed correctly *after* the allowed time limit has expired are scored 0. • No extra credit (bonus point) is awarded for speedy performance. • Items 5 to 9 each have one alternative acceptable response order that is awarded 1 point. • Only one acceptable response is permitted for Items 1 to 4 and 10 to 11.

continued

11. Comprehension	0–1 (Items 1–3) 0–2 (Items 4–18)	• Utilize the general 0- to 2-point scoring criteria and specific examples. • The scoring guide is not all-inclusive and must be used only as a guide. • Score spontaneous improvement in responses. • Degree of understanding expressed by the examinee is scored. • For responses that require two general concepts, only 1 point is earned if both ideas stated by the examinee are included in the same general concept. • Add 1 point to the raw score for each of the unadministered reversal items.
12. Symbol Search	0–60	• Use the Symbol Search scoring template to score responses. • If both "yes" and "no" are marked for the same item, the response is incorrect. • The Symbol Search total raw score is calculated by subtracting the number incorrect from the number correct. • Any items left blank are not included in the score computation. • Any item completed after the 120 seconds time limit should not be counted in the score calculation.
13. Letter-Number Sequencing	0–3 (0 = fail all trials; 1 = pass one trial; 2 = pass two trials; 3 = pass all three trials)	• If a letter or number is omitted in the response, it is incorrect. • Credit is given if letters are given in the correct sequence and then numbers in the correct sequence. • Each of the three trials in an item are worth 1 point. • Practice items are not included in the raw score.
14. Object Assembly	0–8 (Item 1)	• The number of correct junctures (where two adjacent pieces join) must be counted first.

0–12 (Item 2)	• Credit is given for a juncture even if it is separate from the rest of the puzzle.
0–11 (Items 3 and 5)	• If the object is perfectly assembled, bonus points may be awarded on the basis of completion time.
0–10 (Item 4)	• If the object is partially assembled within the time limit, multiply the number of correct junctures by 1 (except for Item 4, which is multiplied by 0.5).
	• No bonus points may be awarded for partial assemblies.

DON'T FORGET

Hardware Requirements for the Scoring Assistant for the Wechsler Scales for Adults

Windows Version

- PC with 486 processor or higher and 8 MB of RAM
- Windows version 3.1 or later, Mirosoft MS DOS version 5.1 or later
- hard disk with at least 10 MB of free disk space
- high-density 3.5 (1.44 MB) disk drive

Macintosh Version

- System 7.1 or later (supports System 7.5 and is accelerated for the Power Macintosh)
- 12-inch screen monitor (640 x 480 pixels) or larger as well as support for PowerBook screen sizes
- 8 MB of RAM (16 MB of RAM on a Power Macintosh)
- hard disk with at least 5 MB of free disk space
- high-density 3.5 (1.44 MB) disk drive

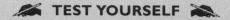 **TEST YOURSELF**

1. **Like the WAIS-R, the WAIS-III scaled scores are determined by comparing an individual's performance with that of the reference group of ages 20 to 34.** True or False?

2. **Unless replacing another subtest, none of the following subtests are used in the calculation of the Verbal IQ or Performance IQ except**
   (a) Letter-Number Sequencing.
   (b) Symbol Search.
   (c) Digit Span.
   (d) Object Assembly.

3. **If Digit Span is a spoiled subtest, which of the following subtests can replace it?**
   (a) Letter-Number Sequencing
   (b) Symbol Search
   (c) Digit Span
   (d) Object Assembly

4. **Beyond what age should Object Assembly no longer be substituted for other Performance subtests?**
   (a) age 54
   (b) age 64
   (c) age 74
   (d) age 84

5. **Which of the following scales are safe to prorate?**
   (a) Full Scale IQ
   (b) Verbal IQ
   (c) Verbal Comprehension Index
   (d) Processing Speed Index

Answers: 1. False; 2. c; 3. a; 4. c; 5. b

Four

HOW TO INTERPRET THE WAIS-III

The process of interpreting a complex measure like the WAIS-III may seem a daunting task when first glancing at the multiple scores that are provided on the record form. There are three IQs and four factor indexes, and each of these scores has corresponding confidence intervals and percentile ranks. In addition, there are seven subtest scaled scores for the Verbal Scale and seven subtest scaled scores for the Performance Scale, each of which also has a corresponding percentile rank. Some subtests even have supplemental scores that can be obtained, such as the cumulative percentage rankings for three Digit Symbol-Coding optional procedures and values for the longest forward and longest backward spans on Digit Span. Taken together, there are more than 50 values to examine and interpret. The goal of this chapter is to help examiners organize these diverse scores in systematic ways, thereby permitting insightful interpretation of a person's WAIS-III profile. This chapter first provides an analysis of each individual subtest, then a framework for step-by-step interpretation of the different "levels" of scores (IQs, factor indexes, scaled scores). Integration of the test scores with each other, and with background and behavioral variables, is the ultimate aim of this chapter.

The general data given about each subtest provide clinical and empirical information that helps to understand each task's unique contribution to the WAIS-III, cognitively, behaviorally, and clinically. However, it is important to keep in mind that the step-by-step fashion of interpretation outlined in this chapter provides a way to test hypotheses that characterize an adolescent or adult's abilities represented in multiple subtests. It is the overlapping, or shared, abilities demonstrated by performance across several subtests that are invaluable in understanding an adult's strong and weak areas of functioning. Looking at individual subtest scores in isolation does not lead to meaningful conclusions about someone's cognitive abilities. Thus, to glean the most valuable information from the WAIS-III, it is necessary to examine the abilities "shared" by many subtests rather than attending only to unique skills tapped by a single subtest.

ANALYSIS OF EACH SUBTEST

The 14 subtests are analyzed in three different categories: empirical, cognitive, and clinical. The empirical analysis category includes reliability, general intelligence, or g, loadings, and subtest specificity. The cognitive analysis summarizes cognitive abilities that each subtest is believed to measure. Finally, the clinical analysis presents factors to consider about each subtest from a clinical perspective.

Empirical Analysis

The empirical analysis of each subtest contains a brief look at reliability and stability coefficients presented in the *WAIS-III and WMS-III Technical Manual* (The Psychological Corporation, 1997), the subtest's g loadings, and the subtest specificities. These data were obtained from the total standardization sample of 2,450 adults aged 16 to 89. However, important differences based on chronological age are noted.

Loadings on the General Factor
General intelligence, or general mental ability (Spearman, 1927), is denoted by *g*. The measurement of *g* may be done by several methods. We report on the loadings on the unrotated first factor in principal components analysis. Factor loadings of .70 or greater are considered "good" measures of *g*, loadings of .50 to .69 are deemed "fair" *g* loadings, and loadings below .50 are usually considered poor. Rapid Reference 4.1 contains data on how well each subtest loads on the *g* factor.

Similar to what has been reported on the WISC-III (Kaufman, 1994), the Verbal Scale tends to hold the best measures of *g*. However, of the Performance subtests, Matrix Reasoning and Block Design also show relatively strong loadings on the general factor. The weakest measures of *g* on the WAIS-III include Digit Span, Digit Symbol-Coding, Object Assembly,

≡ Rapid Reference

4.1 WAIS-III Subtests as Measures of General Ability (g)

Good Measures of g		Fair Measures of g	
Vocabulary	(.83)	Picture Arrangement	(.66)
Similarities	(.79)	Letter-Number Sequencing	(.65)
Information	(.79)	Picture Completion	(.64)
Comprehension	(.77)	Object Assembly	(.62)
Arithmetic	(.75)	Digit Symbol-Coding	(.59)
Block Design	(.72)	Digit Span	(.57)
Matrix Reasoning	(.72)		
Symbol Search	(.70)		

Note. g loading in parentheses. Source: Adapted from Sattler and Ryan (1998).

and Picture Completion, but all of these still are categorized as "fair" g loadings.

The concept of a general intelligence is one whose usefulness has been debated in the intelligence literature. A subtest with a strong g loading should not be interpreted as one that is *the* representation of an individual's overall level of cognitive ability. Rather, as is discussed in the balance of this chapter, there are diverse cognitive abilities represented by an IQ test, all of which need to be understood. The g loadings do represent how well psychometrically the subtests "hang together" as a whole, but they do not provide a theoretical construct that underlies human intellect.

Specificity of Subtests

Each subtest has a proportion of variance that is unique only to it. This uniqueness is somewhat like the inverse of g, as it is a representation of the variance that is not shared with other subtests. Subtest specificity is important to know to determine how feasible it is to interpret the unique abilities or traits attributed to a subtest. It is justifiable to interpret a subtest's unique contributions to the overall test if its unique variance exceeds the error variance and is sufficient in magnitude. About 25% or more of the total variance is

≡ Rapid Reference

4.2 WAIS-III Subtests Categorized by Their Specificity

Ample Specificity	Adequate Specificity	Inadequate Specificity
Digit Span (.50/.10)	Picture Arrangement (.31/.26)	Symbol Search (.21/.23)
Matrix Reasoning (.39/.10)	Block Design (.27/.14)	Object Assembly (.24/.30)
Digit Symbol-Coding (.38/.16)	Information (.23/.09)	
Picture Completion (.35/.17)	Comprehension (.20/.16)	
Letter-Number Sequencing (.34/.18)	Similarities (.20/.14)	
Arithmetic (.30/.12)	Vocabulary (.19/.07)	

Note. Reliable unique variance is the first value in parentheses; subtest error variance follows. Thanks are due Mr. Jason C. Cole for assisting with these computations.

generally considered a sufficient amount to warrant "specific" interpretation, so long as the specific variance exceeds the error variance.

The specificity for each subtest was statistically calculated via an uncomplicated technique. The shared variance for each subtest was obtained (we used the squared multiple correlation), and then this common variance was subtracted from the subtest's reliability coefficient. The result of this calculation is the reliable unique variance (subtest specificity). To determine whether a task's uniqueness should be interpreted, the error variance for the subtest (one minus the reliability) was then compared with the specificity.

The levels of specificity are classified as "ample," "adequate," or "inadequate" in Rapid Reference 4.2. Two values are listed for each subtest: First is the subtest specificity and second is the subtest's error variance. The subtests having the most ample amount of specificity include Digit Span, Matrix Reasoning, Digit Symbol-Coding, and Picture Completion. This information on specificity indicates that most subtests have reliable and interpretable unique characteristics. However, interpretations of unique abilities should not always be made (see the Step by Step: How to Interpret the WAIS-III Profile section on pages 111–146).

Abilities Shared With Other Subtests

Analyses of the numerous abilities that are tapped by each WAIS-III subtest are presented in addition to the empirical data presented on each subtest. Abilities are organized according to the Information Processing Model (Silver, 1993). This model provides a structure containing four components: input, integration, storage, and output. Conceptualizing each subtest in this framework helps to organize the many facets present in all subtests. The Input category contains abilities that involve the type of information that is to be handled (e.g., complex visual stimuli). Abilities categorized under Output are those that represent how individuals express their response (e.g., visual-motor coordination, verbal expression). Processing and memory components are listed together under Integration/Storage, because these abilities are difficult to tease apart in the subtests. For example, consider verbal concept formation, an ability measured by Vocabulary. It is not easy to separate the long-term memory component and learning ability from one's ability to think abstractly to retrieve and formulate an adequate definition of a word.

Wechsler's tests all share the two-category main organization of the subtests (Verbal and Performance). However, Wechsler (1974) and many others have purported that there are alternate organizations of the subtests that may be equally valid. There are many terms listed in the Subtest-by-Subtest Analysis section on pages 86–111 that stem from the useful methods of recategorizing WAIS-III subtests. The next few paragraphs provide a foundation to understand this terminology. The theories underlying the shared abilities of subtests were first presented by pioneers in the field of intelligence such as Cohen (1952); Mayman, Schafer, and Rapaport (1951); and Wechsler (1939). Ban-

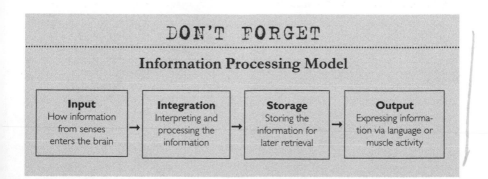

DON'T FORGET

Information Processing Model

Input	Integration	Storage	Output
How information from senses enters the brain	Interpreting and processing the information	Storing the information for later retrieval	Expressing information via language or muscle activity

≡ Rapid Reference

4.3 WAIS-III Subtests as Measures of Crystallized and Fluid Intelligence

Crystallized Intelligence (Gc)

Information
Vocabulary
Comprehension
Similarities
Picture Arrangement

Fluid Intelligence (Gf)

Matrix Reasoning
Block Design
Object Assembly
Similarities
Picture Arrangement
Arithmetic

Note. Picture Arrangement and Similarities include elements of both Gc and Gf.

natyne (1974), Glasser and Zimmerman (1967), and Matarazzo (1972) then provided elaboration and refinement in following years. Neuropsychological theory has also been integrated to enhance our understanding, such as Sperry's (1968) cerebral specialization theory and Luria's (1966) successive and simultaneous dichotomy. Cognitive theories (e.g., Guilford, 1967; Horn, 1989) also provided new perspectives for analyzing the Wechsler subtests. Consult Kaufman (1990, 1994) for in-depth discussions of the various theory-oriented and research-based methods for recategorizing the Wechsler subtests. For overviews, see Rapid References 4.3, 4.4, and 4.5 (Horn, 1989); 4.6 and 4.7 (Guilford, 1967); and 4.8 (Bannatyne, 1974).

The lists of abilities for each subtest should not be thought of as exhaustive. Modified lists may be created by psychologists with different orientations. Any one adult may fail some subtests and succeed on others because of a unique set of variables. In each of the subtests' lists of abilities are skills that are considered prerequisites for success on that task. However, poor performance may be due to a deficiency in an isolated skill. It is important to consider abilities shared by two or more subtests (see Rapid Reference 4.16). These hypothesized abilities should be used flexibly by examiners and adapted as necessary to include individual clinical experience and theoretical beliefs.

≡ Rapid Reference

4.4 WAIS-III Subtests as Measures of Horn's (1989) Broad Visualization, Short-Term Acquisition and Retrieval, and Broad Speediness

Broad Visualization (Gv)	Short-Term Acquisition and Retrieval (SAR or Gsm)	Broad Speediness (Gs)
Picture Completion	Letter-Number Sequencing	Digit Symbol-Coding
Block Design	Arithmetic	Symbol Search
Object Assembly	Digit Span	Object Assembly
Matrix Reasoning		

≡ Rapid Reference

4.5 WAIS-III Factors Corresponding to Horn's (1989) Cognitive Theory

WAIS-III Factor	↔	Horn's Construct
VCI	↔	Gc
POI	↔	Gv and Gf
WMI	↔	SAR (or Gsm)
PSI	↔	Gs

Note. VCI = Verbal Comprehension Index; POI = Perceptual Organization Index; WMI = Working Memory Index; PSI = Processing Speed Index; Gc = Crystallized Intelligence; Gv = Broad Visual Intelligence; Gf = Fluid Intelligence; SAR (or Gsm) = Short-Term Acquisition and Retrieval; Gs = Broad Speediness.

Clinical Considerations

Following the subtest analyses are various clinical suggestions to aid in interpreting each subtest. These clinical points come from clinical experience (our own, as well as generations of Wechsler lore and feedback from colleagues), and the literature. There are several excellent sources from which information has been gleaned: Kamphaus (1993), Kaufman (1990,

≡ Rapid Reference

4.6 Guilford's (1967) Operations and Contents

Operations (Intellectual Processes)	Description
Cognition	Immediate awareness, recognition, or comprehension of stimuli
Memory	Retention of information in the same form in which it was stored
Evaluation	Making judgments about information in terms of a known standard
Convergent production	Responding to stimuli with the unique or "best" answer
Divergent production	Responding to stimuli where the emphasis is on a variety or quality of response (associated with creativity)

Contents (Nature of the Stimuli)	Description
Figural	Shapes or concrete objects
Symbolic	Numerals, single letters, or any coded symbol
Semantic	Words and ideas that convey meaning
Behavioral	Primarily nonverbal, involving human interactions with a stress on attitudes, needs, thoughts, and so on

1994), Reitan and Wolfson (1992), Sattler (1988, 1992), and Zimmerman and Woo-Sam (1985). The clinical considerations are meant to be suggestions of hypotheses to consider, not definitive causes for performance on particular subtests. Each psychologist must employ his or her own theoretical framework to provide the best interpretation of any particular clinical evidence.

Although many have suggested clinical hypotheses about Wechsler profiles, empirical research has not supported hypotheses initially proposed by Rapaport, Gill, and Schafer (1945–46) and other clinicians. This lack of val-

≡Rapid Reference

4.7 Classification of WAIS-III Subtests in Guilford's (1967) Model

WAIS-III Subtest	Cognition	Memory	Evaluation	Convergent-Production
Verbal Comprehension				
Vocabulary	semantic			
Similarities	semantic			
Information		semantic		
Comprehension[a]			semantic	
Perceptual Organization				
Picture Completion	figural		figural	
Block Design	figural		figural	
Matrix Reasoning			figural	figural
Picture Arrangement[a]			semantic figural-behavioral	semantic figural-behavioral
Object Assembly[a]	figural		figural	
Working Memory Index				
Arithmetic	semantic	symbolic		
Digit Span		symbolic		
Letter-Number Sequencing		symbolic		
Processing Speed				
Digit Symbol-Coding			symbolic	symbolic
Symbol Search			figural	figural

Note. Subtests are listed according to Meeker's categorization of Wechsler subtests into the Guilford model. Matrix Reasoning, Letter-Number Sequencing, and Picture Arrangement were modified according to our understanding of the Guilford model.

[a]Not included in the calculation of the WAIS-III factor indexes.

≡ Rapid Reference

4.8 Classification of WAIS-III Subtests According to Bannatyne's (1974) Model

Verbal Conceptualization Ability	Spatial Ability	Sequential Ability	Acquired Knowledge
Similarities	Picture Completion	Arithmetic	Information
Vocabulary	Block Design	Digit Span	Arithmetic
Comprehension	Object Assembly	Digit Symbol-Coding	Vocabulary
	Matrix Reasoning	Letter-Number Sequencing	

Note. Bannatyne's categorization includes the first three subtests listed in each column. Matrix Reasoning and Letter-Number Sequencing represent our classifications based on an understanding of Bannatyne's model.

idation is likely because of the very complicated nature of interpreting pieces of clinical information in isolation. Even two top-notch clinicians may not have exactly the same interpretation of clinical data after testing the same individual (Lipsitz, Dworkin, & Erlenmeyer-Kimling, 1993).

SUBTEST-BY-SUBTEST ANALYSIS

Abilities with an asterisk (*) denote abilities that are unique to the particular subtest being discussed.

Vocabulary: *Abilities Shared With Other Subtests*
Input
> auditory perception of simple verbal stimuli (understanding single words)

Integration / Storage
> Verbal Comprehension (factor index)
> Crystallized Intelligence (Gc) (Horn, 1989)
> cognition of semantic stimuli (Guilford, 1967)

Verbal Conceptualization (Bannatyne, 1974)
Acquired Knowledge (Bannatyne, 1974)
degree of abstract thinking
fund of information
learning ability
long-term memory
verbal concept formation
*language development
*word knowledge

Output
verbal expression

Vocabulary: *Influences Affecting Subtest Scores*
- cultural opportunities at home
- foreign language experience
- intellectual curiosity and striving
- interests
- outside reading
- richness or early environment
- school learning

Vocabulary: *Clinical Considerations*
- Repression may lead to poor performance by pushing out of consciousness any word meanings that are even mildly conflict-laden. Repression may also impair the acquisition of new word meanings as well as recall of specific words on the Vocabulary subtest.
- Similar to Information, high scores relative to other Verbal subtest can reflect intellectual ambitiousness or stress for achievement in one's life.
- The content presented in an adult's or adolescent's response lends itself to analysis regarding the persons fears, guilt, preoccupations, feelings, interests, background, cultural milieu, bizarre thought processes, perseveration, and "clang" associations (moral-floral, perception-reception). Themes in response content may occur also in conjunction with Comprehension or Similarities as well as in spontaneous conversation during the assessment.
- Perseveration is sometimes evident when individuals give the

same opening line for each response ("_____, that's a hard one to define . . .").

- Responses that are overlearned, almost booklike definitions, should be distinguished from those that appear to be responses driven by intellectual vigor and personalization of the responses with current experiences.
- The open-ended nature of the Vocabulary responses makes it possible to glean information about an individual's verbal fluency, not just word knowledge. Some words are easily defined by one-word synonyms, but some individuals may give excessive verbiage in their response or may respond in a roundabout manner.
- Hearing difficulties may become apparent for those individuals who are illiterate (cannot read the visually presented word list) or for those who only focus on the auditory stimuli. Because the words are presented in isolation, there is no context in which to help understand the word.
- Level of abstract thinking can also be evaluated in Vocabulary items. Some responses may be abstract (*Salve* is "something to soothe") or more concrete (*Salve* is an "ointment").

Similarities: *Abilities Shared With Other Subtests*

Input
  auditory perception of simple verbal stimuli (understanding simple words)

Integration/Storage
  Verbal Comprehension (factor index)
  Crystallized Intelligence (Gc) (Horn, 1989)
  Fluid Intelligence (Gf) (Horn, 1989)
  cognition of semantic stimuli (Guilford, 1967)
  Verbal Conceptualization (Bannatyne, 1974)
  degree of abstract thinking
  distinguishing essential from nonessential details
  reasoning (verbal)
  verbal concept formation
  *logical abstractive (categorical thinking)

Output
  verbal expression

Similarities: *Influences Affecting Subtest Scores*
  * flexibility
  * interests
  * negativism ("They're not alike.")
  * overly concrete thinking
  * outside reading

Similarities: *Clinical Considerations*
  * Degree of abstractness should be evaluated; responses may be *abstract* (*table* and *chair* are "furniture"), *concrete* (*pants* and *tie* are "made of cloth"), or *functional* (*map* and *compass* "tell you where you are going").
  * Clinically rich information can be gleaned from the nature of the verbal response: overelaboration, overly general responses, overly inclusive responses, or self-references should be noted. Overelaboration may suggest obsessiveness. Overly inclusive responses may suggest a thought disorder. Self-references are unusual during Similarities and may be indicative of personal preoccupation.
  * Obsessive adults may provide responses that vary in quality by embedding a 2-point response among 1- or 0-point responses. This may lead to unusually high scores, as long as no response spoils the answer.
  * The pattern of responses should be examined. An adult who earns a raw score by accumulating several 1-point responses may differ substantially in potential from an adult who earns the same raw score with some 2-point and 0-point responses. The individual who mixes the 2s and 0s probably has a greater capacity for excellent performance.
  * Creativity may be exhibited in trying to come up with the relationship between two concepts. Sometimes visual imagery may be used. The creativity doesn't invariably mean a wrong response (like Comprehension).
  * Correct responses on the easier items may simply reflect overlearned, everyday associations rather than true abstract thought.

- Individuals who miss the first item administered provide the opportunity to see how they benefit from feedback. The examiner gives an example of a correct answer if the examinee doesn't provide a perfect answer to the first item administered. Adults who catch on quickly to these prompts demonstrate flexibility and adaptability. On the other hand, rigidity may be evident if the adult continues to insist that certain pairs are "not alike."
- Formal learning is less emphasized than "new problem solving" (Horn's fluid classification). The adult's task is to relate to verbal concepts, but the individual concepts tend to be simple and well known.

Arithmetic: *Abilities Shared With Other Subtests*
Input
 auditory perception of complex verbal stimuli (understanding questions)
 mental alertness
Integration/Storage
 Working Memory (factor index)
 Verbal Comprehension
 Fluid Intelligence (Gf) (Horn, 1989)
 Short-Term Acquisition and Retrieval (SAR or Gsm) (Horn, 1989)
 cognition of semantic stimuli (Guilford, 1967)
 memory of symbolic stimuli (Guilford, 1967)
 Acquired Knowledge (Bannatyne, 1974)
 Sequential (Bannatyne, 1974)
 sequential processing
Output
 simple vocal

Arithmetic: *Influences Affecting Subtest Scores*
- attention span
- anxiety
- concentration
- distractibility
- learning disabilities
- attention-deficit hyperactivity disorder

- school learning
- working under time pressure

Arithmetic: *Clinical Considerations*

- Inferring the cause of the error is useful, whether it was computational, reasoning, failure to attend, or misunderstanding the meaning of a question. For example, in response to a question about the number of hours it takes to bike 60 miles at the rate of 15 miles per hour, the answer 7 reflects a computational error, whereas 30 reflects a reasoning error, and 5,000 is bizarre. This type of bizarre response may suggest inattention, lack of comprehension, or a thought disorder. Such an unusual response on Arithmetic should be explored further.
- Testing the limits by removing the time limit and with paper and pencil is often helpful to assess the roles of anxiety and concentration on test performance.
- For retarded adults, the subtest measures a portion of adaptive functioning, as items involve money, counting, and other real-life situations.
- Adolescents or adults who have struggled with mathematics in school may become anxious when asked to respond to school-like Arithmetic questions. Their response to the anxiety and frustration may be clinically interesting: Can they compose themselves? Do they respond with hostility? Do they reject the test?
- It is important to consider when individuals are able to correctly respond to the questions but failed to do so within the time limits. Those who tend to be reflective, compulsive, obsessive, or neurologically impaired may exhibit this pattern of responding.
- Observe for signs of trying to compensate for the auditory nature or memory requirements of the task, for example, "finger writing" on the table or asking for pencil and paper or a calculator.

Digit Span: *Abilities Shared With Other Subtests*
Input
>   auditory perception of simple stimuli (understanding single words)

Integration/Storage
>   Working Memory (factor index)

Short-Term Acquisition and Retrieval (SAR or Gsm) (Horn, 1989)
memory of symbolic stimuli (Guilford, 1967)
Sequential (Bannatyne, 1974)
sequential processing
encoding information for further cognitive processing (Digits
Backward)
facility with numbers
short-term memory (auditory)
*immediate rote recall
Output
simple vocal

Digit Span: *Influences Affecting Subtest Scores*
- ability to receive stimuli passively
- attention span
- anxiety
- distractibility
- flexibility (when stitching from forward to backward span)
- learning disabilities
- attention-deficit hyperactivity disorder
- negativism (refusal to try to reverse digits, to exert effort until the
  more challenging Digits Backward series, or to take a "meaningless"
  task)

Digit Span: *Clinical Considerations*
- Recording responses will help to discern whether failure is due to
  poor sequential ability (right numbers in wrong order) or poor rote
  memory (forgetting digits but otherwise correctly repeating the
  series). Problems with inattention, distractibility, or anxiety may
  be evident in responses that bear little relationship to the actual
  stimuli.
- After the task, testing the limits and questioning whether any strategy was employed can help to differentiate between poor strategy
  generation (e.g., "chunking"), low motivation, anxiety, distractibility,
  sequencing problems, or memory problems.
- Digits Backward, which requires mental manipulation or visualization of the numbers, is more impacted by number ability than is

Digits Forward. Thus those who have better number ability may perform better on Digits Backward.

- The median Digits Forward span stays consistent from ages 16 to 54, with a length of seven digits; after age 54, the length of the forward span remains consistently at six digits. A similar trend is noted in the Digits Backward span, with a median backward span of five digits for 16- to 54-year-olds and a median backward span of four digits for almost all individuals older than 54. For more detailed information on forward and backward spans see Tables B.6 and B.7 in Appendix B of the *WAIS-III Administration and Scoring Manual.*
- Typically adults and adolescents produce forward spans that are two digits longer than backward spans. Longer backward than forward spans occur relatively rarely within the normal population of adults and are therefore noteworthy: less than 4% of the time (averaging across all ages) (Wechsler, 1997, Table B.7). One explanation for a longer backward span is that individuals may find it to be more challenging and worthy of sustaining effort, or individuals may have better skill at representational (high level) tasks than at automatic (overlearned) tasks such as Digits Forward.
- Less than ideal testing conditions may adversely affect performance on this subtest (visual or auditory distractions), and hearing impairment may make one vulnerable to failure).
- Repeating digits seems to be more impaired by state anxiety (or test anxiety) than by chronic (trait) anxiety.
- Impulsivity may be evident when adults begin to respond before the examiner has completed the series of digits, or when the examinee repeats the digits very rapidly.
- Learning ability may be evident when adults make errors on the first trial, but then are able to pass the second trial. Look for this pattern in other subtests as well (Letter-Number Sequencing, Block Design).

Information: *Abilities Shared With Other Subtests*
Input

 auditory perception of complex verbal stimuli (understanding questions)

Integration/Storage
Verbal Comprehension (factor index)
Crystallized Intelligence (Gc) (Horn, 1989)
memory (primarily), mostly of semantic stimuli (Guilford, 1967)
Acquired Knowledge (Bannatyne, 1974)
culture-loaded knowledge
fund of information
long-term memory
range of general factual knowledge
Output
simple vocal response

Information: *Influences Affecting Subtest Scores*
- alertness to the environment
- cultural opportunities at home
- foreign language background
- intellectual curiosity and striving
- interests
- outside reading
- richness of early environment
- school learning

Information: *Clinical Analysis*
- Items are generally nonthreatening and emotionally neutral.
- Rationalizations and excuses may be produced in response to this test (i.e., "That isn't important.")
- Effortless, automatic responding facilitates good performance. Adults or adolescents with chronic anxiety may suffer early failures and depressed scores in general.
- Retrieval difficulties may be revealed on this test when success on harder items is preceded by failure on easy items.
- Alertness to the environment together with formal schooling are the source of most of the factual knowledge needed for success.
- Unnecessary detail and trivial responses may suggest obsessiveness.
- Intellectual ambitiousness can be reflected in high scores and are often coupled with high Vocabulary scores.

- A perfectionistic approach may be evident when no response i[s pre]ferred to an imperfect answer.
- An adolescent's or adult's pattern of responses may be indicative of cultural background. For example questions pertaining to the president of the United States or other famous leaders in America may pose more difficulty than those on general geography or science for individuals who are not originally from the United States.
- Bizarre or odd responses can shed light on an individual's mental state. For example, a response such as "There are 1,000 inches in a yard," or "George Washington is the guy I saw at the supermarket" may indicate a need to explore mental functioning further.

Comprehension: *Abilities Shared With Other Subtests*

Input

auditory perception of simple verbal stimuli (understanding questions)

Integration/Storage

Verbal Comprehension (excluded from factor index)

Crystallized Intelligence (Gc) (Horn, 1989)

cognition of semantic stimuli (Guilford, 1967)

Verbal Conceptualization (Bannatyne, 1974)

common sense (cause-effect relationships)

culture-loaded knowledge

reasoning

social judgment (social intelligence)

*demonstration of practical information

*evaluation and use of past experiences

*knowledge of conventional standards of behavior

Output

verbal expression

Comprehension: *Influences Affecting Subtest Scores*

- cultural opportunities at home
- development of conscience or moral sense
- flexibility (ability to shift from social reasoning to proverb items and ability to give a "second reason")

- negativism ("We shouldn't have to stop at a stoplight if no one is there.")
- overly concrete thinking

Comprehension: *Clinical Considerations*

- A stable and emotionally balanced attitude and orientation is necessary for success on this subtest. Any type of maladjustment may lower scores.
- A high score on Comprehension alone is not enough evidence to interpret strong social adjustment. Corroborating evidence must be obtained from clinical observations, background information, or adaptive behavior inventories.
- Responses offer clues about a disturbed individual's social-adaptive functioning in practical, social situations, but be cautious about generalizing from single-issue questions to the complexities of the real world.
- When responses appear overlearned, stereotypical, or "parroted," test the limits to determine level of real understanding and reasoning ability.
- Like responses to Similarities and Vocabulary, responses to Comprehension may vary in their degree of abstractness. This ability to reason may be especially evident in the explanation of the proverbs. Ability to think in abstract terms (*the grass is always greener* means "you envy what you don't have") is distinct from more concrete types of responses (*the grass is always greener* means "your neighbor is a better gardener").
- Five of the Comprehension items require further questioning if only one response is given and all questions allow querying for clarification of responses. Analyze how individuals respond to follow-up questioning. Do they become defensive? Are they inflexible and unable to move beyond their original response? There are clinically relevant bits of information obtainable from observing the difference between someone who is spontaneously able to produce two concise responses versus someone who needs constant structure and prodding.

Letter-Number Sequencing: *Abilities Shared With Other Subtests*
Input
   auditory perception of simple stimuli (understanding letters and
   numbers)
Integration/Storage
   Working Memory (factor index)
   Fluid Intelligence (Horn, 1989)
   Visualization (Horn, 1989)
   Short-Term Acquisition and Retrieval (SAR or Gsm) (Horn, 1989)
   memory of symbolic stimuli (Guilford, 1967)
   Sequential (Bannatyne, 1974)
   sequential processing
   encoding information for further cognitive processing
   facility with numbers
   short-term memory (auditory)
   learning ability
   planning ability
   *facility with overlearned sequences
Output
   simple vocal

Letter-Number Sequencing: *Influences Affecting Subtest Scores*
   • ability to receive stimuli passively
   • attention span
   • anxiety
   • concentration
   • distractibility
   • flexibility
   • illiteracy or dyslexia (does not know letters and alphabet at an
     automatic level)
   • learning disabilities
   • attention-deficit hyperactivity disorder
   • negativism (refusal to take a "meaningless" task)
   • persistence

Letter-Number Sequencing: *Clinical Considerations*

- Sequencing, poor short-term memory, inattention, distractibility, or anxiety may be causative factors for trouble on Letter-Number Sequencing. Similar to Digit Span, sequencing problems can be evident when the numbers and letters are correctly remembered but in the wrong sequence. Short-term memory may be implicated if part of the sequence is correct but some of the numbers or letters are forgotten.

- Observe the examinee for signs of "stimulus overload," which can lead to frustration. Statements such as "That is too much to remember at once" or "How about just the numbers" can be indicative of an examinee being overwhelmed with the amount of auditory stimuli.

- Digits Backward is more conceptually related to Letter-Number Sequencing than Digits Forward. Both the backward span and Letter-Number Sequencing require the examinee to mentally manipulate or visualize the stimuli. (Some examinees who rely on visualization strategies will close their eyes during the administration of the items and/or during their response.) If strategies were generated to respond to Digits Backward, the examinee may benefit from using those or similar strategies on Letter-Number Sequencing.

- As there are three trials for each item, subjects have an opportunity to develop and test strategies. Test the limits or question the examinee after the test is complete to gather information about any strategies that may have been generated to complete the task.

- Like Digit Span, the skills required for this test are impaired more by state (test) anxiety than by chronic anxiety.

- Whereas number sequences are automatic for most adolescents and adults, the precise alphabetic sequence has not been adequately "overlearned" for many individuals. Note whether some examinees consistently make errors on the letters but get all the numbers right. Do these individuals have reading problems (e.g., illiteracy or dyslexia)?

- Letter-Number Sequencing is a novel task, not likely to be encountered in the real world, and requires a good flexible approach to succeed. Adolescents and adults who do poorly may display problems on other tasks that depend on fluid ability (e.g., Matrix Reasoning) or flexibility (e.g., Similarities).

Picture Completion: *Abilities Shared With Other Subtests*
Input
 visual perception of meaningful stimuli (people and things)
Integration/Storage
 Perceptual Organization (factor index)
 Broad Visual Intelligence (Gv) (Horn, 1989)
 holistic (right-brain) processing
 Cognition and evaluation of figural stimuli (Guilford, 1967)
 Spatial (Bannatyne, 1974)
 simultaneous processing
 distinguishing essential from nonessential details
 visual organization without essential motor activity
 *visual recognition without essential motor activity
Output
 simple motor or vocal (pointing or one-word response)

Picture Completion: *Influences Affecting Subtest Scores*
- ability to respond when uncertain
- alertness to the environment
- cognitive style (field dependence–field independence)
- concentration
- negativism ("Nothing is missing.")
- working under time pressure

Picture Completion: *Clinical Considerations*
- This test typically serves as a good icebreaker, as it is the first test administered. Usually adults find it nonthreatening and enjoyable.
- Although this subtest is timed, usually the 20-second limit is ample time for adults who are neither mentally retarded nor neurologically impaired. Impulsivity may be indicated by extremely quick, incorrect responses. Failure to respond within the limit is of potential diagnostic value, as even reflective individuals typically respond within the limit.
- Verbal responses are far more common than nonverbal responses on this Performance task, especially since the directions explicitly say "TELL me what is missing." Although nonverbal responses are also considered correct, the frequency of such responses should be eval-

uated and may possibly be indicative of word retrieval problems. Verbal responses that are imprecise or vague may also be indicative of word retrieval problems.

- Negativity or hostility may be noted in persistent "Nothing is missing" responses.
- Obsessiveness or concentration problems may be evident in responses that are focused on trivial details of a picture (i.e., brand name on the glasses). Similarly, confabulatory responses (indicating that something *not* in the picture is missing (e.g., feet in the tennis shoes, blood on the knife) are of clinical interest. Giving trivial or confabulatory responses several times during the subtest is of potential diagnostic interest, especially because examiners are instructed to redirect individuals the first time they give a trivial response or a confabulatory response.
- This task appears to be relatively resilient to the impact of brain damage. It is not able to consistently or reliably indicate right cerebral damage, which may perhaps be related to the nature of verbal responding by most adults and "it is entirely possible that the nature of the task is not as heavily demanding of adequate brain functions as are some of the other subtests" (Reitan & Wolfson, 1992, p. 107).

Digit Symbol-Coding: *Abilities Shared With Other Subtests*
Input
   visual perception of abstract stimuli (designs and symbols)
   auditory perception of complex verbal stimuli (following directions)
Integration/Storage
   Perceptual Organization
   convergent production and evaluation of symbolic stimuli (Guilford, 1967)
   Sequential (Bannatyne, 1974)
   sequential processing
   encoding information for further cognitive processing
   facility with numbers
   learning ability
   reproduction of models

short-term memory (visual)

visual sequencing

Output

Processing Speed (factor index)

Broad Speediness (Gs) (Horn, 1989)

paper-and-pencil skill

visual-motor coordination

clerical speed and accuracy

*psychomotor speed

Digit Symbol-Coding: *Influences Affecting Subtest Scores*

- anxiety
- distractibility
- learning disabilities
- attention-deficit hyperactivity disorder
- motivation level
- obsessive concern with accuracy and detail
- persistence
- visual-perceptual problems
- working under time pressure

Digit Symbol-Coding: *Clinical Considerations*

- Visual or motor impairment must be ruled out before interpreting a low score.
- Individuals who have demonstrated perfectionistic or compulsive tendencies prior to Digit Symbol-Coding should be told *during the sample items* that they need to copy the symbols legibly, but not perfectly.
- Changes in rate of responding during the subtest can be related to motivation, distraction, fatigue, boredom, and so forth. Thus, it is a good idea to note the number of symbols copied during each of the four 30-second periods within the 120-second limit.
- Astute observation is key to interpreting scores on this subtest. Include the following in your interpretation of the score: coordination (grip on the pencil), attention-concentration, distractibility, motivation level, visual-perceptual problems (rotating or distorting symbols), perfectionistic tendencies, perseveration (copying the same symbol for a whole line), or anxiety.

- Some individuals appear to have to search for each number in the row of stimulus pairs, seemingly unaware that the 5, for example, is always right before the 6, and this behavior could be indicative of sequencing problems.
- Short-term visual memory deficits may be evident if adults keep referring back to the "key" before copying symbols (or these individuals may be insecure). Those who have memorized several pairs of symbols are likely to have a good visual memory (if they aren't making errors in their response).
- The optional Incidental Learning procedures can be used to help to determine what caused a low coding score. Pairing measures how well an examinee can attend to, process, and remember the symbols and which numbers they are paired with. Free recall measures how many symbols can be recalled regardless of the numbers. Errors in rotation, distortion, or inversion may occur. The copy procedure measures perceptual and graphomotor speed. Thus, performance on each of these supplementary procedures will help to decipher why a subject earned a particular score, whether it be due to memory ability or pure graphomotor speed.

Block Design: *Abilities Shared With Other Subtests*
Input
    visual perception of abstract stimuli (designs and symbols)
    auditory perception of complex verbal stimuli (following directions)
Integration/Storage
    Perceptual Organization (factor index)
    Broad Visual Intelligence (Gv) (Horn, 1989)
    Fluid Intelligence (Gf) (Horn, 1989)
    Spatial (Bannatyne, 1974)
    simultaneous processing
    trial-and-error learning
    reproduction of models
    spatial visualization
    speed of mental processing
    synthesis (part-whole relationships)

*analysis of whole into component parts (analytic strategies)

*nonverbal concept formation

Output

visual-motor coordination

Block Design: *Influences Affecting Subtest Scores*

- cognitive style (field dependence–field independence)
- visual-perceptual problems
- working under time pressure

Block Design: *Clinical Considerations*

- Scores may be substantially lowered by obsessive concern with detail or reflectivity. Bonus points can be earned for quick, perfect performance. There are a total of 24 raw score bonus points that may be earned by quick performance. On average, perfect performance with no bonus points is only equivalent to a scaled score of 11.
- Visual-perceptual problems are often apparent on this subtest. If a low score occurs, the input of the visual material may be related to inaccurate perception rather than problem-solving ability or motor output. Testing the limits can often help to determine whether the adult is having perceptual difficulties or other problems.
- Scores should be interpreted in light of problem-solving approaches that were observed. Some adults use a trial-and-error approach; others have a systematic and planned approach. Factors such as rigidity, perseveration, speed of mental processing, carelessness, self-concept, cautiousness, and ability to benefit from feedback can have an impact on the test.
- Some individuals may have little motivation to try and give up easily; others learn as they take the test and sometimes "catch on" just when they discontinue. In such cases, testing the limits by administering further items can be of great clinical value (although any extra items administered beyond the discontinue rule cannot be counted in the score).
- Performance on this test is vulnerable to any kind of cerebral brain damage (especially right hemisphere). Lesions to the posterior region of the right hemisphere, especially the parietal lobes can strongly impact Block Design.

Matrix Reasoning: *Abilities Shared With Other Subtests*
Input
   visual perception of abstract stimuli
   auditory perception of complex verbal stimuli (following directions)
   distinguishing essential from nonessential detail
Integration/Storage
   Perceptual Organization (factor index)
   Broad Visual Intelligence (Gv) (Horn, 1989)
   Fluid Intelligence (Gf) (Horn, 1989)
   figural cognition (Guilford, 1967)
   convergent production (Guilford, 1967)
   figural evaluation (Guilford, 1967)
   holistic (right-brain) processing
   learning ability
   nonverbal reasoning
   simultaneous processing
   spatial visualization
   synthesis
   reasoning
   *analogic reasoning
   *nonverbal problem solving with no time limit
Output
   simple verbal (word) or nonverbal (pointing)
   visual organization

Matrix Reasoning: *Influences Affecting Subtest Scores*
   • ability to respond when uncertain
   • cognitive style (field dependence–field independence)
   • color-blindness (for some items, the use of several colors may
     confuse color-blind individuals)
   • flexibility
   • motivation level
   • negativism ("None of them go there.")
   • overly concrete thinking
   • persistence
   • visual-perceptual problems

Matrix Reasoning: *Clinical Considerations*

- Since this subtest is not timed, response time may vary widely for adults. Those who are mentally retarded or neurologically impaired may take longer to respond. Impulsivity may be indicated by extremely quick, incorrect responses. Failure to respond within a reasonable amount of time (45 seconds) is of potential diagnostic value, as it may be indicative of reflective style, obsessiveness, or confusion.

- Some items have complex visual stimuli. Individuals with visual-perceptual problems may display "stimulus overload" in attempting to input the multicolored, spatially complex items.

- A holistic processing approach is most common in solving the matrices. Some individuals choose to answer the problem with a trial-and-error approach, testing each of the possible choices one by one. Others may use a more planned approach to the problem, first mentally creating a solution to fill in the question mark and then searching the given responses to see if one matches the solution they had envisioned.

- Perseveration may be apparent on this subtest if an individual repeatedly chooses the same number response for each item (e.g., number 5).

- Color-blindness must be ruled out as a potential cause for poor performance. If such information is not offered spontaneously by the examinee, consider probing for information on color-blindness if there is less difficulty on items that depend on form (e.g., Items 17, 19, 20, 21) than on those that depend on color (e.g., Items 15, 16, 18, 22).

- Indecisiveness (e.g., "It is either 1 or 3") may indicate insecurity or need for feedback.

Picture Arrangement: *Abilities Shared With Other Subtests*

Input

    visual perception of meaningful stimuli (people and things)

    auditory perception of complex verbal stimuli (following directions)

    distinguishing essential from nonessential details

Integration/Storage
 Perceptual Organization (excluded from factor index)
 Crystallized Intelligence (Gc) (Horn, 1989)
 Fluid Intelligence (Gf) (Horn, 1989)
 integrated brain functioning (verbal-sequential and visual spatial/
 synthetic)
 convergent production and evaluation of semantic stimuli (Guilford, 1967)
 simultaneous processing
 planning
 common sense (cause-effect relationship)
 reasoning (nonverbal)
 social judgment (social intelligence)
 speed of mental processing
 synthesis (part-whole relationships)
 visual organization without essential motor activity
 visual sequencing
 *anticipation of consequences
 *temporal sequencing and time concepts
Output
 simple motor

Picture Arrangement: *Influences Affecting Subtest Scores*
 - creativity
 - cultural opportunities at home
 - exposure to comic strips
 - working under time pressure

Picture Arrangement: *Clinical Considerations*
 - Clinical information about social adjustment may be gleaned from Picture Arrangement but only with other corroborating evidence from a similar level of performance on Comprehension and from clinical observations, background information, or data from adaptive behavior scales.
 - An impulsive or reflective cognitive style may be evident during this task. Impulsive adults are likely to jump right in and begin moving the cards before examining the detail in the pictures. Reflective individuals, on the other hand, may carefully study the pictures before

moving any of them. After the cards have been moved, impulsive individuals may begin to pick them up for you to begin the next item, whereas reflective adults are more likely to continue to check their arrangements even after they appear to be done. These styles in solving the problems may also provide information about a trial-and-error versus insightful approach.

- Clinical information may be gathered about an adult's thought processes by testing the limits. After the subtest is completed the cards may be laid out in the order that they were arranged by the examinee, and then you may ask the adult to verbalize the story. It is important *not* to ask for a story explanation during the subtest because it violates the norms and may inadvertently give the person a strategy for solving harder items.

- The drawings on the Picture Arrangement cards are detailed, requiring good visual perception. Therefore, visual acuity and visual perception should be ruled out as possible reasons for a low score.

- Poor performance on some items may be related to cultural background, which may teach different interpretations of situations that depict social situations.

- Individuals with thought disorders may struggle on this task because of its logical, time-dependent, sequential nature.

- Individuals who tend to be manipulative may attempt to look at the letters and numbers on the back of the cards. Also comments may be said in response to the hunt or lunch items that are clinically relevant.

Symbol Search: *Abilities Shared With Other Subtests*
Input
   visual perception of abstract stimuli (designs and symbols)
   auditory perception of complex verbal stimuli (following directions)
Integration/Storage
   Perceptual Organization
   convergent production and evaluation of symbolic stimuli (Guilford, 1967)
   integrated brain functioning (verbal-sequential and visual spatial)
   planning

encoding information for further cognitive processing

learning ability

short-term memory (visual)

spatial visualization

speed of mental processing

*speed of visual search

Output

Processing Speed (factor index)

Broad Speediness (Gs) (Horn, 1989)

paper-and-pencil skill

visual-motor coordination

clerical speed and accuracy

Symbol Search: *Influences Affecting Subtest Scores*

- anxiety
- distractibility
- learning disabilities
- attention-deficit hyperactivity disorder
- motivation level
- obsessive concern with accuracy and detail
- persistence
- visual-perceptual problems
- working under time pressure

Symbol Search: *Clinical Considerations*

- As with many of the Performance subtests, visual impairment should be ruled out before interpreting a low Symbol Search score.
- As was noted in Chapter 2, it is important to be an astute observer during this task, as many observed behaviors can help to interpret the Symbol Search score. Concentration, distractibility, obsessive concern with detail, impulsiveness, reflectivity, motivation level, visual-perceptual problems, or anxiety are just some of the factors that may be inferred to be related to a person's performance on Symbol Search.
- A learning curve may be present on this test. Individuals who begin to answer later items more quickly may have developed a plan or strategy after completing earlier items. To note whether speed of re-

sponding is in fact increasing, you can track how many items were answered during each of the four 30-second intervals during the subtest.

- As this is one of the last subtests administered, the examinee could be fatigued or bored, which should be taken into account as a possible explanation for a low score.
- Visual memory ability can sometimes be inferred from observations on this task. Some adults may look at the target symbols only once and then find the response in the search group, and others may look back and forth several times between the target and search groups before marking yes or no. The repeated referring back and forth between the symbols may be indicative of poor visual memory (or of insecurity).
- After the entire test has been administered, you may test the limits to help discern why certain responses were made. Point to some items answered correctly and some that were wrong, and ask the adult to explain why they chose yes or no.

Object Assembly: *Abilities Shared With Other Subtests*
Input
   visual perception of meaningful stimuli (people and things)
Integration/Storage
   Perceptual Organization (excluded from factor index)
   Broad Visual Intelligence (Gv) (Horn, 1989)
   Fluid Intelligence (Gf) (Horn, 1989)
   holistic (right-brain) processing
   cognition and evaluation of figural stimuli (Guilford, 1967)
   Spatial (Bannatyne, 1974)
   simultaneous processing
   reasoning (nonverbal)
   speed of mental processing
   synthesis (part-whole relationships)
   trial-and-error learning
   ability to benefit from sensory-motor feedback
   anticipation of relationships among parts

Output
Broad Speediness (Gs) (Horn, 1989)
visual-motor coordination

Object Assembly: *Influences Affecting Subtest Scores*
- ability to respond when uncertain
- cognitive style (field dependence–field independence)
- experience with puzzles
- flexibility
- persistence
- visual-perceptual problems
- working under time pressure

Object Assembly: *Clinical Considerations*
- Because of the 15 possible bonus points that are awarded for quick performance, reflectivity or obsessive concern with detail can lower scores substantially. A perfect performance that earns no bonus points yields a scaled score of 11 (when compared with the aged 20 to 34 reference group).
- How individuals manipulate the puzzle pieces is informative. Problem-solving approach may be noted: a trial-and-error versus a systematic and insightful attack, impulsive versus reflective cognitive style, and careless versus cautious approach. Rigidity or perseveration may be evident (trying repeatedly to put the same puzzle piece in the same wrong place). Motor coordination, concentration, persistence, and speed of processing may all be inferred from behaviors and performance on this subtest.
- Also of interest is *when* during the problem-solving process the individual realizes what the object is he or she is trying to assemble. Some adults know what it is immediately after being shown the disassembled object; others are not sure until the figure is together.
- Visual-perceptual problems may be indicated if adults cannot determine what they are assembling. Similarly, input problems may be present if objects are constructed upside down or at an angle.
- Integration problems are demonstrated when separate groups of pieces are assembled, but the individual cannot get the "whole." At

times individuals insist that a piece is missing from the puzzle when they cannot completely integrate the given pieces.

- Output or coordination problems are evident when the adult aligns the puzzle pieces correctly, but too far apart, or inadvertently misaligns a piece or two while adding pieces to complete the puzzle.
- Adults who try to peek behind the screen while the examiner is arranging the puzzle pieces may be revealing impulsivity, insecurity, or a low level of moral development.
- The concrete approaches of some brain-damaged patients may not affect Object Assembly performance (because of the construction of meaningful pictures), although it is likely to impair Block Design performance. However, patients with right posterior cortex damage may have difficulty due to the visual-spatial concepts in the Object Assembly task.

STEP BY STEP: HOW TO INTERPRET THE WAIS-III PROFILE

Examining and interpreting the 50-plus values on the profile page and score conversion page of the WAIS-III record form requires a very systematic plan. Just randomly grabbing interesting-looking scores is not a useful approach. We present an approach that guides you from the most global score to the most specific to determine the most meaningful hypotheses about the examinee's abilities. Using this approach will set up a logical outline after which to pattern your test results and interpretations sections of WAIS-III reports.

This section details nine steps for interpreting WAIS-III profiles. The sequence of steps begins with a look at the most global score (Step 1) and moves through multiple steps that mainly deal first with the separate IQs (Steps 2 to 4), and then the factor indexes (Steps 5 to 7), before addressing strengths and weaknesses in the subtest profile (Steps 8 to 9). Throughout the steps, the interpretability and practical meaningfulness of the IQs and indexes are determined. Although this empirical framework is a simple "cookbook" approach, examiners must know when to deviate from the recipe and use clinical information to reject empirical rules in favor of alternative interpretations of the data. Examiners' knowledge of theory and clinical acumen, along with their conceptual understanding of the instrument, must all be used to create an in-depth understanding of the peaks and valleys of a profile.

Table 4.1 Mike A.'s Wechsler Adult Intelligence Scale—Third Edition (WAIS-III) Profile

Scale	IQ	90% Confidence Interval	Percentile Rank
Verbal Scale	125	120–128	95
Performance Scale	106	100–111	66
Full Scale	118	114–121	88

Factor	Index	90% Confidence Interval	Percentile Rank
Verbal Comprehension	120	114–124	91
Perceptual Organization	111	104–116	77
Working Memory	121	114–125	92
Processing Speed	76	71–86	5

Subtest	Scaled Score	Percentile Rank	Subtest	Scaled Score	Percentile Rank
Vocabulary	14	91	Picture Completion	9	37
Similarities	15	95	Digit Symbol-Coding	5	5
Arithmetic	15	95	Block Design	14	91
Digit Span	13	84	Matrix Reasoning	13	84
Information	12	75	Picture Arrangement	14	91
Comprehension	15	95	Symbol Search	6	9
Letter-Number Sequencing	13	84	Object Assembly	11	63

The next pages walk you through the nine steps and explain how to use the WAIS-III Interpretation Worksheet we have developed (see Appendix). Included in the steps are several "decision boxes" that help to delineate whether you should sequentially proceed through all the steps or skip a step for various reasons. The illustrative samples of how to use the various steps in the WAIS-III Interpretive Worksheet will utilize the data from Mike A.'s profile (see Table 4.1). Mike is a 61-year-old man with concerns about his memory. Mike's profile and another client's are presented as illustrative case reports in the last chapter of this book to demonstrate how the empirical framework is translated into understanding actual clinical cases.

Step 1: Interpret the Full Scale IQ

The WAIS-III Full Scale IQ is the most reliable score obtained on this measure. It has a mean split-half coefficient of .98, a stability coefficient of .96, and a standard error of measurment of about 2 points. Therefore, this most global score should be considered first in the interpretation of the profile. The profile page of the WAIS-III record form has examiners list IQs, confidence intervals, and percentile ranks (conveniently obtained from Wechsler, 1997, Tables A.3 to A.9). The discrepancy analysis page of the record form gives the ability level associated with the different IQ ranges. We recommend examining the qualitative description for the confidence interval, not just the

≡ Rapid Reference

4.9 Step 1: Interpret the Full Scale IQ

Scale	IQ	Confidence Interval (90%)/ 95% (circle one)	Percentile Rank	Descriptive Category
Verbal	125	120–128	95	Superior
Performance	106	100–111	66	Average–High Average
Full Scale	118	114–121	88	High Average– Superior

Note. If there is a significant difference between the component parts of the Full Scale IQ (i.e., the Verbal IQ and the Performance IQ or the Verbal Comprehension Index and the Perceptual Organization Index), the Full Scale IQ should not be interpreted as a meaningful representation of the individual's overall performance.

IQ score alone. For example, if an IQ is 109 and the 90% confidence interval is 105 to 112, then the person is functioning in the Average to High Average level of intelligence. The purpose of this verbal label is to facilitate communication to professionals and laypeople alike, not to pigeonhole the examinee. Rapid Reference 4.9 reviews the scores to examine for Step 1.

Representation of the confidence interval is important because it gives increased meaning to the reader of the case report. The single score representing IQ does not clearly communicate that there is error obtained with the score, but when bands of error are included and reported the IQ is put in perspective. It is notable that the confidence intervals are not always symmetrical. The reason for this stems from the statistical concept of regression to the mean. To correct for regression to the mean, the "true" IQs represented by the confidence intervals show that the IQs are a little closer to the designated mean of 100 than are the actual obtained IQs. It is assumed that people who score high on an intelligence test have benefited from positive chance error (good luck) and those who have low scores suffered from negative chance error (bad luck).

The outcome of the regression to the mean effect is the asymmetrical confidence intervals. When IQs are closest to 100, the regression effects are minimal, leading to symmetrical confidence interval bands. However, the further from the mean of 100 the IQ score is, the more asymmetrical the confidence intervals become. For example a Full Scale IQ of 103 has 90% confidence interval of 100 to 106, but a Full Scale IQ of 143 has a 90% band of 138 to 146. (We consider the 90% confidence interval to be an appropriate band of error for most testing purposes.)

Although the Full Scale IQ is examined first, that does not mean it is the most important score in the profile. In fact, in the steps to follow it may be determined that the Full Scale IQ score is meaningless and rendered uninterpretable. The importance of the Full Scale IQ is diminished if there are large differences between the Verbal and Performance IQs or among the index scores. Other factors such as fatigue, anxiety, or cultural background may also impact the interpretability of the Full Scale IQ.

In some instances the Verbal, Performance, and Full Scale IQs may be fairly similar, and the factor indexes, likewise, may span a narrow range. Even in this case, it is inappropriate to attribute too much value to the Full Scale IQ alone. The global IQ may provide a good summary of an individual's performance, but to truly understand the complex nature of human cognitive functioning many different abilities must be considered separately. Supplemental additional measures are often necessary to capture the spectrum of a person's strong and weak areas.

Step 2: Are the Verbal IQ Versus the Performance IQ (or the Verbal Comprehension Index Versus the Perceptual Organization Index) Significantly Different?

Like all Wechsler measures, the next level of global scores below the Full Scale IQ include the Verbal IQ and the Performance IQ. So the next step in WAIS-III interpretation is to compute the size of the Verbal IQ versus the Performance IQ difference. The direction of the discrepancy does not matter for the purposes of this calculation, but whether the difference is statistically significant is important. The calculation of a discrepancy score will also be performed for the Verbal Comprehension Index versus the Perceptual Organization Index.

The Verbal IQ is more reliable than the Performance IQ (.97 versus .94, on average) and is also more stable (.96 versus .91). The Verbal Comprehension Index and the Perceptual Organization Index are less reliable (.96 and .93) than their respective IQs, and they are also less stable (.95 and .88). The differences in how reliable and stable the IQs are in comparison to the indexes is not surprising, given the fact that the IQs comprise five to six subtests, whereas the Verbal Comprehension Index and the Perceptual Organization Index each comprise only three subtests. Because of these differences, the best number to represent discrepancies between verbal and nonverbal abilities is the difference between Verbal IQ and Performance IQ, if a difference exists. However, if a difference exists between the Verbal Comprehension Index and the Perceptual Organization Index, but not between the IQs, this is important to note and discuss why this difference is present.

Table B.1 in the *WAIS-III Administration and Scoring Manual* gives values for statistical significance between the Verbal IQ and the Performance IQ and also for the Verbal Comprehension Index and the Perceptual Organization Index at the .05 and .15 levels. The .15 level is too liberal for most testing purposes (15% contains too much built-in error). We present difference values at the .01 and the .05 levels, using the averages of all ages. Rapid Reference 4.10

details the process of determining significance and includes the values needed for significance. The overall values for the Verbal IQ versus the Performance IQ discrepancies are 9 points at the .05 level and 12 points at the .01 level. Values for the Verbal Comprehension Index versus the Perceptual Organization Index discrepancy are 10 points at .05 and 13 points at .01.

An appropriate level of confidence for discrepancy scores in most testing purposes is the .05 level. When choosing a band of error, the 90% confidence interval is usually adequate; however, difference scores are more unreliable and should have at least a 95% level of confidence. It is important to remember that the purpose of determining whether significant differences exist in the profile is to generate useful hypotheses. Thus a 99% confidence level is generally too conservative to allow flexible interpretation. Nonetheless, it is up to each individual examiner to decide the level of confidence (and error) that he or she is willing to accept.

If neither a significant Verbal IQ versus Performance IQ or Verbal Comprehension Index versus Perceptual Organization Index discrepancy is found, then you may assume that overall the examinee's verbal and nonverbal skills are fairly evenly developed. In the WAIS-III Interpretation Worksheet, the decision box in Step 2 tells you that you may now skip to Step 6 (to examine the small factors) because Steps 3, 4, and 5 all focus on determining whether the difference is meaningful to interpret (see Rapid Reference 4.10). Obviously, if there is no significant difference, these steps are unnecessary. If any significant discrepancy is found in Step 2, proceed to Step 3.

Step 3: Are the Verbal IQ Versus the Performance IQ (or the Verbal Comprehension Index Versus the Perceptual Organization Index) Differences Abnormally Large?

Step 2 determined whether the differences between scales were large enough to be considered statistically significant. In this step we ask whether these differences are so large that they are considered abnormal or rare among the normal population. The level of significance of a difference tells us nothing about how frequently a discrepancy of a given magnitude occurs in the normal population. In interpreting a discrepancy it is important to understand how common or rare it is. The mean difference between the Verbal IQ and the Performance IQ (disregarding the direction of the difference) is 8.6

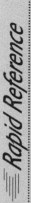

Rapid Reference

4.10 Step 2: Are the Verbal IQ Versus the Performance IQ or the Verbal Comprehension Index Versus the Perceptual Organization Index Significantly Different?

		Difference	**Significant (p < .01)**	**Significant (p < .05)**	**Not Significant**	**Is there a significant difference?**
V-IQ 125	**P-IQ** 106	19	12 or more	9–11	0–8	(YES) NO
VCI 120	**POI** 111	9	13 or more	10–12	0–9	YES (NO)

Step 2 Decision Box

If the answers are both *no*, there are not significant differences between *either* the V-IQ and the P-IQ or the VCI and the POI. ⇨

First explain the meaning of the scales not being significantly different. *Then skip to Step 6.*

If either answer is yes, there is a significant difference between *either* the V-IQ and the P-IQ or between the VCI and the POI. ⇨

Continue on to Step 3.

Note. V-IQ = Verbal IQ; P-IQ = Performance IQ; VCI = Verbal Comprehension Index; POI = Perceptual Organization Index.

points, and the mean Verbal Comprehension Index versus Perceptual Organization Index difference is 9.7 points (Wechsler, 1997, Table B.2). When rounded to the nearest whole number, these mean discrepancies correspond to the size of the verbal-nonverbal difference required for significance at the .05 level. In other words, the average adolescent or adult has a significant difference between his or her verbal and nonverbal intelligence. Similar results with discrepancies of about this size have consistently occurred on all Wechsler scales since their inception.

Given the fact that most normal people have some sort of discrepancy between their Verbal and Performance abilities, it is important to examine how common a discrepancy of a given magnitude is. In the WAIS-III standardization sample, for example, about 27% (more than one out of four) of normal adults had Verbal IQ versus Performance IQ discrepancies that are significant at the .01 level (12 or more points), a magnitude of difference that some clinicians interpret as meaningful in a neurological sense.

However, just because a person has scored significantly higher or lower on one of the IQs does not mean that he or she is "abnormal." Some differences are fairly common in the normal population and provide good information for recommendations, but they do not necessarily indicate problems. Using statistical criteria for determining conventional statistical significance, we determine whether a discrepancy is "real" ($p < .05$ or $p < .01$), as opposed to merely being the result of chance error. However, we must go one step further to determine whether a significant difference is of such magnitude that it is rare or abnormal.

How frequently a discrepancy occurs in the normal population is presented in Table B.2 of the *WAIS-III Administration and Scoring Manual.* The data provided in Rapid Reference 4.11 show the values needed for abnormality for the Verbal IQ versus the Performance IQ discrepancy and for the Verbal Comprehension Index versus the Perceptual Organization Index discrepancy. The extreme 15% of the normal population (corresponding to approximately one standard deviation above the mean) is considered "abnormal" for our purposes.

Note the distinction between *significant* differences and *abnormal* differences: A Verbal IQ versus Performance IQ difference of 12 points is significant at the .01 level, but the discrepancy must be at least 17 points to be considered abnormal. Likewise, the Verbal Comprehension Index versus the

4.11 Step 3: Are the Verbal IQ Versus the Performance IQ or the Verbal Comprehension Index Versus Perceptual Organization Index Differences Abnormally Large?

V-IQ Versus P-IQ Difference

19

Size of Difference Needed for Abnormality

17[a]

Does size meet abnormality criteria? (circle one)

(YES)   NO

VCI Versus POI Difference

9

Size of Difference Needed for Abnormality

19[a]
⇨

Does size meet abnormality criteria? (circle one)

YES   (NO)

Step 3 Decision Box

If *any abnormal differences* are found   ⇨   then this *abnormally large discrepancy* should be interpreted.

Then skip to Step 6.

Explain the *abnormally large* Verbal and Performance differences.

If *no abnormal differences* are found   ⇨   then you must determine if the noted differences are interpretable.

Go on to Step 4.

Note. V-IQ = Verbal IQ; P-IQ = Performance IQ; VCI = Verbal Comprehension Index; POI = Perceptual Organization Index.

[a] Exact point values according to ability level are available in *WAIS-III and WMS-III Technical Manual* (The Psychological Corporation, 1997; pp. 300–309).

Perceptual Organization Index difference of 13 is significant at the .01 level, but it takes a 19-point difference to be considered abnormal. Thus, even though a Verbal IQ versus Performance IQ difference of 12 or 15 points is "real" (i.e., not merely a result of chance error), such discrepancies occur too frequently among normal adolescents and adults to be considered abnormal. Abnormally high Verbal-Performance IQ discrepancies don't begin until the magnitude reaches 17 points. The extreme 10%, 5%, 2%, and 1% can also be determined from Table B.2 in the *WAIS-III Administration and Scoring Manual.* Although we endorse the 15% level of denoting abnormality, once again examiners may choose as abnormal the "extreme percent" that fits best with their own clinical philosophy.

If an abnormally large difference is found between an individual's verbal and nonverbal abilities, then this discrepancy needs to be addressed. Even if there is some scatter found within the IQs or indexes, if an abnormally large difference exists, it should be interpreted. The decision box in Step 3 (see Rapid Reference 4.11) explains that if the size of the discrepancy is *not* abnormal, then Step 4 should be examined to determine if the separate verbal and nonverbal scales are interpretable. However, if *either* the Verbal IQ versus the Performance IQ discrepancy or the Verbal Comprehension Index versus the Perceptual Organization Index discrepancy is indeed abnormal (or if both are abnormal), then Steps 4 and 5 should be skipped. Simply, abormally large discrepancies are too big to ignore for any reason. When a discrepancy is abnormal proceed directly to Step 6.

Step 4: Is the Verbal IQ Versus the Performance IQ Discrepancy Interpretable?

Step 2 determined that there was a significant discrepancy between either the Verbal IQ and the Performance IQ or the Verbal Comprehension Index and the Perceptual Organization Index, but before those discrepancies can be interpreted, further investigation needs to take place. Perhaps the IQ discrepancies are not interpretable because the IQs don't correspond to unitary abilities. In some instances, the "purer" Verbal Comprehension Index and Perceptual Organization Index will give a clearer picture of an individual's verbal versus nonverbal skills than does the discrepancy between the IQ scales. Step 4 helps to determine whether the Verbal IQ versus the Perfor-

DON'T FORGET

Pairs of Factor Indexes

↗ Verbal IQ ↘

Verbal Comprehension Index

Verbal conceptualization, knowledge, and expression: answering oral questions that measure factual knowledge, word meanings, reasoning, and the ability to express ideas in words

Working Memory Index

Number ability and sequential processing: responding to oral stimuli that involve the handling of numbers and/or letters in a step-by-step, sequential fashion and require a good nondistractible attention span for success

↗ Performance IQ ↘

Perceptual Organization Index

Nonverbal thinking and visual motor coordination: integrating visual stimuli, reasoning nonverbally, and applying visual-spatial and visual-motor skills to solve the kinds of problems that are not school taught

Processing Speed Index

Response speed: demonstrating extreme speed in solving an assortment of nonverbal problems (speed of thinking as well as motor speed)

---

mance IQ discrepancy is interpretable in a clinical or practical sense. Note, however, that if Step 3 revealed an abnormally large Verbal IQ versus Performance IQ (or Verbal Comprehension Index versus Perceptual Organization Index) discrepancy, Step 4 (and Step 5 as well) should be skipped.

The Verbal Scale of the WAIS-III is split into a pair of indexes: Verbal Comprehension and Working Memory. The Performance Scale is also divided into two indexes: Perceptual Organization and Processing Speed.

If the Verbal triad of Vocabulary-Similarities-Information (Verbal Comprehension Index) is significantly different from the Arithmetic–Digit Span–Letter-Number Sequencing (Working Memory Index) triad, then the Verbal IQ does not mean very much. It is not a unitary construct. Likewise, if the Picture Completion–Block Design–Matrix Reasoning (Perceptual Organization Index) triad is significantly different from the Performance duo of Digit Symbol-Coding and Symbol Search (Processing Speed Index), then the Performance IQ is not meaningful and is not a unitary construct. Rapid Reference 4.12 provides the discrepancy values necessary for the indexes to be considered significantly different from one another.

If there is variability between the factors making up the IQs, then the IQs are not interpretable. However, even if the pairs of factor indexes do not differ significantly, the IQs still may not be interpretable if significant scatter exists within the Verbal Scale or the Performance Scale. To determine whether each IQ is measuring a unitary construct, the scaled-score range must be examined to determine the amount of subtest scatter. The range is simple to compute: subtract the person's lowest Verbal scaled score from his or her highest Verbal scaled score (to obtain Verbal scale range). Similarly, subtract the person's lowest Performance scaled score from his or her highest Performance scaled score (to obtain Performance scale range). The range of Verbal and Performance scale subtests must each be 8 or more points to be considered abnormal (see Rapid Reference 4.12). When computing these scaled-score ranges, only include the six Verbal scaled scores and the five Performance scaled scores that are used to obtain the Verbal IQ and the Performance IQ, respectively.

Scatter among Verbal subtests indicates that the adult's Verbal IQ represents a summary of diverse abilities and does not represent a unitary entity. If an abnormal amount of scatter is present across subtest scores, it can be assumed that a global verbal ability is not responsible for the individual's scaled scores. Similar logic applies to the Performance IQ. Thus, if unusually large scatter is present in either IQ scale, the discrepancy between the Verbal IQ and the Performance IQ is not very meaningful or interpretable.

To determine when the Verbal IQ versus the Performance IQ discrepancy can be interpreted, four questions must be answered: two about the Verbal scale and two about the Performance scale. (See Rapid Reference 4.12 for an outline of the questions to ask about each IQ scale.) First, the difference between the Verbal Comprehension Index and the Working Memory Index is examined to determine whether the discrepancy is significant (10 point discrepancy necessary at the $p < .05$ level). Next, the amount of scatter in the Verbal Scale is checked (a range of 8 or more points is considered abnormal scatter). A parallel process is undertaken for the Performance Scale. The Perceptual Organization Index versus the Processing Speed Index discrepancy is examined to detect any significant differences (13 points discrepancy neces-

═Rapid Reference

4.12 Step 4: Is the Verbal IQ Versus the Performance IQ Discrepancy Interpretable?

Verbal Scale

A. Is there a significant difference between the VCI and the WMI?

		Difference	Significant (p < .01)	Significant (p < .05)	Not Significant	Is there a significant difference?
VCI 120	WMI 121	1	13 or more ⇨	10–12	0–9	YES (NO)

B. Is there abnormal Verbal scatter?

High Scaled Score of six V-IQ Subtests	Low Scaled Score of six V-IQ Subtests	High–Low Difference	Abnormal Scatter	Not Abnormal	Is there abnormal scatter?
15	12	3	8 or more ⇨	0–7	YES (NO)

Performance Scale

C. Is there a significant difference between the POI and the PSI?

		Difference	Significant (p < .01)	Significant (p < .05)	Not Significant	Is there a significant difference?
POI 111	PSI 76	35	17 or more	13–16 ⇨	0–12	(YES) NO

continued

≡ Rapid Reference

D. Is there abnormal performance scatter?

High Scaled Score of five P-IQ Subtests	Low Scaled Score of five P-IQ Subtests	High-Low Difference	Abnormal Scatter	Not Abnormal	Is there abnormal scatter?
14	5	9	8 or more	0–7	(YES) NO

⇨

Step 4 Decision Box

If *all* Step 4 questions A, B, C, and D are *no* → then the V-IQ *versus* the P-IQ discrepancy is interpretable. → Explain the meaningful difference between V-IQ and P-IQ. *Then skip to Step 6.*

If one or more questions in Step 4 are yes → then the V-IQ *versus* the P-IQ difference should probably *not* be interpreted. ⇨ Examine the VCI *versus* the POI discrepancy in *Step 5.*

Note. V-IQ = Verbal IQ; P-IQ = Performance IQ; VCI = Verbal Comprehension Index; POI = Perceptual Organization Index; PSI = Processing Speed Index.

sary at $p < .05$ level), and Performance scatter is checked (8-point scatter is abnormal).

If either of the two questions about the Verbal Scale indicate significant variability within the scale, then the Verbal IQ does not reflect a unitary construct for the person, and the Verbal IQ should probably not be interpreted. Likewise if significant differences or significant scatter is found in the Performance scale, then the Performance IQ does not reflect a unitary construct for that person, and the Performance IQ probably should not be interpreted.

In summary, if all of the Step 4 questions are answered no, then the Verbal IQ versus the Performance IQ difference provides a meaningful way to denote whether a child differs in verbal versus nonverbal intelligence. If the Verbal IQ versus the Performance IQ difference is statistically significant (see Step 2), then the examinee truly differs in his or her verbal and nonverbal intelligence. If the separate scales are unitary, then the Verbal and Performance IQs merit interpretation. The Verbal Comprehension and Perceptual Organization Indexes are probably best ignored. You should skip Step 5, which examines Verbal Comprehension Index and Perceptual Organization Index, and move ahead to Step 6.

However, if the answer to at least one of the Step 4 questions is yes, then the Verbal-Performance IQ discrepancy is probably *not* interpretable, and the difference between Verbal IQ and Performance IQ should usually not be interpreted (see decision box in Step 4). If the IQs are uninterpretable, for whatever reason, move to Step 5 where the Verbal Comprehension Index and the Perceptual Organization Index will be examined.

Step 5: Is the Verbal Comprehension Index Versus the Perceptual Organization Index Difference Interpretable?

The WAIS-III provides another way to compare verbal and nonverbal abilities, outside the Verbal IQ and the Performance IQ: the Verbal Comprehension Index and the Perceptual Organization Index. The factor indexes are sometimes considered "purer" measures of verbal and nonverbal intelligence. As detailed in the Don't Forget on page 121, the VC factor excludes the subtests that are thought to measure sequential processing, working memory, and number ability and instead measures conceptual thought and verbal expression. The Perceptual Organization factor excludes the two subtests that

Rapid Reference

4.13 Step 5: Is the Verbal Comprehension Index Versus the Perceptual Organization Index Difference Interpretable?

A. Is there significant scatter in the VCI subtests?

High Scaled Score of three VCI Subtests	Low Scaled Score of three VCI Subtests	High-Low Scaled Score Difference	Abnormal Scatter	Not Abnormal	Is there abnormal scatter?
15	12	3	5 or more ⇩	0–4	YES NO

B. Is there significant scatter in the POI subtests?

High Scaled Score of three POI Subtests	Low Scaled Score of three POI Subtests	High-Low Scaled Score Difference	Abnormal Scatter	Not Abnormal	Is there abnormal scatter?
14	9	5	6 or more ⇩	0–5	YES NO

continued

Step 5 Decision Box

If Step 5 questions A and B are *no* ⟹ then the VCI versus the POI discrepancy is interpretable. ⟹ Explain the meaningful difference between the VCI and the POI.

If answer to either question A or B is *yes* ⟹ then the VCI versus the POI discrepancy should *probably not* be interpreted. ⟹ Do not interpret the VCI versus the POI difference.[a]

Note. VCI = Verbal Comprehension Index; POI = Perceptual Organization Index.

[a]*The verbal and nonverbal constructs are not interpretable if you reach this point.*

tap mental and motor speed, and this index does capture one's nonverbal thinking and application of visual-spatial skill.

Just as the IQs were examined to determine whether they were unitary factors, the indexes too need to be checked for scatter or variability. Two questions need to be asked about the factors to ascertain if either factor is compromised by too much scatter: (a) Is there significant scatter in the Verbal Comprehension Index subtests, and (b) Is there significant scatter in the Perceptual Organization Index subtests? As is noted in Rapid Reference 4.13, a 5 or more point range between the highest and lowest Verbal Comprehension Index subtests is considered abnormal, and a 6 or more point range between the highest and lowest Perceptual Organization Index subtests is considered abnormal. The WAIS-III administration manual did not provide these ranges, so we computed them in the following way. The Verbal Comprehension Index and the Perceptual Organization Index each includes three subtests. It is possible to compare pairs of scaled scores within each scale to determine if they are significantly different (data are provided by Wechsler, 1997, Table B.4). For the Verbal Comprehension Index and the Perceptual Organization Index, three pair-wise comparisons are possible (for the Verbal Comprehension Index, these comparisons are Information vs. Similarities, Information vs. Vocabulary and Similarities vs. Vocabulary). We decided that "abnormal scatter" on the Verbal Comprehension Index and the Perceptual Organization Index would correspond to the smallest scaled-score range that ensured significant discrepancies ($p < .05$) between at least two of the three pair-wise comparisons. For the Verbal Comprehension Index, that corresponded to a range of 5 points and, for the Perceptual Organization Index, to a range of 6 points.

If abnormal scatter is found in either the Verbal Comprehension Index or the Perceptual Organization Index (yes answers to either question), then you probably should not interpret the Verbal Comprehension Index versus Perceptual Organization Index discrepancy. Abnormal scatter present in either of these factors indicates that the index cannot be meaningfully interpreted, as it is not a unitary factor. When neither the Verbal-Performance IQ discrepancy nor the Verbal Comprehension–Perceptual Organization Index discrepancy are interpretable, then the verbal and nonverbal constructs are not meaningful for that individual. However, as the decision box in Step 5 indicates, (see Rapid Reference 4.13) if neither the Verbal Comprehension Index nor the Perceptual Organization Index has abnormal scatter, then the two scales are interpretable and so is the significant discrepancy between them.

In either case, the next step in the interpretive process is to investigate the smallest factors on the WAIS-III (Processing Speed Index and Working Memory Index).

Step 6: Determine Whether the Working Memory Index and the Processing Speed Index Are Interpretable

Just as the Verbal IQ, Performance IQ, Verbal Comprehension Index, and Perceptual Organization Index have been examined to determine if they are unitary dimensions, the smallest factors also need to be checked for abnormal scatter. The lowest scaled score of the three Working Memory Index subtests should be subtracted from the highest scaled score on this index to obtain the range of scores. If the scatter is 6 or more points, then the Working Memory Index should not be interpreted as a meaningful, unitary construct. (The same method for inferring abnormal scatter in the Verbal Comprehension Index and the Perceptual Organization Index was used to obtain the 6-point value for the Working Memory Index.) The absolute difference between the Symbol Search scaled score and Digit Symbol-Coding scaled score provides the range of scores on the Processing Speed Index. If the Processing Speed Index scatter is 4 or more points (a significant discrepancy at the .05 level), then this index does not represent a unitary construct and should not be interpreted. Rapid Reference 4.14 reviews the values necessary to determine abnormal scatter on the Working Memory Index and Processing Speed Index.

Step 7: Interpret the Global Verbal and Nonverbal Dimensions as Well as the Small Factors if They Were Found to Be Interpretable

The empirical examination of the IQs and indexes is now complete. We now know what scores we should, or perhaps should not, interpret. But determining what scores to interpret is different from actually interpreting them. That brings us to Step 7, in which we explore a variety of interpretive hypotheses derived from diverse theoretical-, clinical-, and research-based interpretations. The next few paragraphs will outline some of the possible interpretations of these global dimensions; for a more thorough treatment of these hy-

≡ Rapid Reference

4.14 Step 6: Determine Whether the Working Memory Index and the Processing Speed Index Are Interpretable

A. Is the WMI factor interpretable?

Arithmetic	Digit Span	Letter-Number Sequencing	Difference Between High and Low Scaled Score	Abnormal Scatter	Not Abnormal
15	13	13	2	6 or more (do not interpret)	0–5 (do interpret)

⇨

B. Is the PSI factor interpretable?

Symbol Search	Digit Symbol-Coding	Difference Between High and Low Scaled Score	Abnormal Scatter	Not Abnormal
6	5	1	4 or more (do not interpret)	0–3 (do interpret)

Note. WMI = Working Memory Index; PSI = Processing Speed Index.

potheses, consult Kaufman (1990, Chapters 9, 10, and 11; 1994, Chapters 4 and 5).

Horn and Cattell's Fluid-Crystallized Theory

Two broad concepts, Crystallized Intelligence (Gc) and Fluid Intelligence (Gf), have been distinguished by Horn and Cattell (1966, 1967). A person's learning that is dependent on school-acquired knowledge and acculturation is categorized as Gc, whereas Gf reflects one's ability to solve novel problems that do not depend on formal schooling or acculturation (Cattell & Horn, 1978). Horn's original two-construct theory has now been expanded to include roughly eight abilities. The broadening of the Gc-Gf theory is intended to provide "purer" cognitive measures of intelligence. The most recent definitions of Gf emphasize its reasoning component; potentially contaminating variables such as processing speed, visualization, or memory are avoided in "pure" tests of fluid ability (Horn, 1989, 1991; Kaufman & Horn, 1996). The pure Gc factor features knowledge and comprehension, minimizing the effects of short-term memory or fluid reasoning. Some of the additional cognitive factors in the expanded Gc-Gf theory include Short-Term Acquisition and Retrieval (SAR or Gsm), Broad Speediness (Gs), Broad Visualization (Gv), Quantitative Thinking (Gq), and Auditory Intelligence (Ga), and Long-Term Retrieval (TSR or Gln).

The Horn and Cattell theory has frequently been applied to Wechsler's scales (Kaufman, 1994; Matarazzo, 1972). To categorize WAIS-III subtests into Horn's factors we considered the work of Horn (1989, 1991), Kaufman (1994), and Woodcock (1990). Rapid Reference 4.3 categorizes WAIS-III subtests based on their Gc and Gf components. The subtests are then further broken down into some of Horn's expanded factors.

Gv includes "tasks that call for fluent visual scanning, Gestalt Closure, mind's-eye rotations of figures, and ability to see reversals" (Horn, 1989, p. 80). SAR is basically immediate recall of stimuli (Horn & Hofer, 1992). Gs "relates to carefulness, strategies (or metacognition), mood (such as depression), and persistence" (Horn, 1989, p. 84). (See Rapid Reference 4.4 for a list of WAIS-III subtests falling in the Gv, SAR, and Gs categories.)

The four WAIS-III factors can be interpreted within the Horn theoretical framework: The Verbal Comprehension Index is primarily a measure of Gc; the Perceptual Organization Index measures a blend of Gv and Gf; the

Working Memory Index can be interpreted as a measure of SAR; and the Processing Speed Index measures Gs. Because of the considerable impact of bonus points for speedy performance on Object Assembly, this subtest joins the Processing Speed Index subtests on Horn's Gs factor.

Some subtests assess more than one aspect of Horn's theory. For example, Similarities has components of both Gc (word knowledge) and Gf (figuring out the similarity); Arithmetic measures Gf and SAR, and to some extent Gq. Matrix Reasoning falls under both Gv and Gf categories. Although many Matrix Reasoning items require "pure" fluid reasoning ability, spatial orientation and visualization are also demanded for a number of Matrix Reasoning items. This overlap demonstrates how complex the abilities are that underlie the WAIS-III subtests. Because of this complexity, it is often necessary to explore behaviors, background information, and supplementary test scores to determine what is truly "driving" a person's performance on a particular subtest.

Performance > Verbal Profiles

There are many reasons why an individual may have a Performance or Verbal strength on the WAIS-III. Here we present some of the research that gives support for typical Performance > Verbal profiles and Verbal > Performance profiles.

Bilingualism. The Wechsler instruments for adults and children contain a great deal of verbiage in their presentation and in their required responses. Because of this verbal emphasis, examinees who do not speak English as their first language or who are bilingual are sometimes at a disadvantage, especially on the Verbal Scale of the Wechsler instruments. Much research has been done on the topic of multicultural use of the Wechsler instruments (e.g., Helms, 1997). The *WAIS-III and WMS-III Technical Manual* does not include data on the different ethnic groups in the standardization sample, but there are several pertinent studies on the WAIS-R.

In general, Hispanic individuals perform 7 to 9 points higher on the Performance Scale than on the Verbal Scale of the WAIS-R (e.g., Murray, Waites, Veldman, & Heatly, 1973; Whitworth & Gibbons, 1986). Explanations for this Performance > Verbal pattern for Hispanic groups include not only linguistic factors, but also cultural and subcultural factors.

Learning Disabilities. Learning disabled individuals often display Performance > Verbal profiles on Wechsler instruments. This pattern has been noted for both children and adults. Across many studies of adolescents and adults with various learning disabilities, a consistent pattern of a higher Performance IQ than Verbal IQ of about 7 to 19 points is present (e.g., Frauenheim & Heckerl, 1983; Sandoval, Sassenrath, & Penaloza, 1988). This pattern is not that surprising since the Verbal tasks on Wechsler's scales are heavily achievement dependent. Several Verbal subtests tap information taken directly from school-learned knowledge. By definition, individuals with a learning disability are not good achievers. Thus, the Performance > Verbal pattern in learning-disabled individuals may be a reflection of their poor crystallized knowledge. To best understand the cognitive abilities for most adolescents or adults with learning disabilities, the four factor indexes may provide the most useful information. These factors offer a purer measure of Gc (Verbal Comprehension Index) than is reflected by the Verbal IQ, an amalgamation of verbal conceptual and memory tasks.

In samples of college students with learning disabilities, the Performance > Verbal pattern has *not* been consistently found. College students more typically evidence the opposite pattern of Verbal > Performance or have no Verbal-Performance difference (Kaufman, 1990). The Verbal Scale does measure achievement (crystallized abilities), and college students, even if learning disabled, have achieved educationally. This achievement may be facilitated by compensatory strategies that have allowed the students to succeed educationally despite their disabilities.

The WAIS-III was administered to a sample of 24 adolescents diagnosed with a reading disability (The Psychological Corporation, 1997). Looking just at the mean IQs (Verbal IQ of 96.7 and Performance IQ of 102.1), the previously described Performance > Verbal pattern is apparent, although the discrepancy of 5.4 points is smaller than Performance > Verbal differences typically found for the WAIS-R. However, in examining the mean four factor index scores, more information is gleaned. The mean difference between the Verbal Comprehension Index and the Working Memory Index was 6.6 points, and 41.7% of the subjects had a 15-point higher score on the Verbal Comprehension Index than the Working Memory Index. (This is in contrast to 13% of the standardization sample.) The mean Perceptual Organization Index score was also about 6.6 points higher than the Processing Speed Index, with 30.4% of the reading-disabled subjects earning a 15-point higher

Perceptual Organization Index than Processing Speed Index score, about twice the 14% in the standardization sample.

Verbal > Performance Profiles

Depression. Highly educated adults typically earn higher Verbal than Performance IQs, but other variables also are associated with a characteristic Verbal > Performance profile on Wechsler's scales. Depression, for example, often demonstrates itself in the cognitive profile with lower Performance than Verbal IQs (Gregory, 1987; Zimmerman & Woo-Sam, 1973). The reason for the higher Verbal IQ is generally believed to be impaired concentration, psychomotor retardation, anxiety, or low motivation. The pattern can sometimes be evident with as little as a 3-point difference or can be as striking as a 15-point difference (Loro & Woodward, 1976; Pernicano, 1986).

Patients with bipolar disorder have also been shown to obtain a Verbal > Performance pattern on the Wechsler tests (e.g., Nair, Muller, Gutbrodt, Buffet, & Schwartz, 1979). Studies of adults with bipolar disorder being treated with lithium show that the longer patients are on lithium, the lower their scores are on the Performance IQ (Nair et al., 1979). This pattern of performance seems to be due to a mental slowness, rather than poorer accuracy (Kaufman, 1990).

Multiple Sclerosis. Difficulties with motor coordination for various reasons can also lead to the Verbal > Performance profile. If fine motor abilities are compromised, then many of the Performance subtests will not adequately provide an opportunity for an adolescent or adult to express their nonverbal intelligence. Studies have shown that adults with multiple sclerosis (MS) display the expected Verbal > Performance profile, with the Verbal Scale being 5 to 12 points better (e.g., Heaton, Nelson, Thompson, Burks, & Franklin, 1985). The subtests that require the least amount of motor coordination are typically stronger for individuals with MS (i.e., Picture Completion), but the weakest performance is seen on subtests such as Object Assembly and Digit Symbol.

With the addition of Matrix Reasoning to the WAIS-III, there are now two Performance subtests that do not require fine motor skills. Therefore, it is quite possible that WAIS-III research on MS patients will produce Verbal > Performance profiles smaller in magnitude than the ones found on the WAIS and WAIS-R. With the Processing Speed versus Perceptual Organization dichotomy within the Performance Scale, examiners are now able to separate out fine motor skill and speed from perceptual organizational skill, which is quite useful in assessing those with motor difficulties such as those who suffer from MS.

Alcoholism. Patients with intermediate-stage alcoholism have been shown to have a Verbal > Performance profile on the Wechsler instruments. In reviewing the literature, Parsons (1996) noted that sober alcoholic patients are mildly to moderately impaired in "memory and learning, abstracting and problem solving, perceptual-spatial abilities, perceptual motor speed, and information processing speed" (p. 179). However, these same alcoholics usually have verbal abilities that are in the normal range. Barron and Russell (1992) showed that, in alcoholic patients, tasks tapping fluid ability are more impaired than crystallized and overlearned tasks. On the WAIS-III one would therefore predict that alcoholic individuals would evidence a Verbal Comprehension Index > Perceptual Organization Index pattern.

The WAIS-III and WMS-III Technical Manual (The Psychological Corporation, 1997) presented a study with 28 alcoholics who had recently undergone detoxification. Similar to previous research, the sample's WAIS-III Verbal scores were slightly higher than the Perceptual Organization Index and the Processing Speed Index. The average Processing Speed Index (97.7) was 11.3 points lower than the Verbal Comprehension Index (109.0), and the Perceptual Organization Index (102.0) was 7 points lower. The overall apparent deficits were in the same direction as previous research.

Alzheimer's Disease. General intellectual deterioration is one of the hallmarks of individuals with Alzheimer's disease, but the cognitive deficiencies are complex. Nonverbal measures appear to be affected to a greater extent than are verbal measures, commonly leading to a Wechsler profile of Verbal > Performance. Fuld (1984) examined a sample of 46 Alzheimer's patients and found that 52% of the patients had Verbal > Performance profiles of at least 15 points. Fuld also found a profile based on specific subtest scores that was more diagnostic for Alzheimer's patients than the Verbal > Performance profile. The Fuld profile included seven WAIS-R subtests: Information, Vocabulary, Similarities, Digit Span, Digit Symbol, Block Design, and Object Assembly (Fuld, 1984). (The Fuld profile requires verification with the WAIS-III.)

Other researchers have also found the Verbal > Performance profile in patients with Alzheimer's disease (e.g., Brinkman & Braun, 1984). In a sample of 35 individuals with probable Alzheimer's disease, WAIS-III mean Verbal

IQ scores were about 10 points higher (92.2) than Performance IQ scores (81.7) (The Psychological Corporation, 1997). Examination of the mean factor index scores in this sample showed the greatest decrements in the Perceptual Organization Index (84.8) and Processing Speed Index (79.6), and some decrement in the Working Memory Index (87.2), in comparison with the Verbal Comprehension Index (93.0). Although the Verbal > Performance profile is useful in identifying the severity and extent of a patients deficits, this cognitive profile is not good at differentially diagnosing Alzheimer-type dementia from other types of dementia (Nixon, 1996).

Working Memory Factor

The Arithmetic–Digit Span–Letter-Number Sequencing triad forms the WAIS-III Working Memory Index. It is the expanded and more reliable counterpart of the WISC-III Freedom From Distractibility factor. Interpretation of the Working Memory Index score cannot be done on the basis of its name alone; it is best done in light of the behavioral observations, during testing, background information collected on the examinee, and the person's nuances of test performance (e.g., forward versus backward span on Digit Span). The Working Memory Index can be assigned diverse interpretations, including attention, concentration, anxiety, sequencing ability, sequential processing, number ability, planning ability, short-term memory, executive processing or planning, and event visualization. The possible range of interpretations of the Working Memory Index spans both the cognitive and behavioral domains.

Since there are so many possibilities for interpreting the Working Memory Index, how do you decide what it means? Essentially, one must be a good detective and integrate information and data from diverse sources.

DON'T FORGET

Possible Working Memory Index Interpretations

- attention
- concentration
- anxiety
- sequencing ability
- sequential processing
- number ability
- planning ability
- short-term memory
- executive processing or planning
- event visualization

Behavioral explanations sometimes account for a person's low Working Memory Index score, for example, distractibility, inattention, low concentration, hyperactivity, and anxiety. However, before accepting a behavioral interpretation for a low score on Working Memory Index (or any scale or subtest), you must have clinical support. For example, if during a testing session an adult frequently asks you to repeat questions because he or she is unable to maintain attention, this observation would be a good bit of clinical data to support an interpretation of inattention or distractibility. Reasons for referral and background information can also be good sources of information to support interpretations. For example, if a college student who earned a low Working Memory Index came to you for an evaluation of ADHD because he found himself unable to concentrate for more than 5 minutes on homework assignments or class lectures, such background information could provide good corroborating evidence of "short attention span" explanation of his low index. Even that referral information, though, ought to be buttressed by clinical observations of inattention during the administration of at least one Working Memory subtest.

If anxiety is suspected to have influenced the Working Memory Index score, then the examiner should consider whether the referral question alluded to anxiety and whether signs of anxiety were present during the testing. Other subtests may have also been influenced by anxiety, especially highly speeded tasks on the Performance Scale. Excess motor activity, excessive talking, or distractibility can sometimes be manifestations of anxiety during an assessment.

Difficulty with numbers sometimes explains a low Working Memory Index. If computational skills have not been mastered adequately, then behaviors such as counting on fingers or writing with fingers may be observed. Adults with such difficulties may also report a history of struggling in math classes in school or experiencing anxiety about balancing their checkbook or performing daily activities related to numbers (shopping in a supermarket, following recipes). The Arithmetic subtest is where these difficulties may be most apparent, but difficulties may also be noticed on the Digits Backward portion of Digit Span. Digits Forward may be found to be adequate, as it involves simple rote memory, but the backward span may be poorer as it involves manipulation of the numbers and is more complex. Letter-Number Sequencing may also be informative if an examinee can correctly sequence the letters but not the numbers. Also, performance on Digit Symbol-Coding may provide further support for difficulty with symbolic representations (related to numbers). Note also that good number ability can sometimes explain high scores on the Working Memory Index. Consider an accountant who earns a scaled score of 18 or 19 on Arithmetic and has an exceptional backward span for digits.

With the addition of Letter-Number Sequencing to the WAIS-III battery, the Working Memory Index more clearly provides data on the cognitive function of working memory. Letter-Number Sequencing requires an individual to hold letters and numbers in mind, reorganize them, and then repeat them sequentially. These cognitive demands are most like the Digits Backward portion of Digit Span, as they require visualization and manipulation. Repeating digits in a forward order is more of an automatic task and does not strain one's working memory. Arithmetic also requires manipulation and spatial visualization (in addition to knowledge of basic computational facts). Thus, in interpreting the Working Memory Index as a measure of working memory, it is highly advisable to examine the forward and backward portions of Digit Span separately, and then compare these with Arithmetic and Letter-Number Sequencing. Adults with weak working memories may demonstrate poor performance on Digits Backward, Letter-Number Sequencing, and Arithmetic, but they may simultaneously perform adequately on Digits Forward because this rote recall task taps a different skill. If only the total Digit Span scaled score is considered, the dissociation between the forward and backward span will be missed and invaluable information lost. To further verify "memory" hypotheses, memory of Digit Symbol stimuli can be utilized. The supplemental Digit Symbol-Pairing and Free Recall procedures can help to determine how well individuals have held this visual stimuli in their memory.

Processing Speed Factor

The Processing Speed Index, which is comprised of Digit Symbol-Coding and Symbol Search, is the only two-subtest index. Nonetheless, interpretation of this small factor involves the same kind of integration of multiple data sources as was illustrated for Working Memory Index interpretation. Interpretation of the Processing Speed Index may not only be processing speed, as the name suggests, but may also be fine motor coordination, motivation, reflectiveness, compulsiveness, visual memory, planning ability, or working memory.

Symbol Search taps mental speed to a considerable degree, whereas Digit Symbol-Coding primarily measures psychomotor speed. Thus, in interpreting the Processing Speed Index, you need to discern which of these aspects of speed are affecting the score (or whether both are contributing factors). Motor coordination may be observed in how an adolescent or adult holds the pencil during the Processing Speed Index tasks. Awkward grips on the pencil and pencil strokes that are not fluid can be keys to poor visual motor coordination. Also, observe examinees' visual motor coordination during other subtests such as Block Design and Picture Arrangement when they are required to manipulate objects. Visual-perceptual problems may also be evident in the quality of adults' drawing on Digit Symbol-Coding subtest, in the nature of their errors on Block Design and Object Assembly items, and possible figure-ground problems or distortions on Picture Completion items. One of the supplemental Digit Symbol-Coding tasks, Digit Symbol-Copy, helps to determine whether perceptual accuracy and speed are impacting a person's score (while ruling out the effect of memory).

> # DON'T FORGET
> ## Possible Processing Speed Index Interpretations
> - processing speed
> - visual motor coordination
> - motivation
> - reflectiveness
> - compulsiveness
> - visual memory
> - planning ability

Level of motivation, anxiety, perfectionism, and other noncognitive factors may also account for low Processing Speed Index scores. For example, if an examinee is reluctant to try their best to work quickly (perhaps for fear of failing) this limitation can cripple Processing Speed Index scores. Also, some individuals compulsively draw each symbol in Digit Symbol-Coding or draw a perfect diagonal through the Symbol Search boxes. Anxious individuals may have difficulty staying focused on the task, which may reduce their score as well.

Both of the Processing Speed Index subtests measure planning ability, but this ability may be especially apparent in Symbol Search, which requires efficient handling of two abstract symbols simultaneously. Adults with apparently strong planning ability (e.g., high Picture Arrangement) might score significantly higher on Symbol Search than on Digit Symbol-Coding. However, if planning is a deficit area, we would expect the reverse pattern.

A strong visual working memory can enhance the Processing Speed Index score and a poor one can hurt it, because both component subtests depend to a considerable extent on the ability to retain abstract visual stimuli for brief periods of time. On both Symbol Search and Digit Symbol-Coding, if adults can accurately remember the symbol without having to refer back to the key or the target group, they will be able to perform more efficiently. The supplemental Digit Symbol-Incidental Learning procedures (Pairing and Free Recall) provide invaluable information for determining how well a person has memorized the digit-symbol pairs and the symbols themselves. Administer these optional procedures routinely because the obtained scores can be compared with the national norms to permit meaningful interpretation of the results (cumulative percentage obtained from *WAIS-III Administration and Scoring Manual,* Table A.11).

Step 8: Interpret Significant Strengths and Weaknesses of Subtest Profile

Steps 1 to 7 examine the global scores, but in Step 8 we begin to look at the nitty-gritty of an individual's unique subtest profile. It is at this level of examination that we truly begin to understand the uniqueness of each individual and initiate the creation hypotheses about the person's strong and weak areas of cognitive functioning. There are, however, some empirical guidelines to follow before jumping into hypothesis generation.

Step 8 calls for an ipsative comparison of an individual's mean performance on all subtests with each subtest administered. An ipsative comparison examines how well a person is performing on each subtest relative to their own average subtest score. This is different from comparing an individual's subtest scores with the normative group. For example, a person may earn a subtest scaled score of 9, which is performing in the Average range compared to the normative group. However, if that person's own *mean* subtest scaled score is 15, then relative to his or her own performance that subtest scaled score of 9 is low and is a personal relative weakness.

How do you decide which mean to use in Step 8? Rapid Reference 4.15 reviews the rules leading to your choice of means. The simple rule of thumb is this: If an individual's Verbal IQ versus Performance IQ discrepancy is 17

CAUTION

Use All Subtests Administered in Calculation of Mean During Step 8

Mean of	Includes	Total Number of Subtests in Calculation of Mean[a]
All Full Scale subtests	6 Verbal subtests + 5 Performance subtests + Letter-Number Sequencing + Symbol Search + Object Assembly	14
All Verbal Scale subtests	6 Verbal subtests + Letter-Number Sequencing	7
All Performance Scale subtests	5 Performance subtests + Symbol Search + Object Assembly	7

[a]If all of these subtests were not administered, just include *all* that were administered (e.g., 12, 6, or 6).

points or larger, then you should use two separate means (the mean of all Verbal subtests administered and the mean of all Performance subtests administered). However, if the Verbal IQ versus the Performance IQ discrepancy is less than 17 points, you should use the mean of all subtests administered. When the Verbal and Performance IQs differ by an "abnormal" amount, it makes sense to compare scaled scores on the Verbal subtests to the Verbal mean, and, analogously, to compare Performance subtest scaled scores to the Performance mean. If the discrepancy is not unusually large, (less than 17 points), then the Full Scale mean (i.e., the mean scaled score of *all* WAIS-III subtests *administered*) serves as the best point of comparison for every subtest, whether Verbal or Performance.

Once the correct mean or means have been calculated, you should round the mean(s) to the nearest whole number (see Rapid Reference 4.15). This procedure will simplify the next calculations, and likely reduce the chance of making errors, but will not compromise your statistical examination. For the interested reader, Kaufman (1994, pp. 125–128) has provided a detailed review of some of the controversy surrounding the empirical method of calculating strengths and weaknesses based on an individual's own mean score.

4.15 Step 8: Interpret Significant Strengths and Weaknesses of Profile

Determine which mean you should use to calculate strengths and weaknesses.

V-IQ–P-IQ Discrepancy

(After calculating means, round to the nearest whole number.)

0–16	Then use ⇨	mean of all subtests administered.	⇨	Overall Mean ‾‾‾‾‾‾‾	Rounded Mean ‾‾‾‾‾‾‾
17 or more	Then use ⇨	mean of all Verbal subtests administered *and also use*		Verbal Subtest Mean 13.86	Rounded Mean 14
		mean of all performance subtests administered.	⇨	Performance Subtest Mean 10.28	Rounded Mean 10

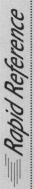

Verbal Subtest	Scaled Score	Rounded Mean	Difference[a]	Difference Needed for Significance	Strength (S) or Weakness (W)	Percentile Rank (See Table 4.6)
Vocabulary	14	14	0	±2	—	91
Similarities	15	14	+1	±3	—	95
Arithmetic	15	14	+1	±3	—	95
Digit Span	13	14	-1	±3	—	84
Information	12	14	-2	±3	—	75
Comprehension	15	14	+1	±3	—	95
Letter-Number Sequencing	13	14	-1	±4	—	84
Performance Subtest						
Picture Completion	9	10	-1	±4	—	37
Digit Symbol-Coding	5	10	-5	±3	W	5
Block Design	14	10	+4	±3	S	91
Matrix Reasoning	13	10	+3	±3	S	84
Picture Arrangement	14	10	+4	±4	S	91
Symbol Search	6	10	-4	±4	W	9
Object Assembly	11	10	+1	±4	—	63

Note. V-IQ = Verbal IQ; P-IQ = Performance IQ.

[a] Use appropriate rounded mean in calculating the "scaled score–mean" difference.

The differences between each of the 14 subtest scores and the rounded mean scaled score should then be calculated. The subtests that are higher than the mean will have a positive valence and those that are lower than the mean will have a negative valence. These difference values should be recorded on the WAIS-III Interpretive Worksheet with the appropriate plus (+) or minus (–) signs (see Rapid Reference 4.15 and Appendix).

The size of the differences necessary for significance are listed in Table B.3 of the *WAIS-III Administration and Scoring Manual* and are summarized in Step 8 of the WAIS-III Interpretive Worksheet (see Rapid Reference 4.15 and the Appendix that begins on page 235). The values presented in the WAIS-III administration manual provide exact values, whereas we present an overview with rounded values. Examiners may use the exact values, although the rounded values are sufficient to calculate strengths and weaknesses and they minimize the risk of clerical error and reduce dependency on tables.

If the difference between each scaled score and the individual's mean is large enough to be statistically significant, then it may be considered a strength (if above the mean) or weakness (if below the mean). The strengths and weaknesses may be denoted by the letters S and W, respectively. If scaled scores do not deviate significantly from the appropriate mean, they should be considered chance fluctuations. Do not interpret nonsignificant differences as strengths or weaknesses per se, but you may use such differences to support hypotheses.

An additional component of Step 8 in the WAIS-III Interpretive Worksheet (see Rapid Reference 4.15) is the translation of scaled scores to percentile ranks. In writing the results section of a report, a metric such as percentile rank is extremely useful in communicating to professionals and laypersons alike. Most people are not familiar with the scaled score's mean of 10 and standard deviation of 3, but they are likely to understand the commonly used percentile rank. The WAIS-III provides percentile ranks for the IQs and indexes but not for the scaled score values, so we provide percentile ranks for the scaled score values in Table 4.6 on page 145.

Step 9: Generating Hypotheses About the Fluctuations in the WAIS-III Profile

The last step in the process of WAIS-III interpretation involves the most crucial part of the process. Step 9, in essence, requires examiners to be good

Table 4.6 National Percentile Ranks Corresponding to Scaled Scores

Percentile Rank	Scaled Score	Corresponding IQ
99.9	19	145
99.6	18	140
99	17	135
98	16	130
95	15	125
91	14	120
84	13	115
75	12	110
63	11	105
50	10	100
37	9	95
25	8	90
16	7	85
9	6	80
5	5	75
2	4	70
1	3	65
0.5	2	60
0.1	1	55

detectives and to use not only evidence provided from analysis of the strengths and weaknesses in a profile but that from observed behaviors, background information, and supplemental testing as well in order to confirm or disconfirm hypotheses. From these interpretations, validated by multiple pieces of data, strong and sensible recommendations can be made for intervention.

As discussed earlier in this chapter, interpretation of Wechsler's Verbal-Performance dichotomy does not provide an adequate explanation for every individual's WAIS-III profile. More than one model is needed to explain the many possible combinations of strengths and weaknesses in the subtest profile. Steps 1 to 8 have provided a framework that navigates you through the global scores down to the empirical determination of relative strengths and weaknesses in the subtest profile. The final step is one that will create meaning from the strengths and weaknesses.

The starting point for creating hypotheses is the discovery of scores that deviate significantly from the examinee's own mean performance. The challenge is to uncover hypotheses regarding abilities shared by two or more subtests or concerning influences that may have affected the test scores. Far too often examiners take the easy road when writing reports and simply regurgitate the textbook definitions of what each single subtest purportedly measures. This type of mindless recitation does not provide useful information about the individual adolescent or adult who was tested. For example, some examiners state that individuals appear to have strong "short-term memory" because an individual had a high score on Digit Span. However, such a statement, when made in isolation, might neglect the relative trouble that was evident on Letter-Number Sequencing and the comments noted by the person's caretaker about forgetfulness throughout the day.

The goal of the detective work involved in deciphering the strong and weak areas in the WAIS-III profile is to find information that is consistent across the entire profile. Specifically, strengths and weaknesses should be supported by two or more subtests and, whenever feasible, by clinical observations, background information, and supplementary cognitive or achievement measures. A subtest-specific hypothesis should only be used when the detective work to find global strengths or weaknesses is futile. At times a profile may be totally flat, evidencing no relative strengths or weaknesses. Examination of such flat profiles does not allow much detective work within the WAIS-III itself. In this case, a wise step to take to uncover more information about an adult's abilities is to administer supplementary subtests that measure abilities not well tapped by the WAIS-III.

INTRODUCTION TO WAIS-III SUBTEST INTERPRETIVE TABLES

The abilities that are believed to underlie each WAIS-III subtest are organized in Rapid Reference 4.16. These tables are useful in facilitating the detective process. The information included in the tables summarizes the material that was included in the subtest-by-subtest analysis at the beginning of this chapter. At a glance, it is possible to see which abilities and influences are shared by at least two WAIS-III subtests.

The subtests organized into the shared abilities (Rapid Reference 4.16) are outlined by the information processing model: Input–Integration/Storage–Output. This psycholinguistic model considers more than just the content of the item. In addition, it asks:

- What type of stimuli does the individual have to respond to?
- How is the information processed and remembered?
- How is the person required to respond?

It is important to consider that some aspect of the properties of the stimulus or the response may affect an adult's performance on certain subtests apart from the specific content or processes inherent in the task.

The shared abilities listed in Rapid Reference 4.16 are, of course, not exhaustive; rather, the information provided is intended to be illustrative and a good guideline. Examiners should utilize this reference as a framework that is open to expansion. The expertise of each examiner and the individuality of each person tested should be incorporated into the detective work involved in profile analysis.

Reliability Coefficients of Shared Abilities

With each cluster of subtests listed are the split-half reliabilities and test-retest reliabilities. These values are based on the average reliabilities presented in the *WAIS-III and WMS-III Technical Manual* and on the average intercorrelations among subtests in each cluster. The formula for a composite was applied (Tellegen & Briggs, 1967). The test-retest and split-half reliabilities differ for most clusters; thus both are provided.

How to Use Information About Shared Abilities

Rapid Reference 4.16 shows how different abilities overlap various subtests. The next question is, what do you do with all that information? Here we provide you with a sequential guide to generate hypotheses. The guidelines pre-

≡ Rapid Reference

4.16 Abilities Shared by Two or More WAIS-III Verbal or Performance Subtests

Ability	Verbal Subtests							Performance Subtests							Reliability[a]	
	I	S	A	V	C	DS	LN	PC	Cd	PA	BD	OA	SS	MR	r_{xx}	r_{12}
Input																
Attention-concentration			A			DS	LN	PC	Cd				SS		.95	.94
Auditory-vocal channel	I	S	A	V	C	DS	LN								.97	.96
Complex verbal directions									Cd	PA	BD		SS	MR	.94	.93
Distinguishing essential from nonessential detail		S						PC	Cd	PA			SS	MR	.94	.93
Encode information for processing			A			DS	LN	PC	Cd				SS		.95	.93
Simple verbal directions								PC				OA			.85	.84
Understanding long questions	I		A		C			PC	Cd	PA	BD	OA	SS	MR	.95	.94
Understanding words		S		V		DS	LN		Cd		BD		SS	MR	.95	.92
Visual-motor channel								PC	Cd	PA	BD	OA	SS	MR	.95	.94
Visual perception of abstract stimuli									Cd		BD		SS		.94	.93
Visual perception of complete meaningful stimuli								PC		PA					.86	.83
Visual perception of meaningful stimuli								PC		PA		OA			.88	.86

Ability	Verbal Subtests							Performance Subtests							Reliability[a]	
	I	S	A	V	C	DS	LN	PC	Cd	PA	BD	OA	SS	MR	r_{xx}	r_{12}
Integration/Storage																
Achievement	I	S	A	V	C										.97	.96
Acquired Knowledge	I		A	V											.96	.95
Cognition		S	A	V				PC			BD	OA		MR	.96	.95
Common sense					C					PA					.86	.82
Concept formation		S		V							BD				.95	.92
Convergent production									Cd	PA			SS	MR	.92	.91
Crystallized Intelligence	I	S		V	C					PA					.96	.95
Culture-loaded knowledge	I				C										.93	.92
Evaluation					C			PC	Cd	PA	BD	OA	SS	MR	.96	.95
Facility with numbers			A			DS	LN		Cd						.94	.92
Figural cognition								PC			BD	OA		MR	.93	.91
Figural evaluation								PC			BD	OA	SS	MR	.94	.92
Fluid Intelligence		S	A							PA	BD	OA		MR	.95	.93
Fund of information	I			V											.95	.95
General ability	I	S	A	V	C						BD			MR	.97	.96
Handing abstract verbal concepts		S		V											.94	.92
Holistic (right-brain) processing								PC				OA		MR	.90	.88
Integrated brain function									Cd	PA	BD		SS		.92	.91
Learning ability				V					Cd				SS	MR	.94	.93

continued

Ability	Verbal Subtests							Performance Subtests							Reliability[a]	
	I	S	A	V	C	DS	LN	PC	Cd	PA	BD	OA	SS	MR	r_{xx}	r_{12}
Integration/Storage (cont.)																
Long-term memory	I		A	V											.96	.95
Memory	I		A			DS	LN								.95	.92
Nonverbal reasoning										PA		OA		MR	.89	.85
Planning ability										PA			SS		.83	.82
Reasoning		S	A		C					PA		OA		MR	.95	.93
Reproduction of models									Cd		BD				.89	.89
Semantic cognition		S	A	V	C										.95	.93
Semantic content	I	S	A	V	C										.97	.96
Sequential			A			DS	LN		Cd						.94	.92
Short-term memory (auditory or visual)						DS	LN		Cd				SS		.93	.91
Simultaneous processing								PC			BD	OA		MR	.93	.91
Social comprehension					C					PA					.86	.82
Spatial								PC			BD	OA			.90	.88
Spatial visualization											BD		SS	MR	.92	.89
Symbolic content			A			DS	LN		Cd						.94	.92
Synthesis										PA	BD	OA		MR	.92	.89
Trial-and-error learning											BD	OA			.86	.83
Verbal concept formation		S		V											.94	.92

Ability	Verbal Subtests							Performance Subtests							Reliability[a]	
	I	S	A	V	C	DS	LN	PC	Cd	PA	BD	OA	SS	MR	r_{xx}	r_{12}
Verbal Conceptualization		S		V	C										.95	.93
Verbal reasoning		S			C										.91	.89
Visual memory								PC	Cd						.88	.90
Visual processing								PC			BD	OA		MR	.93	.91
Visual sequencing									Cd	PA					.85	.85
Output																
Much verbal expression	I	S		V	C										.95	.93
Simple vocal expression	I		A			DS	LN								.95	.92
Visual organization								PC		PA				MR	.86	.83
Visual-motor coordination									Cd		BD	OA	SS		.92	.92
Influences Affecting Scores																
Ability to respond when uncertain								PC				OA		MR	.90	.88
Alertness to environment	I							PC							.91	.92
Anxiety			A			DS	LN		Cd				SS		.95	.93
Attention span			A			DS	LN		Cd				SS		.94	.91
Cognitive style (field dependence)								PC			BD	OA		MR	.93	.91
Concentration			A				LN	PC	Cd				SS		.94	.94
Cultural opportunities	I			V	C					PA					.95	.94

continued

Influences Affecting Scores (cont.)

Ability	Verbal Subtests							Performance Subtests							Reliability[a]	
	I	S	A	V	C	DS	LN	PC	Cd	PA	BD	OA	SS	MR	r_{xx}	r_{12}
Distractibility			A			DS	LN		Cd				SS		.95	.93
Flexibility		S				DS	LN					OA		MR	.94	.91
Foreign language background	I			V											.95	.95
Intellectual curiosity and striving	I			V											.95	.95
Interests	I	S		V											.96	.95
Learning disabilities	I		A	V		DS	LN		Cd				SS		.97	.96
Motivation level									Cd				SS		.88	.91
Negativism		S			C	DS	LN	PC							.95	.92
Obsessive concern with detail and accuracy									Cd				SS		.88	.91
Outside reading	I	S		V											.96	.95
Overly concrete thinking		S			C									MR	.94	.90
Persistence	I						LN		Cd			OA	SS		.91	.90
Richness of early environment	I			V											.95	.95
School learning	I		A	V											.96	.95
Visual-perceptual problems									Cd		BD	OA	SS		.94	.93
Work under time pressure			A					PC	Cd	PA	BD	OA	SS		.95	.94

Note. I = Information; S = Similarities; A = Arithmetic; V = Vocabulary; C = Comprehension; DS = Digit Span; LN = Letter-Number Sequencing; PC = Picture Completion; Cd = Digit Symbol-Coding; PA = Picture Arrangement; BD = Block Design; OA = Object Assembly; SS = Symbol Search; MR = Matrix Reasoning.

[a]r_{xx} = Split-half reliability; r_{12} = test-retest reliability.

sented here should be followed to identify potential strong and weak abilities evident from the WAIS-III profile. Mike A.'s subtest profile is used to demonstrate how to walk through the process.

Guideline 1

Choose one of the strengths (S) or weaknesses (W) determined in Step 8. Write down all shared abilities (and influences affecting performance) that involve this subtest.

We will go through each of these guidelines using Mike A.'s first relative weakness that was found in Step 8: Digit Symbol-Coding. Table 4.2 shows all the possible shared abilities for Digit Symbol-Coding written down together.

Guideline 2

Consider each ability, one by one, to determine how the examinee performed on the other subtest or subtests that also measure the identified abilities. In Step 8, you determined the relative strengths and weaknesses in the subtest profile by considering whether the score deviated significantly from the pertinent mean subtest score. In the process of deciding which abilities explain the strength, less stringent criteria have to be applied. Thus consider whether a person scores above, below, or equal to his or her own mean score on all pertinent subtests for an ability. Record this information on your list of shared abilities by writing the following next to each subtest:

- − (indicating performance below the individual's mean subtest scaled score)
- + (indicating performance above the individual's mean subtest scaled score)
- 0 (indicating performance exactly at the individual's mean subtest scaled score).

Continuing with the example of Mike A.'s relative weakness in Digit Symbol-Coding, Table 4.3 demonstrates how to fill in the empty squares with a +, −, or 0. For example, in the first row, attention-concentration is listed as a hypothesized weak ability. The first blank square is found under the Arithmetic column, and since Mike's Arithmetic scaled score was one point above his Verbal Scale mean scaled score (see Rapid Reference 4.15), a + is placed in the box. Also listed with attention-concentration are Digit Span, Letter-Number Sequencing, Picture Completion, and Digit Symbol-Coding. These

Table 4.2 Example of Partial Shared Ability Worksheet for Digit Symbol-Coding

Ability	Verbal Subtests							Performance Subtests							Strength (S) or Weakness (W)	
	I	S	A	V	C	DS	LN	PC	Cd	PA	BD	OA	SS	MR	S	W
Input																
Attention-concentration			☐			☐	☐	☐	☐				☐		S	W
Complex verbal directions									☐	☐			☐	☐	S	W
Encode information for processing			☐			☐	☐		☐	☐	☐		☐	☐	S	W
Visual-motor channel								☐	☐	☐		☐	☐	☐	S	W
Visual perception of abstract stimuli									☐		☐		☐	☐	S	W
Integration/Storage																
Convergent production									☐	☐			☐	☐	S	W
Evaluation					☐			☐	☐	☐	☐				S	W
Facility with numbers			☐			☐	☐		☐			☐			S	W
Integrated brain function									☐	☐			☐		S	W
Learning ability				☐					☐			☐		☐	S	W

Note. I = Information; S = Similarities; A = Arithmetic; V = Vocabulary; C = Comprehension; DS = Digit Span; LN = Letter-Number Sequencing; PC = Picture Completion; Cd = Digit Symbol-Coding; PA = Picture Arrangement; BD = Block Design; OA = Object Assembly; SS = Symbol Search; MR = Matrix Reasoning.

boxes are filled with the appropriate pluses, minuses, or zeros according to the difference between each of Mike's subtest scores and his mean scaled score. Table 4.3 demonstrates this process further by showing this table partially completed.

Guideline 3

Consider each ability, one by one, to determine whether the ability should be considered a strong or weak ability. In general, shared strengths are those in which a person has scored above his or her own mean score on all pertinent subtests, with at least one discrepancy reaching statistical significance. However, there are exceptions to this global rule for shared abilities that are described in the Don't Forget on page 157. These rules should be considered rules of thumb, rather than rigid principals. There are instances when there is an overabundance of other clinical information from behavioral observations, background information, and supplementary testing data that will support a shared ability as a strength or weakness, even if these rule-of-thumb guidelines are not met. In such instances of multiple sources of information, the rules listed here should not preclude you from interpreting the strength or weakness.

Table 4.3 lists a place for strengths (s) and weaknesses (w) to be circled once the rules of thumb have been applied. In Mike's example of Digit Symbol-Coding shown in Table 4.4, we examine each hypothesized ability to determine which ones may be considered strengths or weaknesses. Attention-concentration ability is considered to be underlying six subtests (Arithmetic, Digit Span, Letter-Number Sequencing, Picture Completion, Digit Symbol-Coding, and Symbol Search). Examination of the pluses, minuses, and zeros filled in, we see that five subtests have minuses (indicating being below the mean) and one has a plus (indicating being above the mean). The rules for accepting and rejecting potential hypotheses tell us that for an ability to be considered a strength when there are five or more subtests, at least four subtests must be below the mean, and only one subtest may be equal to or greater than the mean. Thus, attention-concentration may be considered a weak ability (and the letter *W* is circled on the worksheet).

The next ability to examine with Mike's profile is complex verbal directions. There are five subtests noted to have this underlying ability. On three of the subtests, Mike earned scores that were above his own mean and on two

Table 4.3 Example of Shared Ability Worksheet for Digit Symbol-Coding With Completed –, +, 0

Ability	Verbal Subtests							Performance Subtests							Strength (S) or Weakness (W)
	I	S	A	V	C	DS	LN	PC	Cd	PA	BD	OA	SS	MR	
Input															
Attention-concentration			⊞			□	□	□	□	⊞			□		S W
Complex verbal directions										⊞	⊞		□	⊞	S W
Encode information for processing			⊞			□	□			⊞			□	⊞	S W
Visual-motor channel								□	□	⊞	⊞	⊞	□	⊞	S W
Visual perception of abstract stimuli									□	⊞	⊞		□	⊞	S W
Integration/Storage															
Convergent production								□	□	⊞	⊞	⊞	□	⊞	S W
Evaluation					⊞				□	⊞	⊞	⊞	□	⊞	S W
Facility with numbers			⊞			□	□		□				□	⊞	S W
Integrated brain function									□	⊞	⊞	⊞	□	⊞	S W
Learning ability				⊡					□				□	⊞	S W

Note. I = Information; S = Similarities; A = Arithmetic; V = Vocabulary; C = Comprehension; DS = Digit Span; LN = Letter-Numbering Sequencing; PC = Picture Completion; Cd = Digit Symbol-Coding; PA = Picture Arrangement; BD = Block Design; OA = Object Assembly; SS = Symbol Search; MR = Matrix Reasoning.

DON'T FORGET

Rules for Accepting and Rejecting Potential Hypotheses

Number of Subtests Constituting a Shared Ability	Rule for Interpreting Ability as a Strength (at least one subtest is a significant strength)	Rule for Interpreting Ability as a Weakness (at least one subtest is a significant weakness)
2	• *All* subtests must be above the mean.	• *All* subtests must be *below* the mean.
3 or 4	• *At least two or three* subtests must be *above* the mean, • and *only one* subtest may be *equivalent to* the mean.	• *At least two or three* subtests must be *below* the mean, • and *only one* subtest may be *equivalent to* the mean.
5 or more	• *At least four* subtests must be *above* the mean, • and *only one* subtest may be *equal to* the mean *or less than* the mean.	• *At least four subtests* must be *below* the mean, • and *only one* subtest may be *equal to* the mean *or greater than* the mean.

he earned scores that were below his mean. Thus, because more than one test was above the mean, complex verbal directions cannot be considered as a hypothesized weak ability. However, the next ability, encode information for processing, follows the same pattern as attention-concentration and can be considered a weak ability (and the letter *W* is circled on the worksheet).

Guideline 4

Repeat Guidelines 1, 2, and 3 for every other significant strength that has not been accounted for. Then follow analogous procedures for all significant weaknesses. Shown in Table 4.5 is the next relative strength in Mike's WAIS-III profile—Block Design (Rapid Reference 4.15). After filling in all of the pluses, minuses, and zeros in the Shared Ability Worksheet for Block Design,

Table 4.4 Example of Shared Ability Worksheet for Digit Symbol-Coding With Completed Strength and Weakness Column

Ability	Verbal Subtests							Performance Subtests							Strength (S) or Weakness (W)
	I	S	A	V	C	DS	LN	PC	Cd	PA	BD	OA	SS	MR	
Input															
Attention-concentration			⊞			☐	☐	☐	☐				☐	☐	S (Ⓦ)
Complex verbal directions						☐	☐		☐	⊞	⊞		☐	⊞	S W
Encode information for processing			⊞			☐	☐	☐	☐				☐	☐	S (Ⓦ)
Visual-motor channel								☐	☐	⊞	⊞	⊞	☐	⊞	S W
Visual perception of abstract stimuli									☐	⊞	⊞		☐	⊞	S W
Integration/Storage															
Convergent production								☐	☐	⊞	⊞		☐	⊞	S W
Evaluation					⊞				☐	⊞	⊞		☐	⊞	S W
Facility with numbers			⊞			☐	☐		☐						S W
Integrated brain function									☐	⊞	⊞		☐	⊞	S W
Learning ability	☑												☐	⊞	S W

Note. I = Information; S = Similarities; A = Arithmetic; V = Vocabulary; C = Comprehension; DS = Digit Span; LN = Letter-Numbering Sequencing; PC = Picture Completion; Cd = Digit Symbol-Coding; PA = Picture Arrangement; BD = Block Design; OA = Object Assembly; SS = Symbol Search; MR = Matrix Reasoning.

some hypothesized abilities appear to be possible explanations for Mike's strength in Block Design: concept formation, fluid ability, and synthesis. Before including any of these abilities in Mike's report, it is necessary to consider whether the behavioral observations, background information, and supplemental test data also support these hypotheses. (To see how all of the various strengths and weaknesses are integrated, see Chapter 7, which presents the complete case report written about Mike A.'s WAIS-III profile.)

Guideline 5

If the process of examining shared abilities uncovers no hypothesized strengths or weaknesses, then interpret the unique abilities that are presumably measured by significantly high or low subtests. The primary focus for explaining significant discrepancies in a profile should be on shared abilities that link several subtests, especially when these hypothesized strengths and weaknesses are supported by background information, behavioral observations, and supplementary testing. However, at times no hypothesized strengths or weaknesses are apparent after examining the potential shared abilities. Subtest-specific interpretations may then have to be made. The unique abilities (denoted with an asterisk) are listed in the subtest-by-subtest description of abilities listed earlier in this chapter.

Before interpreting a unique ability on a subtest, one should consider its amount of specificity. Those with "ample" or "adequate" amounts of specificity may be interpreted (see Rapid Reference 4.2). However, even if a subtest score deviates significantly from the mean and if that subtest has "ample" subtest specificity, one should not automatically interpret the unique ability. Only when all hypotheses involving shared abilities prove useless should an examiner acquiesce to an interpretation of a unique and highly specific strength or weakness. When unique abilities are interpreted, it is best to have other supportive evidence from background data, behavioral observations, or supplemental testing.

Table 4.5 Example of Shared Ability Worksheet for Block Design Strength

Ability	Verbal Subtests							Performance Subtests							Strength (S) or Weakness (W)
	I	S	A	V	C	DS	LN	PC	Cd	PA	BD	OA	SS	MR	
Input															
Complex verbal directions									□		⊞		□	⊞	S W
Visual Perception of abstract stimuli											⊞			⊞	S W
Visual-motor Channel								□	□	⊞	⊞	⊞	□	⊞	S W
Integration/Storage															
Cognition	⊞			⊡				□			⊞			⊞	S W
Concept formation			⊞	⊡	⊞			□			⊞			⊞	(S) W
Evaluation					⊞			□	□		⊞	⊞	□	⊞	S W
Figural cognition								□	□	⊞	⊞	⊞		⊞	S W
Figural evaluation								□	□		⊞	⊞	□	⊞	S W
Fluid ability	⊞									⊞	⊞	⊞		⊞	(S) W
General ability	⊞	⊞			⊡			□			⊞			⊞	S W

Note. I = Information; S = Similarities; A = Arithmetic; V = Vocabulary; C = Comprehension; DS = Digit Span; LN = Letter-Numbering Sequencing; PC = Picture Completion; Cd = Digit Symbol-Coding; PA = Picture Arrangement; BD = Block Design; OA = Object Assembly; SS = Symbol Search; MR = Matrix Reasoning.

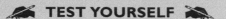

1. **To glean the most valuable information from the WAIS-III, examine**
   (a) mainly a subject's weak areas.
   (b) only the subject's strengths in isolation.
   (c) abilities shared by many subtests.
   (d) only the areas relevant to the referral question.

2. **The subtests that have the most ample amount of subtest specificity include all but which one of the following?**
   (a) Digit Span
   (b) Matrix Reasoning
   (c) Digit Symbol-Coding
   (d) Letter-Number Sequencing
   (e) Vocabulary

3. **The subtest that taps the unique ability of "nonverbal problem solving with no time limit" is**
   (a) Digit Span.
   (b) Matrix Reasoning.
   (c) Digit Symbol-Coding.
   (d) Letter Number Sequencing.
   (e) Vocabulary.

4. **The subtest that taps the unique ability of "speed of visual search" is**
   (a) Digit Span.
   (b) Matrix Reasoning.
   (c) Digit Symbol-Coding.
   (d) Letter-Number Sequencing.
   (e) Symbol Search.

5. **The most reliable scale on the WAIS-III, with a mean split-half correlation of .98, is**
   (a) Verbal IQ.
   (b) Performance IQ.
   (c) Full Scale IQ.
   (d) Verbal Comprehension Index.

continued

6. **An abnormally large discrepancy between Verbal IQ and Performance IQ means the discrepancy is**
   (a) rare among the normal population.
   (b) equivalent to a statistically significant discrepancy.
   (c) at least 50-point discrepancy.
   (d) at least 5-point discrepancy.

7. **If the Working Memory Index or the Verbal Comprehension Index scores do not correspond to unitary abilities, then which of the IQs cannot be interpreted?**
   (a) Verbal IQ
   (b) Performance IQ

8. **If the Perceptual Organization Index or the Processing Speed Index scores do not correspond to unitary abilities, then which of the IQs cannot be interpreted?**
   (a) Verbal IQ
   (b) Performance IQ

9. **Which are the two central constructs of Horn and Cattell's (1967) theory?**
   (a) Verbal and Performance IQ
   (b) Crystallized (Gc) and Fluid (Gf) Intelligence
   (c) Creativity and Practical Intelligence
   (d) Visual and Auditory Memory

10. **Which of these factors will *not* likely lead to a Performance > Verbal profile?**
    (a) bilingualism
    (b) learning disabilities
    (c) depression

11. **Which of these factors will *not* likely lead to a Verbal > Performance profile?**
    (a) alcoholism
    (b) learning disabilities
    (c) depression
    (d) multiple sclerosis

12. **A low score on the Working Memory Index may be interpreted as all of the following except**
    (a) distractibility or attentional difficulties.
    (b) difficulty with numbers.
    (c) poor motor ability.
    (d) excessive anxiety.

13. **A low score on the Processing Speed Index may be interpreted as all of the following except**

   (a) fine motor control difficulty.

   (b) reflective processing style.

   (c) poor visual memory.

   (d) poor nonverbal reasoning.

14. **In calculating an individual's relative strengths and weaknesses in his or her profile, you compare each of the subtest scores to his or her own mean subtest score.** True or False?

15. **The goal of the detective work involved in deciphering the strong and weak areas in the WAIS-III profile is to find information that is consistent across the entire profile.** True or False?

16. **You should always consider unique abilities to explain strengths and weaknesses in the subtest profile before considering any shared abilities.** True or False?

Answers: 1. c; 2. e; 3. b; 4. e; 5. c; 6. a; 7. a; 8. b; 9. b; 10. c; 11. b; 12. c; 13. d; 14. True; 15. True; 16. False

Five

STRENGTHS AND WEAKNESSES OF THE WAIS-III

OVERVIEW OF ADVANTAGES AND DISADVANTAGES OF THE WAIS-III

The Psychological Corporation has made many additions and modifications in its latest version of the WAIS. Because the WAIS-III was about a year old as this book went to press, no published reviews of the test had yet appeared. During the WAIS-III's first year of life we have examined the instrument carefully; used it numerous times in clinical evaluations; and supervised graduate students in its administration, scoring, and interpretations. Based on these diverse experiences, we have identified what we perceive to be its main strengths and weaknesses. We have grouped these strengths and weaknesses into the following areas: test development, administration and scoring, standardization, reliability and validity, and interpretation (see Rapid Reference 5.1, 5.2, 5.3, 5.4, and 5.5).

There are several major strengths that we found on the WAIS-III, but not any weaknesses that we considered *major*. Significant strengths that we feel are important to highlight include the following: excellent standardization sample, high reliability and stability of the IQs, elimination of the reference group from the scaled-score computation, four-factor structure with Working Memory and Processing Speed, addition of Matrix Reasoning and Letter-Number Sequencing to the overall battery, extending the "bottom" by adding reverse items, and enhanced neuropsychological interpretations made possible with supplemental data tables for Digit Span and Digit Symbol-Coding.

The changes made in this latest revision of the WAIS have made it a much stronger instrument. There are several abilities, such as fluid reasoning and working memory, that were not possible to measure with confidence in the earlier versions of the WAIS. With all of these strengths high-lighted, it is also important to note that the WAIS-III does not measure every possible construct that underlies intelligence. As we have emphasized throughout this book, it is important to have many sources of data to truly understand adults and their cognitive abilities. Thus WAIS-III profiles inte-grated with data from supplemental measures, background information, and behavioral observations are interpretable and informative; test scores, in isolation, are not.

≡ Rapid Reference

5.1 Strengths and Weaknesses of WAIS-III Test Development

Strengths	Weaknesses
• The addition of Symbol Search allows a similar four-factor structure for the WISC-III, pro-viding valuable continuity.	• Some of the artwork on the Picture Completion section is too busy and can be distracting (e.g., Items 5, 11, and 24).
• The addition of Matrix Reason-ing enhances the assessment of fluid reasoning on both the Per-formance Scale and Perceptual Organization Index.	• There is great emphasis on the symmetry of items and trivial detail on Picture Completion, which may be subtly biased against disadvantaged individuals (e.g., Items 16, 17, and 21).
• Matrix Reasoning provides opportunity for those exam-inees who are not inclined to perform well on speeded visual-motor tasks to demonstrate their nonverbal abilities on a "power" test.	• Matrix Reasoning colors can be distracting and are potentially unfair to color-blind individuals.
• Artwork, manual with built-in easel, and overall appearance of materials are updated and improved.	
• There is an extension of the age range for which the test was normed from 74 to 89 years.	

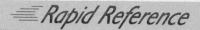

5.2 Strengths and Weaknesses of WAIS-III Administration and Scoring

Strengths

- Scoring rules and reverse rules are consistently implemented.
- Beginning with Picture Completion rather than Information is less anxiety producing for many clients.
- Digit Symbol and other tasks on which the examinee has to use a pencil are all located in one convenient response booklet.
- The record form is well designed with ample space to write responses and to note incorrect block design constructions, and the new rebus symbols are easy to follow.
- The presentation of Vocabulary words a few items at a time is very useful, as it avoids the frustration felt by those with poor vocabularies (who previously had to see the entire list they were going to be administered).
- The presentation of scoring criteria concurrently with the directions for administration for Similarities, Vocabulary, and Comprehension is convenient.
- For Picture Completion, the list of queries to prompt examinees (when they have either named the object pictured, mentioned a part of the picture off of the page, or mentioned an unessential part) has been handily written right on the record form.

Weaknesses

- Some of the Vocabulary, Similarities, and Comprehension items seem to be arbitrarily marked to query (e.g., several 1-point responses on Vocabulary Items 13 and 17, Similarities Items 11 and 15, and Comprehension Items 11 and 12).
- Three verbal tests still require complex judgments to be made in scoring (e.g., Similarities, Vocabulary, Comprehension).
- The Digit Symbol supplementary procedures utilize the word *symbols* whereas the Digit Symbol-Coding directions switch terms and refer mostly to "special marks" or "marks," which can be confusing for low-functioning individuals.
- In the Digit Symbol-Coding response booklet, it is confusing to differentiate the two rows of Pairing from the blank space on which examinees are to respond for Free Recall.
- Because of the need to differentiate colors to determine the correct response on some Matrix Reasoning items, adults and adolescents who are color-blind may be at a disadvantage on these items.
- The proverb items on Comprehension measure a different type of reasoning skill (generalization) than the other items but were still retained in this newest version.
- The artwork in Picture Arrangement contains too many fine details, sometimes obscuring what is important (e.g., Dream and Shark items).

≡ Rapid Reference

5.3 Strengths and Weaknesses of WAIS-III Reliability and Validity

Strengths	Weaknesses
• Split-half reliability coefficients and standard errors of measurement are outstanding for the Verbal IQ, Verbal Comprehension Index, and Full Scale IQ and are excellent for the Performance IQ, Perceptual Organization Index, and Working Memory Index (see Rapid Reference 1.4 in Chapter 1).	• Split-half reliability for Object Assembly at 10 of the 13 age levels is below .75; the four oldest age groups are below .70. For Picture Arrangement, six groups have split-half reliability below .75, and two of those are below .70.
• Overall, split-half reliabilities are excellent for all subtests across the 13 age groups except Object Assembly and Picture Arrangement. Of the split-half reliability values for the Verbal subtests 79% were at or above .85. However, for the Performance subtests, excluding Object Assembly, only 43% of the reliability values were at or above .85.	• Test-retest stability is not excellent for Letter-Number Sequencing, Picture Arrangement, or Object Assembly (average stability coefficients were .75, .69, and .76, respectively).
• WAIS-III is statistically linked to the WIAT and the WMS-III, providing more information about the interrelationships among a wider array of cognitive abilities. Conorming also enables examiners to "predict" an examinee's achievement scores on the basis of his or her IQ.	• The Perceptual Organization and Processing Speed factors do not emerge as separate constructs for the 75- to 89-year-old age group.
• There are strong counterbalanced studies of the WAIS-III with the WAIS-R ($N = 192$) and the WISC-III ($N = 184$).	

continued

Strengths

- The amount of data from validity studies in the WAIS-III
administration manual was
greatly improved from what was
available in WAIS-R manual.
Multiple criterion-validity studies
are presented (e.g., WAIS-III Full
Scale IQ correlated .64 with
Standard Progressive Matrices,
.88 Stanford-Binet-IV Composite, and ranged from .53 to .81
with WIAT composites.

- Construct validity was demonstrated with factor analysis studies. The four-factor structure
was supported for all age
groups except ages 75 to 89. In
the oldest age group, many Perceptual Organization subtests
loaded on the Processing Speed
factor.

≡Rapid Reference

5.4 Strengths and Weaknesses of WAIS-III Standardization

Strengths	Weaknesses
• The standardization sample was well stratified for many key variables.	• Data on the mean IQ and index scores for various ethnic groups are not included in the tables.
• Oversampling was completed to conduct research on educational level and cognitive abilities. An additional 437 individuals were tested so that at least 30 participants would be included in each educational level within each age group.	• The 18- to 19-year-olds performed very similarly to the 20- to 24-year-olds, which raises questions about the norms for the youngest age groups.
• Oversampling was done for African American and Hispanic individuals to perform item bias analyses. An additional 200 individuals from these two ethnic groups were administered the WAIS-III without discontinue rules.	
• Care was taken to ensure that qualified examiners collected the standardization data; only examiners with extensive testing experience were recruited.	
• The standardization sample for older individuals contained more women than men, consistent with census data.	
• Range of Full Scale IQ was extended to 45 to 155 from 46 to 150.	

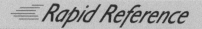

5.5 Strengths and Weaknesses of WAIS-III Interpretation

Strengths

- The new four-factor indexes allow the examiner to more easily interpret cognitive abilities underlying Performance IQs and Verbal IQs.
- The record form contains a new area for calculation of strengths and weaknesses, as well as discrepancy comparisons for the global scales.
- The descriptive categories are conveniently listed right on the record form.
- The comparison between the backward and forward span on Digit Span is encouraged by the record form.
- The new supplemental measures for Digit Symbol-Coding allow easier evaluation of errors on Digit Symbol-Coding. Digit Symbol-Pairing and Free Recall allow further examination of visual memory, and Digit Symbol-Copy allows examination of graphomotor speed without the element of matching the symbol to a digit.
- The removal of the reference group (ages 20 to 34) to determine everyone's scaled scores eases profile interpretation across the age groups and also within each individuals profile (because all subtests have a mean = 10 and SD = 3 for each separate age group, which was not so on the WAIS-R).

Weaknesses

- The technical manual provides little research on minority assessment. When interpreting a profile of a minority individual, it is important to know how other members of a minority group perform, on average, and that data are not available in the manual.
- Caution needs to be exercised in interpreting profiles for gifted individuals because the highest possible scaled score is different for various tests at different ages (e.g., for ages 20 to 34, Picture Arrangement is 17 and Block Design is 19).
- Picture Arrangement may not offer a sufficient floor for low-functioning individuals (e.g., raw score of 0 = scaled score of 5 for ages 85 to 89, a scaled score of 4 for ages 75 to 84, and scaled score of 3 for ages 65 to 74). Some reverse items should have been added.
- The four factors do not perfectly match the WISC-III factors, especially the Verbal Comprehension and Perceptual Organization Indexes, which include three subtests on the WAIS-III, one less than the corresponding WISC-III factors.
- Three-subtest Verbal Comprehension and Perceptual Organization provides limited measurement of these important constructs; no good rationale was provided for eliminating Comprehension and Picture Arrangement; Object Assembly (for ages 16 to 74) would have provided more continuity with WISC-III.

Strengths	Weaknesses
• The *WAIS-III and WMS-III Technical Manual* provides some interpretive guidelines for profile interpretation (The Psychological Corporation, 1997, pp. 181–216). For example, it discusses how to calculate discrepancy scores, how to use the supplementary tables, and how to compare scores on different indexes.	• Replacing Object Assembly with Matrix Reasoning on the Performance Scale alters the meaning of the Performance IQ, perhaps jeopardizing the continuity of the Performance IQ construct from the Wechsler Bellevue-I to WAIS to WAIS-R to WAIS-III. Hence research on this construct for previous adult Wechsler measures may not generalize to the WAIS-III, especially the important neuropsychological research with unilateral brain damage.
• The *WAIS-III and WMS-III Technical Manual* provides guidelines for comparing the WAIS-III and the WMS-III or the WIAT (The Psychological Corporation, 1997, pp. 211–216). It reviews the simple difference method and the predicted difference method for comparing ability with memory or achievement.	
• Addition of Letter-Number Sequencing and the Digit Symbol Supplemental procedures provide excellent new neuropsychological data.	
• The addition of extra items to lower the floor of the test is quite helpful in the assessment of lower functioning individuals.	
• Addition of Symbol Search allows measurement of Processing Speed Index.	
• Addition of Letter-Number Sequencing enhances the Freedom From Distractibility factor, broadening the construct it measures and justifying its new name of Working Memory.	

CAUTION

Abilities Not Measured Well (or at All) by the WAIS-III

- auditory memory for meaningful stimuli
- auditory processing
- creativity[a]
- daily living skills
- facial recognition/processing
- kinesthetic intelligence
- long-term memory for new material
- musical intelligence
- planning ability
- practical intelligence[a]
- receptive vocabulary
- spatial memory
- visual closure

[a]From Robert Sternberg's (1985) triarchic theory, the WAIS-III measures analytic abilities, but includes no measurement of the other two components of intelligence: creativity and practical intelligence.

✍ TEST YOURSELF ✍

1. **Each of the four WAIS-III factor indexes comprises exactly the same subtests as the WISC-III indexes.** True or False?
2. **The addition of Matrix Reasoning enhances assessment of**
   - (a) crystallized ability.
   - (b) processing speed.
   - (c) fluid reasoning.
   - (d) visual motor coordination.
3. **The WAIS-III age range for the normative sample was extended to**
   - (a) 69.
   - (b) 79.
   - (c) 89.
   - (d) 100.
4. **When assessing individuals who are color-blind, caution should be used on what subtest?**
   - (a) Block Design
   - (b) Matrix Reasoning
   - (c) Picture Arrangement
   - (d) Picture Completion
5. **The colorful nature and fine detail on some of the artwork is something that is considered a weakness on which two subtests?**
   - (a) Block Design and Matrix Reasoning
   - (b) Object Assembly and Block Design
   - (c) Matrix Reasoning and Object Assembly
   - (d) Picture Completion and Picture Arrangement
6. **The split-half reliability coefficients are strong for all subtests except for which of the following two?**
   - (a) Object Assembly and Picture Arrangement
   - (b) Matrix Reasoning and Object Assembly
   - (c) Picture Arrangement and Picture Completion
   - (d) Picture Completion and Matrix Reasoning
7. **The WAIS-III was conormed with which tests?**
   - (a) Woodcock-Johnson—Revised and Differential Abilities Scale (WJ-R and DAS)

continued

(b) Peabody Picture Vocabulary Test—Revised and Stanford Binet—Fourth Ed. (PPVT-R and SB-IV)

(c) Wechsler Individual Achievement Test and Wechsler Memory Scale—Third Ed. (WIAT and WMS-III)

(d) Developmental Test of Visual Motor Integration and Bender-Gestalt Visual Motor Test (VMI and Bender)

8. **For which age group do the Perceptual Organization factor and the Processing Speed factor *not* emerge as separate constructs?**

(a) 75–89

(b) 69–74

(c) 19–20

(d) 16–17

9. **Because the 18- to 19-year-olds performed very similarly to the 20- to 24-year-olds, questions are raised about the norms for the youngest age groups.** True or False?

10. **It is possible to look up supplemental scores from tables provided in the WAIS-III administration manual on which of the following?**

(a) Digit Span

(b) Digit Symbol—Free Recall

(c) Digit Symbol-Pairing

(d) Digit Symbol-Copy

(e) all of the above

11. **Like the WAIS-R, the WAIS-III uses the reference group of 20- to 34-year-olds to determine everyone's scaled scores.** True or False?

Answers:: 1. False; 2. c; 3. c; 4. b; 5. d; 6. a; 7. c; 8. a; 9. True; 10. e; 11. False

Six

CLINICAL APPLICATIONS OF THE WAIS-III

I n this chapter, we will focus on four common clinical applications of the WAIS-III: (a) assessment of learning disabilities (LDs), (b) utility for understanding attention-deficit hyperactivity disorder (ADHD), (c) assessment of mental retardation, and (d) interpretation of age-related differences in abilities.

APPLICATION OF THE WAIS-III IN ASSESSMENT OF LEARNING DISABILITIES

An LD is diagnosed when an individual's achievement on standardized tests is substantially below what would be expected for his or her age and level of intelligence (American Psychiatric Association, 1994). There are several statistical methods used to determine whether a significant difference exists between achievement and cognitive aptitude. The most common is the simple discrepancy model that requires a discrepancy of more than 1.5 or 2 standard deviations between achievement and IQ (Siegel, 1990). Another method is the regression model, which, though psychometrically sound, is not used as frequently in clinical settings (Feagans & McKinney, 1991). The regression model uses a formula to determine a predicted score based on the correlation between a cognitive ability score and the achievement score, and then compares the actual achievement ability score with this predicted score.

Information in the area of cognitive functioning of adults with learning disabilities is limited (Gregg, Hoy, & Gay, 1996). Part of the difficulty leading to the paucity of information is related to the poor definition and assessment methods of academic achievement for adults, which can in turn lead to difficulty in determining what assessment criteria to follow. Morgan, Sullivan, Darden, and Gregg (1997) recently investigated college students with and without LDs. They found that the WAIS-R global scales were highly correlated with the scales of another adult intelligence scale, the Kaufman Adolescent and Adult Intelligence Test (KAIT). The KAIT has three major scales: Crystallized, Fluid, and Composite. Subjects performed similarly on the WAIS-R Verbal Scale and the KAIT Crystallized Scale but performed more poorly on the Fluid Scale than the Performance Scale. The students with an LD did not exhibit a distinct profile from those without an LD.

The Wechsler scales have been widely used in the assessment of LDs. The Wechsler profile most commonly associated with LDs is the ACID profile (*A*rithmetic, *C*oding [Digit Symbol-Coding], *I*nformation, and *D*igit Span). The ACID subtests are typically the lowest scores in the profile of individuals with LDs (Gregg, Hoy, & Gay, 1996). After examining six studies that utilized the ACID profile, Kaufman (1990) concluded that "the ACID system does not seem to contribute anything over and above the Bannatyne groupings, so I suggest that it be dropped from consideration, except for research purposes" (p. 452). Although the ACID profile is found to fit many samples of learning-disabled adolescents and adults, on an individual basis the profile may not be diagnostic. For example, Johnson and Blalock (1987) found that in their sample of 93 learning-disabled adults, only 11 of the cases had their lowest scores in the ACID subtest quartet.

The general findings from data reported in the *WAIS-III and WMS-III Technical Manual* (The Psychological Corporation, 1997) on a sample of learning-disabled adults was discussed in Chapter 4 of this book. The 46 adults diagnosed with an LD who were administered the WAIS-III were found to have depressed subtest scores on ACID subtests. Specifically, 24% exhibited a "partial ACID profile" and 6.5% exhibited a full ACID profile, both of which are proportions greater than seen in the normal population. However, the WAIS-III results obtained from the learning-disabled adult population suggest the discrepancies among index scores (discussed in Chapter 4) appear to be a stronger way to characterize an LD. In the learning-disabled group, the Working Memory Index was significantly lower than the Verbal Comprehension Index, and the Processing Speed Index was significantly lower than the Perceptual Organization Index for about 30% to 40% of the subjects. In light of these findings using the index scores, a profile combining the Working Memory Index and the Processing Speed Index may be useful in examining LDs. A SCALD profile (*S*ymbol Search, *C*oding, *A*rithmetic, *L*etter-

Number Sequencing, *D*igit Span) may be useful to investigate by clinicians and researchers working with learning-disabled adults.

Using Bannatyne's (1974) Spatial, Sequential, and Acquired Knowledge groupings (see Rapid Reference 4.8) can provide useful information in interpreting a profile of an adolescent or adult with an LD. Low scores on the four ACID subtests may reflect low Sequential ability (Digit Span and Coding) and Acquired Knowledge (Arithmetic and Information), as defined by Bannatyne (Kaufman, 1990). In a learning-disabled group, the typical pattern of performance is higher Spatial abilities than Sequential abilities or Acquired Knowledge. However, with college students, Acquired Knowledge may not emerge as a weakness, and Verbal Conceptualization may be at a level similar to Spatial ability (Kaufman, 1990). Bannatyne's categories do not correspond perfectly to the WAIS-III indexes, so the individual subtests in each category should be examined. According to previous findings on the Wechsler scales, we would expect that adults with an LD would show the strongest performance on Picture Completion, Block Design, and Object Assembly (Bannatyne's Spatial ability) and lower performance on Arithmetic, Digit Span, Digit Symbol-Coding, (and Letter-Number Sequencing, which is our addition to Bannatyne's triad of Sequential ability subtests). Low performance on Information, Arithmetic, and Vocabulary (Bannatyne's Acquired Knowledge) may also be found. Similarities, Vocabulary, and Comprehension (Bannatyne's Verbal Conceputalization) may be strong scores for college-educated adults with an LD.

APPLICATION OF THE WAIS-III FOR ATTENTION-DEFICIT HYPERACTIVITY DISORDER

ADHD is characterized as a persistent pattern of inattention and/or hyperactivity-impulsivity that is more frequent and severe than is typically observed in age-matched peers (American Psychiatric Association, 1994). The diagnosis of ADHD is most commonly made in childhood, but in recent years the diagnosis has often been made in adulthood as well (although there must be evidence that some symptoms were present before age 7). Further, there is evidence that about 30% to 60% of children diagnosed with ADHD continue to have the disorder as adults (Barkley, 1996; Gittleman, Mannuzza, Shenker, & Bongura, 1985). Thus the topic of ADHD is of prime interest for the clinical assessment of adolescents and adults, not just children.

Barkley's (1997) model of cognitive deficits associated with ADHD posits that the key impairment in ADHD is a deficit in response inhibition. This deficit is presumed to lead to secondary impairments in the following abilities: working memory, internalizing of speech, self-regulation of affect-motivation-arousal, and reconstitution. Each of these abilities is partially dependent on inhibition to work effectively. Because of these secondary impairments, Barkley's model posits that the person's motor control is decreased as the executive functions controlling these actions are impaired.

The factor indexes that are most related to the impaired abilities in ADHD are Working Memory and Processing Speed. Symbol Search and Digit Symbol-Coding (Processing Speed Index), when placed together with Arithmetic and Digit Span, are known as the SCAD profile (Kaufman, 1994). Kaufman (1994) presented data on the SCAD profile using the WISC-III that showed that groups of children with ADHD or LDs have a larger deficit on the SCAD subtests, relative to their performance on Perceptual Organization subtests than do normal samples. However, differential diagnosis cannot be made on the basis of this Wechsler profile alone (Kaufman, 1994; Schwean & Saklofske, 1998).

The WAIS-III technical manual has provided data obtained from a sample of 30 adolescents and adults diagnosed with ADHD (mean age 19.8). Similar to the SCAD profile discussed with the WISC-III, the ADHD group earned significantly lower Working Memory Index scores (mean = 97.1) than Verbal Comprehension Index scores (mean = 105.4) and lower Processing Speed Index scores (mean = 93.4) than Perceptual Organization Index scores (mean = 100.9). Of the ADHD sample, about 30% had Working Memory Index scores that were at least 1 standard deviation lower than their Verbal Comprehension Index scores, in contrast with 13% of the WAIS-III standardization sample. Examination of the Processing Speed Index scores in the ADHD sample showed that about 26% of the group had scores that were at least 1 standard deviation lower than their Perceptual Organization Index scores, in contrast with 14% of the standardization sample.

On individual subtests, the ADHD sample performed poorest on Letter-Number Sequencing, Symbol Search, and Digit Symbol-Coding (The Psychological Corporation, 1997). Lower performance on these subtests is consistent with Barkley's (1997) theory, which hypothesized that executive functions such as working memory are impaired in ADHD. These results are also consistent with those found on the WISC-III (Schwean & Saklofske, 1998).

Although the preliminary data on the WAIS-III with an ADHD sample are intriguing, test scores on IQ tests alone cannot be used to diagnose ADHD; they can, however, be an important part of the diagnostic process. A thorough clinical interview, behavioral observations made during testing, and administration of measures that are pertinent to criteria from the *Diagnostic and Statistical Manual of Mental Disorders* (4th ed.) (American Psychiatric Association, 1994) for ADHD (e.g., behavioral rating scales) are also essential aspects of the diagnostic process. Low scores on Working Memory Index and Processing Speed Index can be integrated with behavioral information and background information to determine if executive functions are impaired. For example, if subjects appear to answer impulsively, are distracted by extraneous stimuli, or seem to lose focus, these data should be integrated with interpretation of the Working Memory Index and Processing Speed Index. It is critical to get information from settings other than the testing environment (e.g., work, school, etc.) to determine whether difficulty was noted during the testing was also present in other circumstances. Once a persistent pattern of behavior can be established that supports the obtained scores, the diagnosis of ADHD can be more justifiably made.

APPLICATION OF THE WAIS-III TO MENTAL RETARDATION ASSESSMENT

The diagnosis of mental retardation is typically made on the basis of data from a standardized instrument measuring cognitive ability and a measure of adaptive functioning. To be categorized as mentally retarded, a person must have an IQ of less than 70 in addition to having significantly impaired adaptive functioning (American Psychiatric Association, 1994). However, states vary in their definitions of mental retardation; consequently, some of the studies in the literature that used mentally retarded populations did not strictly adhere to these criteria in their diagnosis. This inconsistency in applying diagnostic criteria may explain some of the variability shown in the results of various studies. The data available on the characteristic WAIS-R profile of individuals who are mentally retarded do not yield a consistent Verbal-Performance profile. Several studies support a Performance > Verbal profile in the developmentally disabled populations, but there are also those that support a Verbal > Performance profile. In a summary of 14 studies, Zimmerman and Woo-Sam (1973) found that 10 of the samples had Performance > Verbal profiles and 4 of the samples had Verbal > Performance profiles. In more recent studies with subjects with mild mental retardation, small standard deviations in the IQs were found, as are typically shown, and a Verbal > Performance pattern was reported (Mandes, Massimino, & Mantis, 1991). Leslie Atkinson (Atkinson, 1992; Atkinson & Cyr, 1988) has reported that in her investigation of mentally retarded populations the factor structure of the WAIS-R was similar to that reported with the normative data, and she also reported data that allow a clinician to examine pair-wise comparisons of subtests using data specific to this unique population.

The most recent studies with individuals diagnosed as mentally retarded are presented in the WAIS-III technical manual. Samples of 46 mildly mentally retarded and 62 moderately mentally retarded adults were administered the WAIS-III. Individuals who were diagnosed with mild mental retardation earned a mean Verbal IQ of 60.1, a Performance IQ of 64.0, and a Full Scale IQ of 58.3. Those diagnosed with moderate mental retardation earned a mean Verbal IQ of 54.7, a Performance IQ of 55.3, and a Full Scale IQ of 50.9. In both groups there was very little variability, which is typical of all mentally retarded samples. Examination of factor index scores provided a similar picture of a small range of scores (the largest difference between the indexes was 3.4 points). The general impairment across the scores was similar to that reported in earlier studies.

As mentioned in Chapter 5, the revisions made from the WAIS-R to the WAIS-III did improve the floor of the test to make it more appropriate for the assessment of adults with mental retardation. The WAIS-III's Verbal IQ Scale and Verbal Comprehension Index are both heavily loaded with questions that tap crystallized abilities (those that are school learned). Since many individuals with mental retardation may not have had the same educational background as nondisabled individuals (because many schools place individuals with mental retardation in a "vocational-track" rather than "academic-track" curriculum), the Verbal subtests may not provide the most helpful data in terms understanding cognitive processes to make appropriate recommendations. Supplementing the WAIS-III with a test that measures one's ability to apply crystallized knowledge to everyday situations, for example, the Kaufman Functional Academic Skills Test (Kaufman & Kaufman, 1994), may be more helpful than the WAIS-III Verbal Scale in understanding how a person can function adaptively in society. A measure such as the Vineland Adaptive Behavior Scales (Sparrow, Balla, & Cichetti, 1984) can also provide additional information about other domains of adaptive functioning including communication, daily living skills, and socialization.

APPLICATION OF THE WAIS-III ACROSS THE LIFE SPAN

Age Trends in Working Memory

The WAIS-III technical manual has summarized research on working memory abilities in aging populations (The Psychological Corporation, 1997, pp. 187–188). On the Digits Forward task, the average adult can recall between five and nine digits (Miller, 1956). Only a small number (8%) of adults show a decrease in their performance (Benton, Eslinger, & Demasio, 1981). The backward repetition of digits has been shown to be more affected by aging. In normally functioning adults, the backward span is generally one digit less than the forward span (Costa, 1975). After age 70, however, the discrepancy becomes greater because the backward span is significantly shortened (Lezak, 1995). Thus, given previous research, one may expect to find that the WAIS-III standardization sample would show larger discrepancies for the last four age groups (70 to 74, 75 to 79, 80 to 84, and 85 to 89) in comparison with the discrepancies in the sample under age 70.

The data from the WAIS-III standardization sample do not seem to follow this same pattern described in the research (e.g., Costa, 1975; Lezak, 1995). Across the sample, the forward-backward discrepancy is reasonably consistent. The youngest group (ages 16 to 17) has the largest difference between their forward and backward spans with a difference of 1.84 digits between their longest forward and longest backward span. The oldest age group shows the smallest difference of 1.59, on average, between the forward and backward spans (Table 6.1). The length of the longest forward span decreased by about one digit from ages 16 to 17 through ages 85 to 89, and the length of the longest backward span decreases by slightly less than one digit across this age range. The relative consistency in the WAIS-III Forward and Backward Digit Span data from ages 18 to 69 is what you would expect given what has

Table 6.1 Age Trends in Backward Versus Forward Span

	Mean		
Age Group	Difference Between Longest Digits Forward and Digits Backward Spans	Longest Forward Span	Longest Backward Span
16–17	1.84	6.72	4.88
18–19	1.62	6.66	5.04
20–24	1.70	6.80	5.10
25–29	1.64	6.68	5.04
30–34	1.74	6.61	4.87
35–44	1.70	6.63	4.93
45–54	1.78	6.57	4.79
55–64	1.80	6.35	4.55
65–69	1.80	6.28	4.48
70–74	1.75	6.14	4.40
75–79	1.75	6.06	4.31
80–84	1.64	5.89	4.25
85–89	1.59	5.69	4.10

Note. Data adapted from Tables B.6 and B.7 in *WAIS-III Administration and Scoring Manual*, by D. Wechsler, 1997, pp. 212–213.

been previously shown in the literature, but the data from ages 70 to 89 also show relative consistency with the rest of the younger age groups, which is somewhat contrary to what you would expect given earlier research findings.

INTERPRETATION OF GAIN SCORES

Wechsler's scales for children and adults have long been known to produce substantial gains from test to retest, with this "practice effect" especially large for Performance IQ. Gain scores over an interval of several weeks or months have averaged about 2 to 3 points for Verbal IQ, 9 to 10 points for Performance IQ, and 6 to 7 points for Full Scale IQ (Kaufman, 1990, 1994; Matarazzo & Herman, 1984). The larger gains on the Performance Scale probably reflect the fact these tasks are only "novel" the first time they are administered. On subsequent administrations, the tasks are more familiar, and many examinees undoubtedly remember the strategies they used to solve the items (such as arranging the Block Design cubes to match the target stimuli), even if they don't recall specific items.

The impact of this practice effect on interpretation is to anticipate higher IQs on a retest simply because of the effects of practice, not because of real gains in intellectual functioning. Or, at least, an individual's gains should be substantially higher than "normal" or "baseline" gains before inferring improved intelligence. Another by-product of the gains concerns the differential practice effects for Verbal IQ versus Performance IQ. Because the Performance IQ will improve much more than the Verbal IQ on a retest, examiners can easily be misled by the magnitude of a person's Verbal-Performance IQ discrepancy on a retest. On the WAIS-R, for example, adults improved by about 8½ points on Performance IQ and 3 points on Verbal IQ (Wechsler, 1981), for a net Performance > Verbal gain of 5 to 6 points. On the WISC-III, the differential is even more extreme. Performance IQ improves by a whopping 12½ points compared with just 2½ points for Verbal IQ, yielding an enormous Performance > Verbal gain of 10 points. Clinically, WISC-III examiners might see a nonsignificant 7-point Performance > Verbal profile on the first test jump to a substantial 17 points on the second test. Conversely, a significant Verbal > Performance profile of 13 points on the first test might diminish to a trivial 3 points on the second test. In both instances, the Verbal-Performance IQ discrepancy on the retest is totally misleading and does not accurately portray the person's true difference between verbal and nonverbal abilities.

On the WAIS-R retest, data were presented in the manual for two subsamples totaling 119 subjects, one ages 25 to 34 and one ages 45 to 54 (Wechsler, 1981). The differences in gain scores for the two age groups were unremarkable, allowing Matarazzo and Herman (1984) to merge the data for their in-depth investigation of adults' WAIS-R IQ gains. For the WAIS-III, more than three times as many retest subjects were obtained ($N = 394$, interval averaging about 5 weeks; see The Psychological Corporation, 1997, pp. 58–61), with four age groups represented (16 to 29, 30 to 54, 55 to 74, and 75 to 89).

Rapid Reference 6.1 summarizes the gain scores for the 14 subtests, three IQs, and four factor indexes. The inclusion of a substantial sample of retest cases across the entire WAIS-III age range permitted an analysis of gain scores by age. The two youngest age groups did not differ notably in their gain scores, mirroring the results of the two similarly aged retest samples for the WAIS-R. However, when data for the two WAIS-III retest groups within the 16- to 54-year range are analyzed alongside the two older age groups (55 to 89), age trends are apparent. After age 54, the gain scores drop steadily, owing primarily to a decrease in the Performance IQ gain. Whereas the Performance IQ gain is the anticipated size (about 8 points) for ages 16 to 29 and 30 to 54, it is about 6 points for ages 55 to 74 and 4 points for ages 75 to 89. Perhaps adults ages 55 and above do not benefit as much from the experience with the novel Performance tasks on the first testing, as do children and younger adults, and therefore did not learn well (or simply not remember) the strategies that they applied the first time around. Alternatively, maybe the life experience of the older two samples is such that no cognitive task is truly novel, even on the first testing. Whatever the reason, the increase in WAIS-III Full Scale IQs from the first to second testing show an age-related pattern, as follows.

Age Group	Gain Score on Full Scale IQ
16–29	6 points
30–54	5 points
55–74	4 points
75–89	3 points

Furthermore, the substantial Performance > Verbal gain that has been axiomatic for Wechsler retests applies only to adults ages 16 to 54 on the WAIS-III. At those ages, expect a Performance > Verbal gain of 5 to 6 points. For ages 55 to 74, the Performance > Verbal gain is 3 to 4 points, and at ages 75 to 89, it is a mere 1 to 2 points. These age-related differences need to be internalized by WAIS-III examiners. When retesting elderly individuals (age 75 and older), especially, do not expect the substantial gains that have long been associated with Wechsler's scales. Even the Performance IQ and Perceptual Organization Index are only likely to improve by about 3 to 4 points; expect increases of only about 2 to 4 points on the IQ scales and 1 to 3 standard score points on the factor indexes. When an elderly adult gains 7 or 8 points (about ½ standard deviation) in Full Scale IQ on a retest, such a gain may be noteworthy because it is substantially higher than the average gain of 3 points for that age group. In contrast, such gains on the Full Scale are probably nothing more than a reflection of the practice effect for young and middle-aged adults, whose average gain is 5 to 6 points.

Typically, decreases in IQs on a retest are considered a cause for some concern, because such losses have been shown to be rare within the normal population (Kaufman, 1990; Matarazzo & Herman, 1984). That axiom requires modification in view of the WAIS-III data. When a person age 75 or older scores lower on any IQ scale or factor index on a retest, such a decrease may reflect normal variability around the relatively small average gain scores found for these individuals. As a rule of thumb for examiners, losses in IQs or index scores on a retest for adults ages 75 to 89 years should be at least ½ standard deviation (7 or 8 points) below the initial value before inferring loss of function. For adults below age 75, decreases of 4 or 5 points on a retest are likely to denote loss of function, a generalization that is consistent with the results of Matarazzo and Herman's (1984) WAIS-R study.

Rapid Reference 6.1 lists the subtests in order of their median gain score across the age span. Largest gains (of at least 1 scaled-score point) were found for three Performance subtests—Picture Completion, Object Assembly, and Picture Arrangement. Although the gain scores for these three subtests were substantially smaller than their median values for the sample of 75- to 89-year-olds (ranging from 0.7 to 0.9), they remained the subtests with the largest gain scores for the oldest sample. For the total retest sample, the smallest gains (0.2 point) were for two Verbal subtests (Vocabulary and Comprehension) and the newest member of the Performance Scale, the untimed Matrix Reasoning subtest. The very small gains on Matrix Reasoning are undoubtedly partially responsible for the smaller Performance IQ gains, in general, for the WAIS-III relative to the WAIS, WAIS-R, and other Wechsler scales.

One final point is worth noting. Even though the gain scores, especially for young and middle-aged adults, may seem substantial, this practice effect does not detract from the fact that the WAIS-III is quite a stable test battery. Mean test-retest reliability coefficients for the three IQs across the four age

≡ Rapid Reference

6.1 WAIS-III Test-Retest Gains Across the Age Span

Subtest/Scale/Index	Point Gain From First to Second Testing — Age Group 16–29	30–54	55–74	75–89	Median Gain Score
Picture Completion	2.3	2.4	1.6	0.9	2.0
Object Assembly	2.3	1.6	1.0	0.8	1.3
Picture Arrangement	1.2	1.2	1.2	0.7	1.2
Digit Symbol-Coding	1.2	1.1	0.8	0.6	1.0
Information	0.5	0.6	0.5	0.6	0.6
Block Design	1.0	0.7	0.2	0.3	0.5
Similarities	0.6	0.3	0.4	0.7	0.5
Arithmetic	0.6	0.3	0.3	0.5	0.4
Digit Span	0.5	0.4	0.4	−0.1	0.4
Letter-Number Sequencing	0.1	0.7	0.3	0.5	0.4
Symbol Search	1.0	0.5	0.5	−0.2	0.3
Comprehension	0.4	0.1	0.1	0.3	0.2
Matrix Reasoning	0.1	0.3	0.2	−0.1	0.2
Vocabulary	0.2	0.1	0.2	0.4	0.2
Verbal IQ	3.2	2.0	2.1	2.4	2.2
Performance IQ	8.2	8.3	5.7	3.7	7.0
Full Scale IQ	5.7	5.1	3.9	3.2	4.5
Verbal Comprehension Index	2.5	2.1	1.9	3.2	2.3
Perceptual Organization Index	7.3	7.4	4.0	2.7	5.6
Working Memory Index	2.9	3.1	2.2	1.3	2.6
Processing Speed Index	6.0	4.6	3.8	1.3	4.2

Note. Subtests are listed in order of their median gain scores across the 16–89 year range. Data are adapted from Tables 3.6, 3.7, 3.8, and 3.9 of the WAIS-III and WMS-III Technical Manual (The Psychological Corporation, 1997). Copyright © 1997 by The Psychological Corporation. Used by permission. All rights reserved.

groups are as follows: Verbal IQ (.96), Performance IQ (.90), and Full Scale IQ (.96).

AGING AND INTELLIGENCE

A few differences between elderly individuals and those who have accumulated fewer birthdays have been noted. The small practice effect, just discussed, is one key difference; also important is the steady decrease in the size of the practice effects with increasing age when examining data for ages 30 to 54, 55 to 74, and 75 to 89. A second age-related finding concerns Object Assembly, which is very unreliable for age 75 and above (mean split-half coefficient = .58, test-retest coefficient = .68). Consequently, Object Assembly is considered an alternate Performance subtest only for ages 16 to 74 years.

A third age-related difference concerns the WAIS-III factor structure. Whereas the four designated factors emerge in robust form for most of the age groups, that robustness is not evident for ages 75 to 89. Instead, the Perceptual Organization factor is a trivial dimension for the elderly sample, defined by barely meaningful loadings of about .40 by Matrix Reasoning and Block Design. The Processing Speed factor, by contrast, included loadings of about .50 to .60 by the two Processing Speed subtests as well as three other Performance subtests. The only Performance subtest *not* to load meaningfully on that dimension was Matrix Reasoning (Object Assembly was excluded from the analysis). From a clinical perspective, the Performance Scale does not divide into two subscales for elderly individuals in the same way that it subdivides for other age groups. Rather, it hangs together as a solid unit, with a single exception: Matrix Reasoning splits off. Because of the known loss of speed in older individuals, as well as visual-motor coordination, the Performance Scale may be primarily a measure of visual-motor speed for adults ages 75 and older. The maverick subtest, Matrix Reasoning, demands no visual-motor coordination and is the only untimed Performance subtest.

When one thinks of aging and IQ, however, the focus is more on changes in abilities with age rather than on factor structure, subtest reliability, or practice effects. Such changes have been the subject of considerable research and controversy, with Schaie (1983) and his colleagues arguing for the maintenance of adult intelligence across virtually the entire life span, in contrast with Horn (1989) and his colleagues who insist that crystallized (school-related) abilities maintain through old age whereas fluid (novel problem solving) skills peak in late adolescence and then decline rapidly throughout the adult life span. We agree with Horn's position for reasons outlined elsewhere (Kaufman, 1990, Chapter 7). Furthermore, Horn's contentions are to a considerable extent based on research with Wechsler's adult scales, so his theoretical and neuropsychological arguments conform to clinical applications of Wechsler's Verbal Scale (akin to crystallized thinking) and Performance scale (often associated with Fluid Intelligence). In contrast, Schaie's data are largely based on the group-administered Primary Mental Abilities Test, which includes no tasks that require visual-motor coordination.

It has been observed for years from cross-sectional investigations of Wechsler's scales (usually based on analysis of scores earned by different age groups comprising the standardization samples) that test scores generally are lower for the older age groups than the younger ones, with the greatest age-related declines associated with Performance subtests. Wechsler (1958) accepted these sobering data, stating, "What is definitely established is . . . that the abilities by which intelligence is measured do in fact decline with age" (p. 142). However, Wechsler and other early clinicians and researchers failed to consider that the age groups may have differed on other key variables besides age, perhaps contaminating the data. The control of numerous cohort variables associated, for example, with differences in growing up in the 1920s, during World War II, or during the computer age, became the goal of Schaie and other investigators of aging and intelligence (e.g., Birren & Morrison, 1961). And one of the most prominent cohort variables requiring control was educational attainment. To illustrate with data from the WAIS (Wechsler, 1955) standardization sample, 48% of adults aged 25 to 34 were high school dropouts, compared with 60% of those in the 35- to 44-year-old group and nearly 80% of adults aged 55 to 64. Since education correlates substantially with IQ, about .60 to .70 (Kaufman, 1990; Matarazzo, 1972), how could one be certain that the lower scores by older rather than younger samples were due exclusively to chronological age when the true culprit might be the known differences in educational attainment? When educational attainment was controlled statistically, the WAIS and WAIS-R results conformed closely to Horn's predictions for Crystallized and Fluid Intelligence (Birren & Morrison, 1961; Kaufman, Reynolds, & McLean, 1989). Verbal intelligence was a "maintained" ability that increased into the decade of the 60s before declining slightly as people passed their 70th birthdays. Nonverbal intelligence, as depicted by Performance IQ, was what Horn termed a "vulnerable" ability; it peaked in the early 20s and then declined steadily and dramatically between ages 25 and 74. For a more thorough theoretical and practical treatment of the topic of aging on the WAIS, WAIS-R, and other intelligence tests, consult Kaufman (1990, Chapter 7) and Kaufman and Horn (1996).

The publication of the WAIS-III across the expanded age range of 16 to 89 years raised interesting questions about differences in human cognitive abilities across the life span. The mere availability of a revised instrument with a new sample of adults tested in the mid-1990s led to the immediate question of whether the age differences in abilities that have been observed on Wechsler's adult scales for previous generations apply as well to changes for the present generation. The extended upper age limit from the WAIS-R's 74 years to the WAIS-III's 89 years permitted a more in-depth understanding of IQ changes during old age. The addition of Matrix Reasoning to the battery permitted the investigation of age changes on a prototypical measure of fluid reasoning (Horn, 1989), in contrast to the traditional Performance subtests, which, at best, assess both Fluid Intelligence and Broad Visualization (Horn & Hofer, 1992; Kaufman, 1994) and, at worst, measure only visualization and not fluid reasoning at all (Woodcock, 1990). Furthermore, the inclusion of the four factor indexes in the WAIS-III profile permitted the study of age differences on skills that are more homogeneous and therefore more "pure" than the global IQ scales.

The WAIS and WAIS-R derived scaled scores, and hence sums of scaled scores, from a reference group of 20- to 34-year-olds, whereas the WAIS-III uses the more sensible method of deriving scaled scores and their sums separately by age group. Despite the clinical superiority of the new method, the old method had a singular advantage for researchers: It permitted comparisons of abilities across age groups, because a common yardstick (ages 20 to 34) was used for everyone. To conduct analyses of age-related changes on the WAIS-III, scaled scores derived from the reference group were needed for each subtest at each age. And to control for educational attainment, mean scores on each WAIS-III subtest and scale, by age, were needed for each educational attainment category (i.e., 0 to 8 years of schooling, 9 to 11 years, 12 years, 13 to 15 years, and 16+ years). As was true for the WAIS and WAIS-R standardization samples, the WAIS-III standardization was also characterized by quite different educational attainments for different age groups (The Psychological Corporation, 1997, Table 2.6). For example, the percentage of adults with less than 9 years of schooling was 4.5 for the 30- to 34-year-olds, 17.5 for the 65- to 69-year-olds, and 32.0 for the 80- to 84-year-olds.

The Psychological Corporation kindly made the pertinent unpublished standardization data available to Kaufman (1998, 1999a, 1999b). The remainder of this section reports the key results of his analyses and their clinical and theoretical applications. Ages 16 to 19 are excluded from these analyses because those in this group have not nearly completed their formal education. In addition, only their parents' educational attainment was available, preventing any type of meaningful control of education for these older adolescents.

1. *As was true for the WAIS and WAIS-R, the WAIS-III Verbal IQ was maintained across most of the adult life span.* Verbal IQ, when controlled for education and compared with a common yardstick, increased steadily from 20 to about 50, peaking at ages 45 to 54, and then declining slightly in the 70s and 80s (Figure 6.1). The mean for ages 80 to 84 is almost identical to the mean earned by adults in their early 20s. These results parallel findings for the WAIS-R, with one notable exception: The peak Verbal IQ was earned by adults of about age 60 on the WAIS-R as opposed to age 50 on the WAIS-III. The peak at age 60 is consistent with Horn's (1989) research findings with subjects tested on a variety of instruments (not just Wechsler's scales) in the 1960s and 1970s. However, the peak at about age 50 is consistent with education-controlled data obtained for adults on the KAIT (Kaufman & Kaufman, 1993) and the Kaufman Brief Intelligence Test (Kaufman & Kaufman, 1990), both of which were standardized within the last decade (Kaufman & Horn, 1996; Wang & Kaufman, 1993). When interpreted in the context of Kaufman's (1998, 1999a, 1999b) recent WAIS-III data, the earlier peak in Verbal IQ (and, by inference, in crystallized intelligence) seems to represent a real generational shift from the recent past to the present. Explanations for the shift are not obvious.

2. *Like previous findings with Wechsler's scales, even when adjusted for educational attainment, Performance IQs peaked early and declined rapidly and steadily across the remainder of the life span.* Mean Performance IQ peaked at ages 20 to 24 on both the WAIS-R (Kaufman et al., 1989) and WAIS-III (Kauf-

man, 1998, 1999a, 1999b) and the mean reference-group IQs are remarkably similar for the two instruments at virtually every age. When the results of the separate subtests are analyzed, it is apparent that steep declines characterize all seven subtests. Though the slopes are most extreme for the highly speeded Processing Speed subtests, they are also quite steep for Matrix Reasoning (the purest measure of fluid ability that does not require a stopwatch), Picture Completion (primarily a measure of Broad Visualization), and Block Design (a clear-cut blend of fluid reasoning and visualization). These data support Horn's contentions about the vulnerable nature of both fluid and visualization abilities. Figure 6.1 shows a graph of the education-adjusted "reference-group" mean Verbal IQs and Performance IQs for the adult age groups in the WAIS-III standardization sample (unadjusted means for ages 16 to 17 and 18 to 19 are included for comparison). Visual inspection of the graph reveals the very different aging patterns for the two major constructs assessed by the WAIS-III. Relative to a common yardstick (and to adults in general, regardless of age), it is apparent that adults of 65 and older have an average Verbal > Performance discrepancy of about 20 points. Although this relative discrepancy will not "show" in their actual profiles (because their obtained IQs are based only on norms for their age group), this underlying difference in abilities should be understood well by clinicians, especially those who routinely test elderly patients. It is important to remember that the data in the graph are cross-sectional in nature and that inferences about development are tenuous at best when based on such data. Interestingly, though, a longitudinal investigation of the WAIS and WAIS-R produced Performance IQ age-related declines that mirrored almost exactly the declines observed in cross-sectional studies (Kaufman, 1990, pp. 212–221).

3. *When adjusted for education and based on the reference group norms, mean Full Scale IQs remain remarkably constant for adults between the ages of 20 and 54 years.* As noted, Verbal IQ increases with advancing age until the 50s, at the same time that Performance IQ has begun its inevitable descent. The net result is a mean Full Scale IQ that is astonishingly stable for the five age groups between 20 to 24 and 45 to 54 years. For each age group, the adjusted mean Full Scale IQ rounds to 99 or 100 (range = 98.9 to 100.0). Even for the next two age groups (55 to 64 and 65 to

Figure 6.1 Mean WAIS-III "Reference Group" Verbal and Performance IQs for Adults Ages 16 to 17 Through 85 to 89 Years.

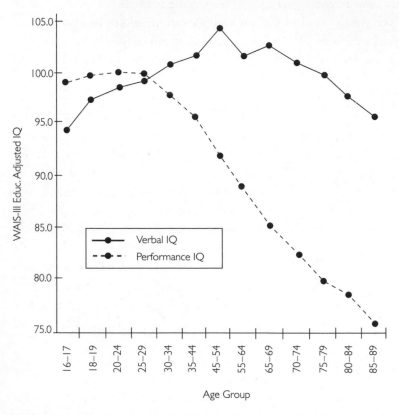

Note. Values are adjusted for educational attainment. Values for ages 16 to 19 are unadjusted. Standardization data of the Wechsler Adult Intelligence Scale—Third Edition. Copyright © 1997 by The Psychological Corporation. Used by permission. All rights reserved.

69), mean Full Scale IQs are 97 and 95, respectively. So regardless of the distinct characteristic aging profile for the predominantly crystallized Verbal IQ and the decidedly fluid Performance IQ, their merger produces an atheoretical combination that yields almost the identical mean value for young and middle-aged adults. In fact, even *without* the education adjustment, mean reference-group Full Scale IQs were nearly identical for ages 20 to 54 years (range = 98.5 to 100.1), owing to the fact that educational attainment was fairly similar for these separate age groups (see The Psychological Corporation, 1997, Table 2.6). Therefore, if Full Scale IQ is used as the criterion of intelligence, as it often is in research studies and sometimes is in clinical practice, then no age group between the 20s and 50s can be said to be smarter than any other. On the WAIS-R, this generalization only held for ages 20 to 34 years, with or without a correction for education (Kaufman et al., 1989).

4. *The four factor indexes change with increasing age in quite different ways.* Figure 6.2 displays separate graphs for each factor index, depicting mean standard scores (education adjusted and based on reference group norms) for the 11 age groups between 20 to 24 and 85 to 89 years; unadjusted values for ages 16 to 19 are also shown. The Verbal Comprehension Index includes three subtests, all of which seem to measure Horn's crystallized, or Gc, ability. The three Perceptual Organization Index subtests seem to measure Broad Visualization, or Gv (Picture Completion); fluid reasoning, or Gf (matrix analogies); or an amalgam of Gv and Gf (Block Design). The Working Memory Index includes three subtests— Digit Span and Arithmetic, which form the WISC-III Freedom From Distractibility Index and the new Letter-Number Sequencing subtest. The Freedom From Distractibility Index has been viewed by Horn (1989) as a measure of SAR (Gsm), or short-term memory. The Processing Speed Index comprises two highly speeded subtests, which, from Horn's theory, measure Broad Speediness, or Gs. The four WAIS-III factor indexes seem to measure Gc, Gf/Gv, SAR (Gsm), and Gs, respectively. As indicated, Gc is an ability that is maintained throughout most of the adult life span, whereas the other three are vulnerable to the effects of aging (Horn & Hofer, 1992). From Horn's (1985, 1989) theory and research and from subsequent research on measures of Horn's abilities (e.g., Kaufman, Kaufman, Chen, & Kaufman, 1996), the most extreme decrease in abilities with increasing age occurs for Gs and the smallest amount of decrease for a vulnerable ability occurs for SAR (Gsm). The graphs of the four indexes differ from each other in ways that are entirely consistent with Horn's theoretical speculations and that conform with the results of prior research. Note in Figure 6.2 that the

graphs converge prior to age 30 before following their distinct paths toward old age. Even at ages 45 to 54, when the Verbal Comprehension Index peaks (mean = 105.9), the means for the Perceptual Organization Index and the Processing Speed Index are already 12 to 14 points lower.

5. *Similarities demonstrates aspects of both crystallized and fluid intelligence in its relationship to age.* Similarities displays increasing education-adjusted mean scores through ages 45 to 54 (like most measures of Gc), but it declines with increasing age to a far greater extent than the other Verbal Comprehension Index subtests or Comprehension (data not shown here). The mean scores on Similarities do not decline to the extent of the Performance subtests, but quite clearly older adults do not perform as well on this task as they do on other measures of verbal comprehension and expression. For example, adults in their 70s earn education-adjusted mean scores of about 11 to 11½ on Vocabulary and Information, but only 9½ on Similarities; for those in their 80s, the difference is 10½ to 8½. The crystallized components of Similarities concern the language abilities that are required, whereas the fluid reasoning component comes in when the examinee tries to find the common category that unites the two verbal concepts. The fact that the concepts are not obscure but tend to be simple (e.g., everyday words like "praise" and "fly"), even in the hardest items, enhances the fluid nature of Similarities.

6. *The new Letter-Number Sequencing subtest, though on the Verbal Scale, displays a profile of mean scores across the age range that is highly similar to Performance subtests.* The stimuli are read to the examinee on the Letter-Number Sequencing subtest, and the response is oral, but those seem to be the only similarities between this new task and other Verbal subtests. Figure 6.3 displays separate graphs for Letter-Number Sequencing and the other two subtests that constitute the Working Memory Index, revealing mean scaled scores (education adjusted and based on reference group norms) for the 11 age groups between 20 to 24 and 85 to 89 years; unadjusted values for ages 16 to 19 are also shown. Despite factor-analytic evidence that supports the meaningfulness of the Working Memory Index construct for all age groups, the graphs shown here reveal that each component subtest has its own characteristic aging curve. The progression of mean scores from late adolescence through old age reveals a pattern for Letter-Number Sequencing that is closely

Figure 6.2 Mean "Reference Group" Indexes on the Four WAIS-III Factors for Adults Ages 16 to 17 Through 85 to 89 Years.

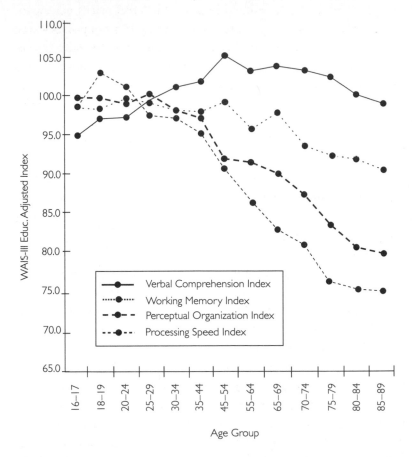

Age Group

Note. Values are adjusted for educational attainment. Values for ages 16 to 19 are unadjusted. Standardization data of the Wechsler Adult Intelligence Scale—Third Edition. Copyright © 1997 by The Psychological Corporation. Used by permission. All rights reserved.

similar to the vulnerable pattern shown in Figure 6.1 for Performance IQ, and, in addition, is almost identical to the pattern for each of the seven Performance subtests. Letter-Number Sequencing may therefore have components of both fluid ability and visualization. The fluid aspect would appear to be reflected in the novelty of the task and visualization is undoubtedly a strategy that adults commonly employ to facilitate the recall of the numbers and letters in their proper sequence. Similarly, visualization has been inferred to be a key mediating strategy for repeating Digits Backward (Costa, 1975). Whereas Figure 6.3 shows an aging pattern for Digit Span that is consistent with the vulnerability posited by Horn for SAR (Gsm) tests, it is quite clear from the graphs that Letter-Number Sequencing demonstrates a far more extreme vulnerability than Digit Span, resembling that of Gf and Gv abilities. And Arithmetic, although considered a measure of SAR (Gsm) by Horn (with some fluid reasoning required as well), nonetheless displays an aging pattern consistent with maintained abilities, notably Gc. One other interesting feature of Figure 6.3 concerns the peak performance on Letter-Number Sequencing, which occurs at ages 16 to 17; the only other WAIS-III subtest that shows a similar early peak is Matrix Reasoning. In clinical practice, mean scaled scores will necessarily average 10 for each age on each Working Memory Index subtest (because conventional scaled scores for the WAIS-III are age based). Nevertheless, prudent clinicians will be aware that the *quality* of the performance is quite different after the 30s when abilities are compared with "adults in general." Relative to all adults, middle-aged and elderly individuals perform best on Arithmetic, worst on Letter-Number Sequencing, and at an intermediate level on Digit Span. In contrast, though the data are not shown here, the Perceptual Organization Index is composed of subtests that share very similar age-by-age patterns, as is the Processing Speed Index. The Verbal Comprehension Index includes two subtests that share a similar age-by-age "maintained" pattern (Vocabulary, Information) and one with a somewhat "vulnerable" pattern (Similarities).

7. Matrix Reasoning evidences the same aging pattern as Object Assembly, the subtest it replaced in the regular Performance and Full Scales. Object Assembly requires quick, efficient visual-motor problem solving for success; offers bonus points for quick, perfect performance; and places a heavy premium on visual-spatial ability. Matrix Reasoning, which replaced Object Assembly in the regular WAIS-III battery, demands no speed or coordination and is a prototypical measure of Horn's Gf ability (Horn & Hofer, 1992), which is less dependent on Broad Visualization. This subtest substitution, therefore, raises the possibility that what Performance IQ measures may be different from the WAIS-R to the WAIS-III, espe-

Figure 6.3 Mean "Reference Group" Scaled Scores on the Working Memory Index Subtests for Adults Ages 16 to 17 Through 85 to 89 Years.

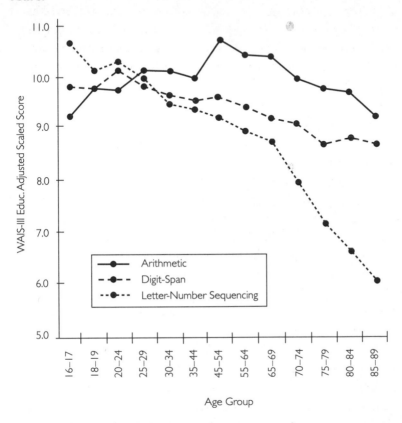

Age Group

Note. Values are adjusted for educational attainment. Values for ages 16 to 19 are unadjusted. Standardization data of the Wechsler Adult Intelligence Scale—Third Edition. Copyright © 1997 by The Psychological Corporation. Used by permission. All rights reserved.

cially across the life span. Therefore a logical question is whether the new Matrix Reasoning subtest and the old Object Assembly subtest display similar or different patterns of mean scores across the wide age range. In fact, an examination of the education-adjusted reference-group scaled scores (data not shown here) indicates almost identical means for each age group on these two subtests. For 10 of the 11 age groups between 20 to 24 and 85 to 89 the means are within 0.2 of each other, a remarkable degree of consistency (by way of contrast, that degree of similarity was found for only 4 of the 11 age groups when comparing Object Assembly with Block Design). Although the similar aging patterns for Matrix Reasoning and the subtest it replaced do not ensure that the two subtests measure the same ability, the finding is nonetheless reassuring regarding the continuity of one aspect of the Performance construct from the WAIS-R to its successor.

8. *The aging pattern for Performance IQ resembles the pattern for Perceptual Organization Index during its period of stability, but it resembles the pattern for Processing Speed Index during its period of decline.* The reasons for the steady rapid decline on Wechsler's Performance subtests and Performance IQ across the age range have been debated for years, with some researchers attributing the decline primarily to speed (Botwinick, 1977) and others stressing a decline in fluid ability (Horn, 1985). The new organization of the WAIS-III permits an investigation of this issue because the Perceptual Organization Index emphasizes nonverbal problem solving whereas the Processing Speed Index stresses speed of responding. Figure 6.4 depicts separate graphs for Performance IQ and the two factor indexes that are composed solely of Performance subtests: Perceptual Organization and Processing Speed. The graphs show mean standard scores (education adjusted and based on reference group norms) for the 11 age groups between 20 to 24 and 85 to 89 years; unadjusted values for ages 16 to 19 are also shown. Interestingly, the graph for Performance IQ overlaps greatly with the graph for Perceptual Organization Index from ages 16 to 44, the ages during which Performance IQ is rather stable. However, during the period of rapid decline (ages 55 and older), the Performance IQ graph overlaps more nearly with the aging pattern for the Processing Speed Index. The implication is that the steady decline in Performance IQ with age is a function of fluid (and visualization) ability as well as speed, with the latter variable assuming primacy during the senior citizen years.

The main points summarized here from Kaufman's (1998, 1999a, 1999b) work need to be well understood by clinicians. Because the IQs, indexes, and scaled scores revealed in a person's WAIS-III profile are derived relative to his or her age peers, the important age-related results will not be readily evident. The average 70- or 80-year-old has a Verbal > Performance profile of about

Figure 6.4 Mean "Reference Group" Standard Scores (IQ/Index) on the WAIS-III Performance Scale, Perceptual Organization Factor, and Processing Speed Factor for Adults Ages 16 to 17 Through 85 to 89 Years.

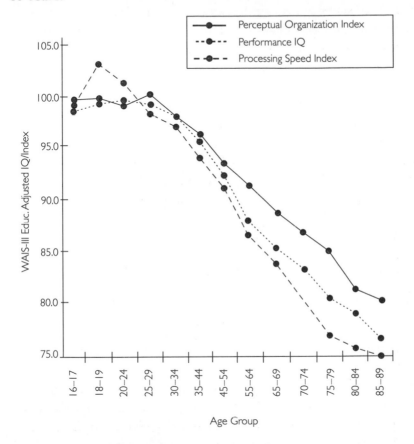

Note. Values are adjusted for educational attainment. Values for ages 16 to 19 are unadjusted. Standardization data of the Wechsler Adult Intelligence Scale—Third Edition. Copyright © 1997 by The Psychological Corporation. Used by permission. All rights reserved.

20 points when IQs are derived from reference-group norms and adjusted for education. In real clinical life, however, the means for these elderly samples are set at 100 for all IQs and indexes and at 10 for all scaled scores. It is, therefore, imperative for clinicians to internalize the age-related findings so that their qualitative test interpretations will not be obscured by the quantitative

data. The young adult, relative to the older adult, must solve many more Performance items correctly to achieve the same Performance IQ, Perceptual Organization Index, or Processing Speed Index. Conversely, the life experiences of middle-aged individuals give them an advantage over adolescents and young adults on the Verbal subtests. Because the age range of the WAIS-III is so large relative to previous editions of Wechsler's adult scale, and because elderly adults are more prevalent within the population and are assessed with far greater frequency than in previous years, it is more important than ever that examiners who routinely evaluate adolescents and adults of all ages be intelligent consumers of the research on aging and intelligence.

🔖 TEST YOURSELF 🔖

1. **Along with the WAIS-III, what other type of test is essential to administer to diagnose a learning disability?**
   (a) projective personality instrument
   (b) adaptive behavior scale
   (c) achievement measure
   (d) creativity test

2. **The term *ACID profile* is an acronym for what four subtests?**
   (a) Arithmetic, Comprehension, Information, Digit Symbol-Coding
   (b) Arithmetic, Coding, Information, Digit Span
   (c) Arithmetic, Comprehension, Information, Block Design
   (d) Picture Arrangement, Coding, Information, Digit Span

3. **When assessing a learning-disabled adult, you may expect to see which of the following patterns of Bannatyne's abilities?**
   (a) Spatial stronger than both Sequential and Acquired Knowledge
   (b) Spatial and Sequential stronger than Acquired Knowledge
   (c) Acquired Knowledge stronger than Spatial and Sequential
   (d) Sequential stronger than Acquired Knowledge and Spatial

4. **The WAIS-III factor index most similar to Bannatyne's Spatial Ability is**
   (a) Perceptual Organization Index
   (b) Verbal Comprehension Index
   (c) Working Memory Index
   (d) Processing Speed Index

5. **The diagnosis of ADHD can be definitively made on the basis of a WAIS-III profile alone.** True or False?

6. **Which two factor indexes might you expect to be lower in an ADHD client's profile?**

   (a) Perceptual Organization Index and Verbal Comprehension Index

   (b) Verbal Comprehension Index and Processing Speed Index

   (c) Working Memory Index and Processing Speed Index

   (d) Processing Speed Index and Perceptual Organization Index

7. **If an individual's Full Scale IQ is lower than 70, there is sufficient evidence to make the diagnosis of mental retardation.** True or False?

8. **Which of the following best describes what is typically seen in the profile of an individual who is mentally retarded?**

   (a) a consistent Performance > Verbal pattern

   (b) no consistent Performance > Verbal or Verbal > Performance pattern

   (c) a consistent Verbal > Performance pattern

   (d) a consistent Full Scale IQ > Performance IQ pattern

9. **Which type of additional test is essential to administer to confidently make the diagnosis of mental retardation?**

   (a) projective personality instrument

   (b) adaptive behavior scale

   (c) achievement measure

   (d) creativity test

10. **Which of the following is the pattern seen in gain scores noted from the first to second WAIS-III testing?**

    (a) Subjects aged 16 to 29 have larger gain scores than do subjects aged 75 to 89.

    (b) Subjects aged 75 to 89 have the largest gain scores.

    (c) Subjects aged 16 to 89 have approximately equal gain scores.

    (d) Subjects aged 55 to 74 typically have the largest gain scores.

11. **Which of the two factor indexes show the greatest gains in the second testing?**

    (a) Verbal Comprehension Index and Perceptual Organization Index

    (b) Perceptual Organization Index and Processing Speed Index

    (c) Verbal Comprehension Index and Working Memory Index

    (d) Working Memory Index and Processing Speed Index

continued

12. **Which of the following clients is *least* likely to show subtantial gains on the WAIS-III IQ scales if tested for a second time after 4 or 5 weeks?**

(a) Charlie, age 18

(b) Lucinda, age 39

(c) Josh, age 39

(d) Maria, age 76

13. **Which of the Working Memory Index subtests show an aging pattern that is closely similar to the vulnerable pattern shown for Performance IQ?**

(a) Digit Span

(b) Letter-Number Sequencing

(c) Arithmetic

(d) none of the above

14. **Mildred was tested on the WAIS-III at ages 55 and 85. Which of the following would you expect to see occur in her Digits Forward versus Digits Backward Digit Span performance across this age span?**

(a) an increase in forward-backward span discrepancy by four digits

(b) a decrease in forward-backward span discrepancy by four digits

(c) relative consistency in this discrepancy between ages

(d) an increase in forward-backward span discrepancy by eight digits

Answers: 1. c; 2. b; 3. a; 4. a; 5. False; 6. c; 7. False; 8. b; 9. b; 10. a; 11. b; 12. d; 13. b; 14. c

Seven

ILLUSTRATIVE CASE REPORTS

This chapter includes the case studies of two adults who were referred for psychoeducational evaluation. The WAIS-III profile of Mike A. was presented in Chapter 4 to exemplify how to progress through the steps of interpretation; here the culmination of his case is presented in the first case report. The second case report examines the profile of a 31-year-old female law student, Laura O., who was referred for a suspected learning disability.

Chapters 1 through 6 of this book have reviewed the key features of the WAIS-III and how to administer, score, and interpret the instrument. The goal of this chapter is to bring all of these other facets of the book together and illustrate how the WAIS-III may be utilized as part of a comprehensive test battery. Specifically, the case reports will demonstrate how hypotheses are cross-validated with behavioral observations, background information, and supplemental tests. The basic outline of the report includes the following: information on the examinee, the reason for the referral, some background information, observations on the appearance and behavior of the examinee, the test to be administered, the test results and interpretations, a summary, recommendations, the examiner's signature, and a psychometric summary of scores. The summary portion of the reports demonstrates how to translate results of the tests into effective recommendations.

203

> ## DON'T FORGET
>
> ### Pertinent Information to Include in Identifying Information Section
>
> - name
> - date of birth
> - age
> - grade in school (if applicable)
> - date(s) of testing
> - date of report
> - examiner's name

Case Report: Mike A., Age 61, Possible Memory Impairment

Wechsler Adult Intelligence Scale—Third Edition (WAIS-III) Profile

Scale	IQ	90% Confidence Interval	Percentile Rank
Verbal Scale	125	120–128	95
Performance Scale	106	100–111	66
Full Scale	118	114–121	88

Factor	Index	90% Confidence Interval	Percentile Rank
Verbal Comprehension	120	114–124	91
Perceptual Organization	111	104–116	77
Working Memory	121	114–125	92
Processing Speed	76	71–86	5

Subtest	Scaled Score	Percentile Rank	Subtest	Scaled Score[a]	Percentile Rank
Vocabulary	14	91	Picture Completion	9	37
Similarities	15	95	Digit Symbol-Coding	5 (W)	5
Arithmetic	15	95	Block Design	14 (S)	91
Digit Span	13	84	Matrix Reasoning	13 (S)	84
Information	12	75	Picture Arrangement	14 (S)	91
Comprehension	15	95	Symbol Search	6 (W)	9
Letter-Number Sequencing	13	84	Object Assembly	11	63

[a](S) indicates a significant relative strength, $p < .05$; (W) indicates a significant relative weakness, $p < .05$.

Kaufman Functional Academic Skills Test (K-FAST)

	Standard Score	90% Confidence Interval	Percentile Rank
Composite	115	108–121	84
Subtests			
Arithmetic	121	110–129	92
Reading	111	103–118	77

Reason for Referral

Mike A. is a 61-year-old Caucasian male who referred himself for a psychoeducational evaluation because of concern about his memory. Mike is the vice president of a major mortgage banking company and is very successful in his work. However, he has become concerned about his memory in the last few months because he has started to forget about his appointments, paperwork deadlines, and returning client phone calls. He hoped that this psychoeducational evaluation could provide a preliminary evaluation of his memory skills and also provide him with recommendations to help him improve this aspect of his cognitive functioning.

Background Information

Mike is married and has two adult daughters, ages 31 and 35, who are self-sufficient. His wife, age 59, is a homemaker and Red Cross volunteer. Mike began his professional career in real estate and shortly afterward formed a mortgage bank-

> **DON'T FORGET**
>
> **Pertinent Information to Include in Reason for Referral Section of Report**
>
> **A. Who Referred the Client**
> 1. List name and position of referral source.
> 2. List questions of referral source.
>
> **B. Specific Symptoms and Concerns**
> 1. Summarize current behaviors and relevant past behaviors.
> 2. List any separate concerns that the client has.

DON'T FORGET

Pertinent Information to Include in Background Information

Present in paragraph form the information you have obtained from all sources, including referral source, client, family members, social worker, teachers, medical records, etc. Only state pertinent information, not needless details.

The following information may be included.

- current family situation (spouse, children, siblings, etc.) (*no gossip*)
- other symptoms
- medical history (including emotional disorders)
- developmental history
- educational history
- employment history
- previous treatment (educational or psychological)
- new or recent developments (including stressors)
- review of collateral documents (past evaluations)

ing company with two other colleagues. Mike has been in the mortgage banking business for the past 32 years and does not currently have plans for retirement in the near future. He holds two titles in his company: vice president and branch manager. Mike is frequently invited to give speeches at mortgage banking conferences, seminars, and community events. He is very well known and well respected in his district. Mike reported a high level of satisfaction with his career and remarked that although it can be extremely stressful and frustrating at times, it is also very stimulating and rewarding for him. He stated that he has excellent relationships with his coworkers and the employees that he manages have all worked for him for a very long time.

Mike provided the examiner with information about his educational history. He reported that he graduated from high school and went directly to attend college. Unfortunately, he had to withdraw after 1 year due to financial difficulties. He made every effort to enroll in some city college courses and extension classes over the next few years, but he never received his college degree. Mike remarked that he wished that he could have finished college but that he "had no choice" in the matter and is thankful that a degree was not necessary to achieve success in his line of work.

Mike's medical history is unremarkable. He stated that he is nearsighted and is required to use contact lenses for his distance vision. He reported that he noticed his hearing has deteriorated in the last 10 years, but he attributes it to a natural and expected consequence of getting older and the effects of heredity since many of his relatives have hearing problems. Despite his noted possible hearing loss, Mike has not had his hearing tested by a physician and wears no corrective hearing devices. Mike has had no major illnesses, injuries, or hospitalizations. Mike began smoking cigarettes on a daily basis at age 20, but quit smoking at the age of 45. Mike reported daily use of alcohol in small quantities; he enjoys a cocktail in the evening before dinner. Mike stated that he is dissatisfied with his current weight and appearance and would like to eat healthier and have time to exercise. He stated that his pattern of caffeine use is abnormally high; he speculated that on an average day, he generally consumes 15 cups of coffee. He remarked that he feels he is now "immune" to caffeine's effects, and he just likes to drink it for the taste. Mike reported that dinner is the only meal that he eats; therefore he consumes a very large quantity of food right before he goes to bed.

Mike reported no history of learning problems in his family but noted his uncle suffered from major depression in late adulthood and was hospitalized for many years. Mike commented that his mother is alive and well at the age of 90.

Mike stated that his hobbies include playing golf, water-skiing, and visiting the cattle and horses at his ranch. When asked what he believed to be his strengths and weaknesses, Mike stated that his strengths are his strong belief and commitment to ethics and honesty as well as his dedication to working hard to provide for his family. He reported that his weakness is a lack of good organization.

Appearance and Behavioral Observations

Mike A., a 61-year-old Caucasian male, stands about 6 feet, 2 inches tall, is 20 to 30 pounds overweight, and appears much younger than his stated age. He arrived for the evaluation dressed professionally in nice slacks and a button-down shirt. He appeared clean-shaven and well groomed.

DON'T FORGET

Pertinent Information to Include in Appearance and Behavioral Characteristics

- Talk about significant patterns or themes you see going on during testing.
- Sequence information in order of importance, rather than in order of occurrence. (Don't just do a chronological list.)
- Describe the behavioral referents to your hypotheses (specific examples).
- Describe what makes this client unique. (Paint a picture for the reader.)

Suggested areas to review (note only significant behavior):

Appearance
- size: height and weight
- facial characteristics
- grooming and cleanliness
- posture
- clothing style
- maturity: Does the person look his or her age?

Behavior
- speech articulation, language patterns
- activity level (foot wiggling, excessive talking, nail biting, tension, etc.)
- attention span/distractibility
- cooperativeness or resistance
- interest in doing well
- How does the client go about solving problems?
  - Does the client use a trial-and-error approach?
  - Does the client work quickly or reflectively?
  - Does the client check his or her answers?
- How does the client react to failure or challenge?
  - Does client continue to work until time is up?
  - Does client ask for direction or help?
  - Did failure reduce interest in the task or working on other tasks?
  - When frustrated, is the client aggressive or dependent?
- What is the client's attitude toward self?
  - Does he or she regard self with confidence, have a superior attitude, feel inadequate, or appear defeated?

- How did client strive to get approval and respond to your praise of effort?

Validity of test results

- "On the basis of John's above behaviors, the results of this assessment are considered a valid indication of his current level of cognitive and academic ability."
- Or if not, state why.

Mike was pleasant and cooperative throughout the administration. During the intake interview, he provided succinct answers about his background and history, and he seemed eager to begin the testing. Mike's easygoing manner and strong social skills made rapport extremely easy to establish during the interview, and this relationship was maintained throughout the test administration.

Mike's verbal responses were very articulate and his answers appeared well thought out. During a task in which he was required to give word definitions, Mike provided long, expressive answers. On a task in which he speculated about the similarity between two common objects, Mike provided elaborate answers of how the two objects were alike. When responding verbally to questions, Mike's speed of language expression was slower than average. He tended to emphasize each syllable of a word. His manner of speaking could be due to his familiarity and skill in public speaking engagements where he must speak slowly and clearly enough for all of his audience to hear him.

Mike used a reflective problem-solving approach during the evaluation. He applied a verbal mediation approach to work out mathematical problems, and he deliberated about his answers on other tasks before giving his final answer. On tasks that required a high level of concentration, such as memory subtests, Mike frequently closed and squinted his eyes in an effort to focus. He worked slowly and precisely on motor tasks as he was more concerned with his accuracy than with his speed.

When Mike felt challenged by certain items, he provided his answers and then qualified them by saying "That is a guess." He appeared to be a little frustrated by his failures, but they did not affect his performance or interest in working on other tasks. Mike showed a high level of self-confidence and pride regarding his success on certain difficult items. For example, when reproducing designs using blocks, Mike was very proud of himself when he

he most difficult items. He worked diligently on these
ess was achieved, he responded with an enthusiastic
the design.

e's above stated behaviors, the results of this assess-
alid indication of his current level of cognitive ability
and functional academic skill.

Tests Administered

- Wechsler Adult Intelligence Scale—Third Edition (WAIS-III)
- Kaufman Functional Academic Skills Test (K-FAST)

Test Results and Interpretation

Mike was administered the Wechsler Adult Intelligence Scale—Third Edition (WAIS-III), which is an individually administered test of a person's intellectual ability and cognitive strengths and weaknesses. The WAIS-III is
comprised of 14 separate subtests and measures both verbal skills and specific nonverbal abilities such as constructing designs with blocks and arranging pictures to tell a story. On the WAIS-III, Mike earned a Full Scale
IQ of 118, which classifies his intelligence in the High Average range and
ranks him at the 88th percentile when compared with other adults his age.
The chances are 9 out of 10 that his true Full Scale IQ falls within the
range from 114 to 121. However, because there was a significant difference
of 19 points between the Verbal and Performance components of his Full
Scale IQ, the Full Scale IQ of 118 is rendered meaningless and cannot be
interpreted as an accurate representation of Mike's overall performance.
Furthermore, this Verbal versus Performance discrepancy was found to be
abnormally large, occurring in less than 9% of normal adults. Mike's Verbal IQ of 125 (95th percentile; Superior range) was significantly larger
than his Performance IQ of 106 (66th percentile; Average range), indicating that he demonstrated his intelligence better via verbal comprehension
and expression than nonverbally with pictures and concrete materials. Because Mike's Full Scale IQ is not interpretable based on the large Verbal IQ
versus Performance IQ difference, an examination of the components of
the WAIS-III is required to achieve a clearer representation of his cognitive abilities.

DON'T FORGET

Pertinent Information to Include in Test Results and Interpretation

- Use paragraph form.
- Put numbers in this section, including IQs and index scores with confidence intervals and percentile ranks. When discussing performance on subtests use percentile ranks (most people aren't familiar with a mean of 10 and standard deviation of 3); do *not* include raw scores.
- Tie in behaviors with results to serve as logical explanations or reminders wherever appropriate.
- With more than one test, find similarities in performances and differences (discrepancies), and try to hypothesize if you have enough information to say.
- Support hypotheses with multiple sources of data, including observed behaviors.
- Do not contradict yourself.
- Be sure that you are describing the subtests, not just naming them. Remember, the reader has no idea what "Picture Completion" means.
- Describe the underlying abilities that the task is tapping.
- Talk about the person's abilities, not the test.
- Be straightforward in your writing. Avoid being too literary, and do not write in metaphors.

The Performance scale of the WAIS-III is composed of the Perceptual Organization Index and the Processing Speed Index. A significant and striking difference of 35 points was found between Mike's Perceptual Organization Index (111; 77th percentile) and his Processing Speed Index (76; 5th percentile). This very large discrepancy indicates that Mike performs much better on tasks that emphasize nonverbal reasoning than on those that test his visual-motor processing speed. This unusually large discrepancy also means that Mike's Performance IQ represents nothing more than the statistical average of very diverse abilities.

Mike scored in the Low Average to Borderline range of cognitive functioning on the two timed subtests that make up the Processing Speed Index—coding and copying symbols in one task (5th percentile) and searching for target symbols in an array of stimuli in another task (9th percentile). One possible explanation for his poor performance on these subtests is that his methodical and deliberate approach to these items depressed his speed of response. To achieve a high score on the Processing Speed Index, examinees must be able to work very quickly while also taking care not to make errors. Mike was more concerned with his accuracy than his speed; therefore, his Processing Speed Index was lowered. In addition, the Processing Speed Index tasks tend to be more tedious than other Performance subtests that require reasoning and may have not been as mentally challenging for Mike.

Mike's poor performance on the highly speeded visual-motor tasks of the Processing Speed Index may have negatively impacted his Performance IQ because one of the Processing Speed Index subtests is utilized in the calculation of the Performance IQ. Thus the abnormally large discrepancy noted between the Verbal IQ and the Performance IQ may be significantly related to Mike's extremely poor performance (5th percentile) on the Processing Speed Index subtest that requires rapid copying of symbols. When the effect of this low score on the Processing Speed Index subtest of digit copying is "removed" from the Performance IQ, the extreme difference between his verbal and nonverbal abilities is lessened. This effect can be observed by examining measures of verbal conceptualization and nonverbal reasoning that do not include tasks specific to memory and processing speed. For example, Mike received scores of 120 and 111 on his Verbal Conceptualization Index and his Perceptual Organization Index, respectively. These index scores indicate that Mike performs similarly on verbal conceptualization tasks (91st percentile) and nonverbal reasoning tasks (77th percentile) when processing speed and memory are excluded.

The Verbal Scale of the WAIS-III comprises the Verbal Comprehension Index and the Working Memory Index. Mike received standard scores of 120 (91st percentile) and 121 (92nd percentile), respectively, on these indexes. The negligible difference between indexes indicates that he performs about equally well on all verbal tasks, regardless of whether they depend on acquired knowledge and verbal expression or the use of working memory to perform operations with numbers. Thus, although Mike expressed concern about his memory abilities as his reason for referral, he performed in the High Average to Superior range of intellectual functioning on tasks requiring him to utilize his short-term auditory memory, working memory, and mental visualization skills. His scores on these tasks ranged from the 84th percentile (on tasks requiring him to remember auditorally presented strings of numbers and repeat them forward and backward, and to track and orally repeat sequences of letters and numbers in the correct order) to the 95th percentile (on a task of mental arithmetic).

Further understanding of Mike's memory and overall abilities are found through investigation of his individual strengths and weaknesses. As discussed earlier, his score on the Processing Speed Index supports a relative weakness in processing speed. Further information can be gleaned about Mike's relatively low Processing Speed Index (76) when it is compared with his Working Memory Index (121). A significant difference of 45 points exists between these two indexes. This striking discrepancy supports the idea that Mike does very well (92nd percentile) on tasks that require memory skills in performing various operations with auditorally presented numbers and letters, which contrasts sharply with potential deficits in his visual memory ability that may also be reflected in the low scores on Processing Speed Index subtests.

On the Processing Speed Index task in which Mike reproduced symbols that were paired with corresponding numbers in a key, he frequently checked back to the key because he could not remember which symbols corresponded with which numbers. Likewise, on a task in which he searched for target symbols among an array of stimuli, Mike examined both the target pairs and the search groups several times before determining if either of the two target symbols existed in the search groups. Mike's performance on these two subtests may be due in part to his nearsightedness reported in the intake interview, but it could also be indicative of poor visual memory skills. These two Processing Speed Index tasks not only require an individual to work quickly to achieve a high score but can also be influenced by one's short-term visual memory. This hypothesized deficit in visual memory is further supported by the fact that: (a) no motor deficits were observed during the evaluation; (b) he performed relatively poorly (37th percentile) on a Performance subtest that measures long-term visual memory (finding the missing part of pictures); and (c) on supplemental WAIS-III tasks, Mike was able to remember a relatively small number of number-symbol pairs and symbols alone. In fact, his level of recall on these supplemental tasks is typical for only about 10% of people his age.

In contrast to Mike's relatively weak ability to process information quickly and remember visual information is his relatively strong ability to synthesize and integrate information through nonverbal reasoning. Mike is able to assemble separate elements together to form a coherent whole, both spatially and temporally. His strengths were exemplified by his superior performance (91st percentile) on a task that required him to reproduce designs with blocks, on a task that required him to arrange picture cards temporally to create a meaningful story, and on an abstract analysis task that required him to complete a series of incomplete grid patterns and demands well-developed reasoning ability. Mike's intense concentration and the methodical approach he adopted to these tasks were noted by the examiner. His approach was also consistent on a task in which Mike put puzzle pieces together to form whole, common objects and supported his hypothesized strength in synthesis. Rather than determining what the pieces would form as a whole and working backward, Mike instead concentrated on fitting the separate pieces together in small groups and then joining them together to create the whole object.

Mike's strengths in reasoning and synthesis were further noted by his performance on the Arithmetic subtest of the Kaufman Functional Academic Skills Test (K-FAST). The K-FAST is an individually administered test of achievement for adolescents and adults. The K-FAST is not an IQ test but is instead intended to be an achievement-based test that yields a composite score of Functional Academic Skills and subtest scores on Arithmetic and Reading. Mike performed in the Above Average range on the K-FAST, earning a Functional Academic Skills composite standard score of 115 (84th percentile). There is a 90% chance that this composite score lies somewhere between 108 and 121. On the Arithmetic subtest, Mike earned a standard score of 121 (92nd percentile), which was consistent with his performance on a WAIS-III measure of mathematical ability (95th percentile). The Arithmetic subtest of the K-FAST required Mike to synthesize the material presented with his previous learning and apply his skills to realistic situations. On the K-FAST Reading subtest, Mike earned a standard score of 111 (77th percentile), indicating that his ability to utilize his reading skills in applied situations is equally well developed with his arithmetic skills. Overall, his K-FAST performance was entirely consistent with his Verbal scores on the WAIS-III.

Summary and Conclusions

Mike A. referred himself for a psychoeducational evaluation to assess his overall cognitive abilities, specifically his memory. Recent events such as forgetting appointments and deadlines led him to be concerned about a potential deficit in his memory abilities. Mike is a 61-year-old Caucasian man who has been in the mortgage banking business for many years. During the evaluation he was cooperative, verbally expressive, and methodical and reflective in his processing of information.

> ## DON'T FORGET
>
> ### Pertinent Information to Include in Summary and Diagnostic Impressions
>
> - Information to be summarized should be stated earlier in the body of the report.
> - Include summary of referral, key background, or behavioral observation points.
> - Summarize the most important interpretations of global scores and strengths and weaknesses.
> - Defend your diagnosis if one is made.

Mike performed in the High Average to Superior range of intellectual functioning on the WAIS-III but showed significant variability in his cognitive profile. The significant and abnormally large discrepancy between his Verbal IQ score of 125 and Performance IQ score of 106, renders his Full Scale IQ score of 118 meaningless and warrants interpretation of other components of the test. Generally, this discrepancy indicates that he expresses his intelligence better through verbal comprehension and expression than nonverbally with pictures and concrete materials.

The 35-point discrepancy found between his Perceptual Organization Index and his Processing Speed Index indicates that Mike performs better on nonverbal tasks that require nonverbal reasoning than on performance tasks of visual processing speed. Mike tended to use a laborious, methodical approach on certain performance tasks and, consequently, had a slower motor speed. Mike's Verbal Comprehension and Working Memory Index scores were almost identical, indicating that he performs equally well on all types of verbal tasks including those dependent on acquired knowledge (Verbal Comprehension Index) as well as tasks of auditory memory and numerical ability (Working Memory Index).

A significant relative strength was noted in Mike's ability to use nonverbal reasoning and integrate and synthesize information. Mike is able to consider many parts of separate elements at the same time and assemble them together to form a coherent whole. This strength was evidenced by several subtests of the WAIS-III Performance Scale as well as Mike's performance on Arithmetic subtests of the WAIS-III and K-FAST. Mike manifested weak abilities in his psychomotor speed and speed of visual searching. He also appeared to have relatively weak visual memory skills, which were in contrast to his relatively strong auditory memory and working memory skills.

Overall, Mike is an intelligent, distinguished 61-year-old man who is very successful in his mortgage banking career. It is evident that he remains at a high level in his cognitive and intellectual functioning. Though his referral reason was a concern pertaining to his memory abilities, the battery of tests administered only revealed a potential weakness in his visual memory. Further evaluation of his visual memory is necessary to reveal the exact nature and level of memory impairment.

Recommendations

The following recommendations have been made to assist Mike with his areas of concern:

1. Mike should be referred to a licensed clinical psychologist or neuropsychologist who can perform further memory tests necessary for an in-depth evaluation of this area of his cognitive functioning. For example, the Wechsler Memory Scale—Third Edition (WMS-III) could provide a clearer understanding of his verbal, visual, and general memory skills.

2. As Mike expressed concern specifically about forgetting appointments and deadlines, he is encouraged to keep a date planner (organizer) and write down his appointments and paperwork deadlines each day. He should also keep a list of phone calls that he needs to return, and check them off as he completes these calls. As he writes these lists and records the appointments, he should verbalize them aloud in order to capitalize on his stronger auditory memory. He may also want to consider obtaining a computerized calendar program that can provide auditory reminder messages of appointments and meetings. These sub-

tle changes will help him to better organize his activities and help him remember all of his important events.

3. Mike should have a complete physical examination performed by his primary care physician. His hearing needs to be checked thoroughly since he has recently noted some hearing problems. Although he already wears corrective lenses for his vision, he should obtain an ophthalmological reevaluation to rule out any further uncorrected vision problems that could be impinging on his day-to-day functioning. His relatively unhealthy lifestyle (poor eating habits and lack of exercise) also needs to be addressed. Perhaps his physician can design a nutritional diet and exercise regimen that will fit into Mike's lifestyle and gradually help him to improve his health and self-confidence with his physical appearance.

Megan Lucas　　　　　*Liz Lichtenberger, Ph.D.*
Examiner　　　　　　　*Supervisor*

CAUTION

Common Errors to Avoid in Report Writing

- including inappropriate detail
- using unnecessary jargon or technical terms
- using vague language
- using abstract statements
- not supporting hypotheses with adequate data
- making gross generalizations from isolated information
- inserting value judgments
- discussing the test itself rather than the person's abilities
- using poor grammar
- presenting behaviors or test scores without interpreting them
- failing to adequately address reasons for referral
- failing to provide confidence intervals or otherwise denote that all obtained test scores include a band of error
- giving test results prematurely (e.g., in the Appearance and Behavioral Characteristics section).

Case Report: Laura O., Age 31, Possible Learning Disability

Wechsler Adult Intelligence Scale—Third Edition (WAIS-III) Profile

Scale	IQ	90% Confidence Interval	Percentile Rank
Verbal	111	107–115	77
Performance	119	112–124	90
Full Scale	115	111–118	84

Factor	Index	90% Confidence Interval	Percentile Rank
Verbal Comprehension	120	114–124	91
Perceptual Organization	118	111–128	88
Working Memory	90	85–96	25
Processing Speed	103	95–110	58

Verbal Subtest	Scaled Scores[a]	Percentile Rank	Performance Subtest	Scaled Scores[a]	Percentile Rank
Vocabulary	16 (S)	98	Picture Completion	12	75
Similarities	11	63	Digit Symbol-Coding	13	84
Arithmetic	10	50	Block Design	12	75
Digit Span	9	37	Matrix Reasoning	15 (S)	95
Information	13	84	Picture Arrangement	12	75
Comprehension	11	63	Symbol Search	8	25
Letter-Number Sequencing	6 (W)	9			

[a](S) indicates a significant relative strength, $p < .05$; (W) indicates a significant relative weakness, $p < .05$.

Kaufman Adolescent and Adult Intelligence Test (KAIT)

Subtest	Scaled Score	Percentile Rank
Logical Steps	12	75
Auditory Comprehension	15	95
Mystery Codes	11	63
Auditory Delayed Recall	15	95

Woodcock Johnson Revised (WJ—R): Achievement

Broad Scale	Standard Score	Percentile Rank
Broad Reading	120	90
Broad Math	102	56
Broad Written Language	111	77

Subtest	Standard Score	Percentile Rank
Letter-Word Identification	109	72
Passage Comprehension	131	98
Calculation	111	77
Applied Problems	97	42
Dictation	95	36
Writing Samples	145	99.9

Reason for Referral

Laura O. is a 31-year-old Caucasian female who was referred for a psycho-educational evaluation by her university to better understand her academic difficulties. Laura was concerned about her performance on her final exams because she did not have enough time to complete them. She also stated that it takes her much longer than her law school classmates to read through the course material. She would like to be assessed for a possible learning disability and also to use the information from the evaluation to maximize her performance at school by learning ways to improve her study skills and reading speed.

Background Information

Laura is a full-time, 1st-year law student. Although she has excelled in academics for most of her life, she reported that she is now struggling. She stated that she believes her difficulties arise not because the material in the program is complex but rather because she must read and learn large quantities of complex material in a short amount of time. Thus she does not have enough time to read supplementary materials to improve her understanding of the subject matter. Laura indicated that one reason she may read slowly is because she has a difficult time concentrating because of "intrusive thoughts." Additionally, she indicated having problems comprehending lectures, which she feels may indicate an auditory processing problem. It should be noted that Laura reported that although she was unable to complete a large portion of her final exam questions, other students had plenty of time to answer all the test questions as well as review their answers. Even though Laura believed she had failed her exams, when the grades were released, she reported that she had passed all of her courses and had received A's and honors on exams with the least time constraints.

Laura reported that she was diagnosed with obsessive-compulsive disorder (OCD) in college and has been depressed most of her life. Currently her symptoms include trichotillomania (hair pulling), excessive checking of electrical outlets, excessive weighing of herself, repetitive phone calling, and intrusive thoughts. In the past Laura has taken medication for her OCD and depression under the consultation of a psychiatrist; however, she indicated that she has not taken medication for over 5 years. She recently began seeing a counselor for adjustment issues and depression. In a telephone interview, her counselor told a Psychoeducational Assessment Services staff member that Laura was exhibiting symptoms of depression, including excessive sleeping, lack of motivation, body image issues, and ruminative thinking about how others do not like her. However, she stated that during the past 2 weeks, Laura has been taking better care of herself, making friends, and exercising. Her counselor referred her to a psychiatrist for medication treatment. Laura reported that there is a history of OCD and depression in her family (her mother, sisters, and aunt all have OCD). Her mother has been hospitalized several times for her condition. Laura stated she has never been hospitalized.

Laura reported that she had mononucleosis in the sixth grade, underwent an appendectomy in the seventh grade, and has had a history of high fevers and ear infections. She stated that when she had mononucleosis she had a fever of 104°, which resulted in a weight loss of 15 pounds, hair loss, and "jumpiness." On three occasions, once in college and twice in high school, she reported experiencing "temporary blindness" because of these excessively high fevers. Also while in college, she reported being very thin and that she did not have a menstrual cycle for 1 year. She stated that she has not had a hearing exam since junior or senior high school.

Laura started kindergarten a year early, was a junior high honors student and high school valedictorian; received National Merit commendation; and earned a 3.16 grade point average in college as an English major. However, while attending college, Laura considered herself a "slacker." She stated that she played more than she should have and did not study because of family problems that were emotionally stressful for her. Additionally, she did not have to deal with the pressure of timed tests, as all of her assignments and tests were essay or take-home papers.

Laura was raised in Montana and is the second youngest of four children. All of the children in her family were "heavily tutored" by their mother at home, and all of them graduated from college and have been "high achievers." Laura has had stable relationships in her adult life but is currently single and living alone off campus. She reported that she left a 3-year relationship to move to California for law school. In addition to ending that relationship, she stated that the move and leaving her family and support system have contributed to problems adjusting. Laura stated that starting law school in California is the first thing she has done by herself. She does not have friends in California and said she feels isolated from other law students because she is older than most of the students. Laura said she relaxes by skating, walking, and watching television, although during final exams she does not have time to do these activities.

Appearance and Behavioral Observations

Laura presented as an attractive Caucasian female with shoulder-length, dark brown hair. She was dressed neatly and casually in pants and T-shirt, which was appropriate for the setting. Laura appeared comfortable during the intake interview. She was quite verbal and articulate, and it appeared easy for her to discuss her current and past problems, although she stated that it was embarrassing. Her eye contact was good and she presented in a lively and engaging manner during the interview, making it easy to establish rapport.

Throughout the testing, Laura appeared anxious about performing well. For instance, she would continually ask the examiner to repeat instructions to verify that she understood the directions. She also made comments about tasks that she predicted would be difficult for her. For example, on a task in which she was required to copy abstract pictures using colored blocks, she explained that she could not do well on problems with spatial relations. In response to hearing that she would be solving math problems, she said, "Let me get my fingers out" and appeared quite distressed that she was not allowed to use pencil and paper to help her solve the problems. On arithmetic problems where Laura was allowed to use paper and pencil, she was still frustrated and openly voiced her intolerance for the more difficult problems, stating "I can't do any of these. . . . I haven't done math in 14 years. I don't remember it. I'm not going to guess." Further, when tasks became more difficult, she anxiously rubbed her hands through her hair or tapped her nails on the table as she thought through her answers. Consistent with her diagnosis of OCD, Laura demonstrated a tendency toward perfectionism, which was evidenced in both her checking and rechecking her answers in addition to her continual erasing of her responses. In fact, on a task that required her to write brief sentences on a given topic, she seemed dissatisfied with her efforts and erased her sentences numerous times, taking an extremely long time to finish the task.

Laura appeared more relaxed on tasks that required the use of verbal abilities, such as defining words and giving factual information, than on those requiring nonverbal skills (assembling cut-up picture puzzles or assessing number abilities. On verbal tasks she eloquently stated her answers, seemed confident in her abilities, and even made jokes about items she did not know. Moreover, she used verbal mediation to help her work on math problems, talking her way through the problems. She also used her fingers to draw on the table or count, when not allowed to use paper and pencil.

Laura's problem-solving approach demonstrated a reflective and an overly cautious style. For example, when asked to identify what was missing in a picture of a pie, she stated that she did not know what was missing but that she would have put another hole in the crust, which was the correct response. When asked if that was her answer, she responded that she did not know what was missing. Similarly, when given verbal arithmetic problems, Laura would say the correct answer but then hesitate to commit to the answer, responding "I'm still thinking about it," thus exceeding the time limit. Her reflective and systematic approach to problem solving was displayed throughout the testing in that she would take long pauses before responding to both verbal and nonverbal problems. On an untimed visual analogy task, she took a sequential approach by eliminating choices and covering them with her fingers until only one response was left. Then she would double-check that response before committing herself to her answer. Furthermore, she seemed to ignore the timed nature of tasks, not attempting to work quickly. For instance, when identifying codes associated with a set of pictorial stimuli and then figuring out the code for a novel pictorial stimulus, she carefully and meticulously checked each code before responding, even though she was asked to work as quickly as possible. On another task in which she was to attend to logical premises and then respond to a question by making use of the logical premise, when asked what her response was after 30 seconds, she stated, "I don't know yet" and was unwilling to take a guess.

While Laura stated her dislike for visual-spatial and visual-motor tasks, she continued to work diligently and with a high level of determination on these tasks. However, on tasks requiring short-term auditory memory (without visual cues), she appeared extremely frustrated and her perseverance waned. For example, when asked to repeat a string of numbers in the same order in which she had heard them, she became increasingly upset as the span of numbers increased. As the problems became more complex, Laura asked to have them repeated a second time and ran her hands through her hair over and over again. Thus she became more anxious as items became more complex, and this anxiety seemed to interfere with her attention.

Laura appeared to be highly motivated and put forth her best effort on all the tasks presented to her. Therefore, even though she appeared quite anxious, the results of this evaluation are deemed a valid estimate of her current cognitive and emotional functioning.

Tests Administered

- Wechsler Adult Intelligence Scale—Third Edition (WAIS-III)
- Woodcock Johnson—Revised (WJ-R): Tests of Achievement
- Kaufman Adolescent and Adult Intelligence Test (KAIT)—selected subtests
- Rorschach Inkblot Test
- clinical interview
- Thematic Apperception Test
- Sentence Completion
- telephone interview with Laura's psychiatrist
- telephone interview with Laura's counselor

Tests Results and Interpretations

Cognitive Functioning

Laura performed in the High Average range of intelligence on the Wechsler Adult Intelligence Scale—Third Edition (WAIS-III), earning a Verbal IQ of 111 (between 107 and 115 with 90% confidence), a Performance IQ of 119 (between 112 and 124 with 90% confidence), and a Full Scale IQ of 115 (between 111 and 118 with 90% confidence). However, there were significant differences within the scales comprising Laura's verbal and nonverbal abilities, making it is more meaningful to examine separately her performance on these scales rather than look at the midpoint of highly discrepant skills. Thus the best measures of her cognitive functioning are her performance on the Verbal Comprehension Index (standard score of 120) and the Perceptual Organization Index (standard score of 118), which place her overall cognitive functioning in the High Average to Superior range compared with her peers.

Two indexes make up the Verbal Scale: the Verbal Comprehension Index and Working Memory Index. Laura earned a standard score of 120 (91st percentile) on the Verbal Comprehension Index, which is in the Superior range, and a standard score of 90 on the Working Memory Index (25th percentile), which is in the Average range. The 30-point difference between her Verbal Comprehension Index and Working Memory Index is statistically significant and striking and suggests that she performs much better when solving problems requiring verbal comprehension and knowledge than when solving problems that require short-term auditory memory. However, it should be noted that anxiety as well as auditory processing affect one's performance on the tasks that make up the Working Memory Index.

The Performance Scale also comprises two indexes: the Perceptual Organization Index and the Processing Speed Index. There was a significant difference between Laura's performance on the Perceptual Organization Index, in which she obtained a standard score of 118 (88th percentile), and her performance on the Processing Speed Index (standard score of 103, 58th percentile), suggesting that her High Average visual-spatial and visual-motor abilities are better than her Average skills in clerical speed and accuracy. This discrepancy is not surprising given her slow and highly perfectionistic approach to solving problems in which she disregarded the timed nature of the tasks. In fact, she avoided making any errors on these tasks.

On the WAIS-III, Laura demonstrated several strengths and weaknesses. She showed a significant strength in defining vocabulary words (98th percentile), indicating her superior word knowledge skills. When combined with her good performance on a test of general factual knowledge (84th percentile), Laura's exceptional fund of information is observed. These strengths are consistent with her academic history, as she was an English major, and also with her strong verbal skills evidenced in the ease and fluidity with which she spoke. Laura also demonstrated a significant strength in solving visual analogy problems (95th percentile), suggesting superior visual-spatial and novel problem-solving abilities. It is important to note that this task was not timed and that Laura spent a great deal of time solving the problems. Laura displayed a significant weakness in performing a task requiring complex auditory memory in rearranging and organizing a string of numbers and letters (9th percentile) and also achieved only the 37th percentile in a test of digit recall, both of which indicate Below Average short-term auditory memory skills.

Because Laura reported having problems with auditory processing and with slow completion of exams and reading material, she was administered selected subtests from the Kaufman Adolescent and Adult Intelligence Test (KAIT) to further explore these areas. To assess her short- and long-term auditory memory and comprehension, she was administered a subtest in which she was required to listen to audiotaped news stories. She was then required to answer questions about the news stories both directly after hearing the stories and approximately 30 minutes later. On both the immediate and delayed recall portion of these tasks, Laura performed at the 95th percentile, indicating superior auditory comprehension and auditory memory abilities. These scores also indicate that she does not have problems with auditory processing, as she was easily able to understand the spoken words in the news stories. Her good auditory memory on the KAIT contrasts with the weakness in this area that she displayed on the WAIS-III. The KAIT task required recall of meaningful and interesting stimuli (news stories) in contrast to the symbolic, nonmeaningful stimuli employed in the WAIS-R memory tasks. Her auditory memory therefore may be excellent for meaningful stimuli but weak for stimuli that are not meaningful. Furthermore, her low scores on the symbolic subtests on the processing speed score may reflect not only her perfectionism but also a more pervasive weakness in short-term memory for nonmeaningful stimuli (extending to the visual-motor channel).

To assess her abilities to quickly solve novel problems, she was administered two tasks from the KAIT: one in which she was given logical premises and was to answer questions applying these premises and another in which she was shown identifying codes associated with a set of pictorial stimuli and then asked to "crack" the code for a novel pictorial stimulus. As was stated previously, Laura worked slowly and diligently on the tasks, and she performed in the Average range on both tasks (75th and 63rd percentile, respectively). Because she did significantly better on a novel problem-solving task on the WAIS-III when there were no time constraints, it is likely that the timed nature of these tasks coupled with her overly perfectionistic approach negatively impacted her performance.

To assess Laura's academic achievement, she was administered the Woodcock Johnson—Revised: Tests of Achievement (WJ-R: Achievement), which contains three global measures of reading, math, and writing abilities, in addition to dividing each of these broad areas into smaller components. On the global scales, Laura performed in the Average to Well Above Average range; however, she demonstrated unusually large discrepancies within the broad areas of reading and writing, rendering these global scores meaningless. Thus it is important to examine separately her performance on each of the two components that make up the global score. On the Broad Math scale, Laura earned a standard score of 102 (56th percentile), indicating Average skills in both computation of mathematics problems (77th percentile) and in applying mathematical concepts to word problems (42nd percentile). Within the Broad Reading scale, Laura earned a standard score of 131 (98th percentile) in her reading comprehension, which was significantly better than her standard score of 109 (72nd percentile) in her ability to pronounce isolated words. Further, on the Broad Written Language scale, she earned a standard score of 145 (99.9th percentile) in her written expression, whereas she earned a standard score of 95 (36th percentile) in her spelling and grammar usage. It is important to mention that Laura took a great deal of time both reading the passages during reading comprehension as well as in formulating her written responses in the written expression task, indicating that her perfectionistic stance compels her to read and reread or write and reformulate her written responses until she is absolutely certain she knows what is expected of her and has responded to the best of her ability.

Social and Emotional Functioning
Because Laura exhibited much anxiety during the evaluation and because she has a history of OCD and depression, assessment of her social and emotional functioning was conducted to determine how these and associated emotional issues are impacting her academic performance.

Laura is a sensitive woman who is currently experiencing a great deal of stress, including the academic demands of law school, being socially isolated, and feeling depressed. Moreover, she stated that when she is under stress, the OCD symptoms she experiences worsen. Thus she is experiencing increasing obsessive and intrusive thoughts and compulsive behaviors, which interfere with her ability to concentrate. Although much of the stress Laura is experiencing stems from situational demands, she also appears to be prone to frequent and intense experiences of depression.

Results from the Rorschach Inkblot Test indicate that Laura has low self-esteem and perceives herself much less favorably when comparing herself with others, although this perception is largely based on imaginary rather than real experience. This inference is consistent with her counselor's assessment of Laura that she does not feel she is good enough. Furthermore, her self-value seems to be largely related to how well she performs and achieves. Thus, when her perception of herself as a high achiever is threatened, such as performing poorly at school, it leads to anxiety and decreased self-esteem, which serve to exacerbate her depression. Anxiety about her performance was evidenced both in completing cognitive tasks as well as on a task in which Laura completed incomplete phrases. She completed "My greatest fear . . . is failure" and "My greatest worry is . . . not succeeding, even if I really try."

As was stated previously and observed throughout the evaluation, Laura demonstrated a marked tendency toward perfectionism. She also tends to merge her feelings with her thinking during problem solving or decision making, even when it would be more efficient not to do so. Thus it is likely that both her excessive worrying about her performance and her problem-solving style (intermingling feelings and thinking) interfere with her ability to concentrate and affect the speed at which she works. In fact, this interference was seen during the testing, in which Laura tended to check and recheck her work and was unwilling to make a decision or respond quickly.

Laura also seems to be confused by emotions, possibly feeling both positively and negatively about the same situation. Further, she seemed to actively avoid appearing "down" or depressed, while at the same time admitting to these feelings. On the Thematic Apperception Test, a task in which she was shown ambiguous picture cards and asked to tell stories about the pictures, she often avoided the inherent negative affective theme. For example, for a picture in which a woman is slouched down with what looks like a gun next to her, Laura stated, "Susie . . . couldn't find her keys. . . . She thought she'd look under the couch . . . and found her keys." For another picture in which a woman appears to be strangling another woman, she created the following story: "[Jacqueline has] been living at home with her mom because her mom has Alzheimer's . . . and other health problems. . . . This evening . . . her mom was really disoriented . . . and seemed afraid so Jacqueline was reaching around to hug and comfort her mom." Thus, on pictures that typically evoke themes of depression or aggression, Laura apparently denied the negative themes and focused on positive or neutral emotions. In contrast, when completing incomplete phrases, she completed "I feel . . . sad," openly admitting her depressed mood. Results from the Rorschach Inkblot Test demonstrate many indicators of Laura's depression and self-criticism and also suggest that one way in which Laura copes with these intense negative feelings is to distance herself from them.

Laura appears to be much more introspective than most people, spending more time thinking about her own conflicts and perceived defects, which in turn interfere with her ability both to reach out to others and to understand their struggles. Moreover, she appears to be quite cautious about interpersonal relations, not anticipating being close to others. This caution probably makes her feel increasingly socially isolated, which, again, exacerbates her depression.

Summary and Diagnostic Impression

Laura, a 31-year-old 1st-year law student, was referred for an evaluation by her university to better understand her current academic difficulties, specifically her extremely slow working time, and to determine if she has a learning disability. During the evaluation, Laura appeared quite anxious about performing well and displayed a desire for her responses to be perfect. Because it seemed more important to her that her responses be perfect, she took an extremely long time to complete tasks, even disregarding the fact that some tasks were timed. Moreover, it is likely that her anxiety about performing well interfered with her ability to attend and concentrate, thus further slowing her down.

Laura's overall cognitive functioning ranged from the Average to Superior range. On the WAIS-III, the best estimates of her abilities were her Above Average to Superior Verbal Comprehension Index of 120 and Perceptual Organization Index of 118. She demonstrated significant discrepancies among the various abilities measured on the WAIS-III, specifically displaying Average performance in her working memory and processing speed skills. Moreover, she showed two significant strengths on the WAIS-III, in her fund of verbal information and fluid ability, and one significant area of weakness, in her short-term auditory memory for nonmeaningful information. Laura's auditory comprehension skills were assessed to determine if there was an auditory processing problem, and she displayed superior auditory comprehension and memory skills, indicating that she does not have a learning disability in her processing of spoken words. Laura's speed of problem solving was further assessed using selected subtests from the KAIT. She performed in the Average range on these tasks, indicating that her ability to solve novel problems is negatively impacted when she must work under strict time constraints.

Consistent with Laura's history of strong academic performance in high school and college, her performance on the WJ-R Tests of Achievement indicated that her academic functioning is in the Average to Well Above Average range. On the Broad Math scale, Laura earned a standard score of 102, which is in the Average range compared with her peers. Within the Broad Reading scale, Laura earned a standard score of 131 (Well Above Average) in her reading comprehension and a standard score of 109 (Average) in her ability to pronounce isolated words. On the Broad Written Language scale, she earned a standard score of 145 (Well Above Average) in her written expression, whereas she earned a standard score of 95 (Average) in her spelling and grammar usage. In both instances, Laura performed much better in the comprehension or reasoning aspects of reading and writing than in the basic "building-block" skills that underlie areas of achievement. Despite her relative weakness in acacemic achievement, Laura's overall academic achievement places her in the Above Average range as does her cognitive functioning, indicating that her achievement is consistent with her cognitive abilities and that she does not have a learning disability. Thus Laura has the cognitive capabilities to succeed in law school. However, there are emotional issues that are currently interfering with her ability to demonstrate these skills.

Laura is currently experiencing a great deal of stress associated with the academic demands of law school, adjusting to a new social environment in which she has no social support, and increasing symptoms of depression and OCD. Her excessive anxiety about her performance and not making mistakes coupled with her perfectionistic and ruminative thinking impede her ability to work quickly and efficiently. In effect, Laura appears not to trust that she will cover all of the necessary information to perform well if she works quickly or does not check her work. Thus she works slowly to ensure that she has not "missed" crucial information. Furthermore, her anxiety about performing well and her depression affect her ability to concentrate and take in information. Thus she must review information already read because she has not properly attended to it.

Laura's depression and negative self-image, social isolation, and introspective nature keep her from reaching out and creating a supportive network, which might alleviate at least some of the stress she experiences. Rather, she seems to be caught in a cycle in which she spends much of her time reflecting about her own negative features and anticipating that relations with others will not be positive, which serve to exacerbate her depression and maintain her ruminative thinking.

Recommendations

The following recommendations have been made to assist Laura with her educational difficulties.

1. It is recommended that Laura continue to participate in individual psychotherapy. Therapy that focuses on alleviating depressive symptoms, managing OCD symptoms, and increasing her self-esteem may be beneficial.

2. Laura recently met with a psychiatrist and was prescribed medication to treat her OCD and depressive symptoms. It is strongly recommended that Laura continue to meet with her psychiatrist to discuss the effectiveness of medication management.

3. To help with Laura's social isolation and provide a safe and supportive environment for her to practice social skills, Laura might benefit from joining group therapy. Therapy groups are available at the counseling center at no to minimal cost to students.

4. Laura's complaints that she reads and completes work much more slowly than her classmates appears to be due to her anxiety about her performance and tendency toward perfectionism. Thus she may benefit from the following.

a. To help her increase the speed at which she reads, she should designate a certain amount of time to be spent in each sitting (e.g., 30 minutes), as opposed to however long it takes to complete the reading assignment. If she finds that her mind is wandering or she is having many intrusive thoughts, she should take a break until she is better able to concentrate rather than continue to reread the same information.

b. Laura lacks confidence that if she works quickly or reads material only once, she will not be able to respond well enough. To increase her confidence in her abilities, she will need to practice reading material one time (not necessarily faster) and practice responding to questions quickly. Although it would not be wise to "practice" these skills on her law school exams, she could practice during the course of the semester. For instance, she could go through old LSAT workbooks and do the practice tests, reading the information only once and answering questions without allowing herself time to think about every possible perspective to each item. She may want to compare her performance on a practice test in which she did not force herself to respond quickly.

c. Laura may also benefit from practicing reading materials only one time and test herself on how much she has retained. If she finds herself spontaneously trying to reread the information, she should consciously tell herself to stop and continue with the next page or reading assignment.

Debra Broadbooks, Ph.D.   *Carren J. Stika, Ph.D.*   *Lynda B. Brooks, M.A.*
Associate Director   *Clinical Supervisor*   *Examiner*
Psychoeducational
Assessment Services

🪶 TEST YOURSELF 🪶

1. **In the referral section of the report, you should be sure to include all of the following except**
   - (a) the name and position of the person who referred the client for testing.
   - (b) the specific referral question.
   - (c) the previous test scores.
   - (d) the a summary of current behaviors/problems relevant to the referral concern.

2. **It is especially important to include the details that you have heard from gossip in the Background section of the report.** True or False?

3. **The information in the Appearance and Behavioral Characteristics section of the report should be sequenced in**
   - (a) the order of occurrence of the behaviors.
   - (b) the order of importance.
   - (c) alphabetical order.
   - (d) reverse chronological order.

4. **In addition to describing important features of the subject's appearance and pertinent behaviors, the Appearance and Behavioral Characteristics section of the report should include**

   (a) test results.

   (b) a statement about the validity of the test results.

   (c) brief recommendations.

   (d) summary of the referral question.

5. **It is good practice to mention any of the following types of scores in the Test Results and Interpretation section of the report except**

   (a) percentile ranks.

   (b) confidence intervals.

   (c) raw scores.

   (d) standard scores.

6. **It is often a good idea to include test results in the Summary and Conclusions section of the report that were not mentioned previously in the report.** True or False?

7. **List four common errors that examiners typically make in report writing.**

   (a) _____

   (b) _____

   (c) _____

   (d) _____

Answers: 1. c; 2. False; 3. b; 4. b; 5. c; 6. False; 7. See Caution box on page 217.

Appendix WAIS-III Interpretive Worksheet

Step 1: Interpret the Full Scale IQ

Scale	IQ	Confidence Interval 90% / 95% (circle one)	Percentile Rank	Descriptive Category
Verbal				
Performance				
Full Scale				

Note: If there *is a significant difference* between the component parts of the Full Scale IQ (i.e., the Verbal IQ and the Performance IQ or the Verbal Comprehension Index and the Perceptual Organization Index), the Full Scale IQ should *not* be interpreted as a meaningful representation of the individual's *overall* performance.

Step 2: Are the Verbal IQ Versus the Performance IQ or the Verbal Comprehension Index Versus the Perceptual Organization Index Significantly Different?

			Difference			Is there a significant difference?	
V-IQ	P-IQ		Significant (*p* < .01)	Significant (*p* < .05)	Not Significant		
			12 or more	9–11	0–8	YES	NO

			Difference			Is there a significant difference?	
VCI	POI		Significant (*p* < .01)	Significant (*p* < .05)	Not Significant		
			13 or more	10–12	0–9	YES	NO

Step 2 Decision Box

If the answers are both no, there are not significant differences between *either* the V-IQ and the P-IQ *or* the VCI and the POI.

⇨ First explain the meaning of the scales not being significantly different. *Then skip to Step 6.*

If either answer is *yes*, there is a significant difference between either the V-IQ and the P-IQ or between the VCI and the POI.

⇨ *Continue on to Step 3.*

Step 3: Are the Verbal IQ versus the Performance IQ or the Verbal Comprehension Index Versus the Perceptual Organization Index Differences Abnormally Large?

V-IQ Versus P-IQ Difference

Size of Difference Needed for Abnormality		Does size meet abnormality criteria? (circle one)
17[a]		YES NO

VCI Versus POI Difference

Size of Difference Needed for Abnormality		Does size meet abnormality criteria? (circle one)
19[a]		YES NO

⇨

[a]Exact point values according to ability level are available in *WAIS-III and WMS-III Technical Manual* Appendix D (The Psychological Corporation 1997) p. 300–309.

Step 3 Decision Box

If *any abnormal* differences are found	⇨	then this *abnormally* large discrepancy should be interpreted.
If *no abnormal* differences are found	⇨	then you must determine if the noted differences are interpretable.

⇨ Explain the *abnormally* large Verbal and Performance differences. *Then skip to Step 6.*

⇨ *Go onto Step 4.*

⇨

Step 4: Is the Verbal IQ Versus the Performance IQ Discrepancy Interpretable?

Verbal Scale

A. Is there a significant difference between the VCI and the WMI?

VCI	WMI	Difference	Significant ($p < .01$)	Significant ($p < .05$)	Not Significant	Is there a significant difference?
			13 or more	10–12	0–9	YES NO

⇨

B. Is there abnormal verbal scatter?

High Scaled Score of six V-IQ Subtests	Low Scaled Score of six V-IQ Subtests	High–Low Difference	Abnormal Scatter	Not Abnormal	Is there abnormal scatter?
			8 or more	0–7	YES NO

⇨

Performance Scale

C. Is there a significant difference between the POI and the PSI?

POI	PSI	Difference	Significant (p < .01)	Significant (p < .05)	Not Significant	Is there a significant difference?
			17 or more	13–16	0–12	YES NO

⇨

D. Is there abnormal performance scatter?

High Scaled Score of five P-IQ Subtests	Low Scaled Score of five P-IQ Subtests	High-Low Difference	Abnormal Scatter	Not Abnormal	Is there abnormal scatter?
			8 or more	0–7	YES NO

⇨

Step 4 Decision Box

If *all step 4* questions A, B, C, and D are *no*   ⇦   then the V-IQ versus the P-IQ discrepancy is interpretable.   ⇨   Explain the meaningful difference between the V-IQ and the P-IQ. *Then skip to Step 6.*

If one or more questions in step 4 are *yes*   ⇦   then the V-IQ versus the P-IQ difference should probably *not* be interpreted.   ⇨   Examine the VCI versus the POI discrepancy in *Step 5.*

Step 5: Is the Verbal Comprehension Index Versus the Perceptual Organization Index Difference Interpretable?

A. Is there significant scatter in the VCI subtests?

High Scaled Score of three VCI Subtests	Low Scaled Score of three VCI Subtests	High–Low Scaled Score Difference	Abnormal Scatter	Not Abnormal	Is there abnormal scatter?	
			5 or more	0–4	YES	NO

⇨

B. Is there significant scatter in POI subtests?

High Scaled Score of three POI Subtests	Low Scaled Score of three POI Subtests	High–Low Scaled Score Difference	Abnormal Scatter	Not Abnormal	Is there abnormal scatter?	
			6 or more	0–5	YES	NO

⇨

Step 5 Decision Box

If Step 5 questions A and B are *no*	⇧	then the VCI versus the POI discrepancy is interpretable.	⇧	Explain the meaningful difference between the VCI and the POI.
If answer to either question A or B is *yes*	⇧	then the VCI versus the POI discrepancy should probably *not* be interpreted.	⇧	Do not interpret the VCI versus the POI difference.[a]

[a]The verbal and nonverbal constructs are not interpretable if you reach this point.   ⇨

Step 6: Determine Whether the Working Memory Index and the Processing Speed Index Are Interpretable

A. Is the WMI factor interpretable?

		Difference Between High and Low Scaled Score		
Arithmetic	Digit Span	Letter-Number Sequencing	Abnormal Scatter	Not Abnormal
			6 or more (do not interpret)	0–5 (do interpret)

⇩

B. Is the PSI factor interpretable?

	Difference Between High and Low Scaled Score		
Symbol Search	Digit Symbol-Coding	Abnormal Scatter	Not Abnormal
		4 or more (do not interpret)	0–3 (do interpret)

⇩

Step 7: Interpret the Global Verbal and Nonverbal Dimensions as Well as the Small Factors If They Were Found to be Interpretable

Review the information and procedures presented on pages 129–140.

⇩

Step 8: Interpret Significant Strengths and Weaknesses of Profile

1. Determine which mean you should use to calculate strengths and weaknesses.

V-IQ–P-IQ Discrepancy

(After calculating means, round to the nearest whole number)

				Rounded Mean
0–16	Then use ⇨	mean of all subtests administered.	⇨ Overall Mean	
17 or more	Then use ⇨	mean of all Verbal subtests administered *and also use*	⇨ V-IQ Mean	Rounded Mean
		Mean of all Performance subtests administered	⇨ P-IQ Mean	Rounded Mean

Verbal Subtest	Scaled Score	Rounded Mean	Difference[a]	Difference Needed for Significance	Strength or Weakness (S or W)	Percentile Rank (See Table 4.6)
Vocabulary				±2		
Similarities				±3		
Arithmetic				±3		
Digit Span				±3		
Information				±3		
Comprehension				±3		
Letter-Number Sequencing				±4		

(continued)

Performance Subtest	Scaled Score	Rounded Mean	Difference[a]	Difference Needed for Significance	Strength or Weakness (S or W)	Percentile Rank (See Table 4.6)
Picture Completion				±4		
Digit-Symbol Coding				±3		
Block Design				±3		
Matrix Reasoning				±3		
Picture Arrangement				±4		
Symbol Search				±4		
Object Assembly				±4		

[a]Use appropriate *rounded mean* in calculating the "scaled score–mean" difference.

Step 9: Generating Hypotheses About the Fluctuations in the WAIS-III Profile

Review the information presented on pages 144–146, which details how to reorganize subtest profiles to systematically generate hypotheses about strengths and weaknesses.

Note. V-IQ = Verbal IQ; P-IQ = Performance IQ; VCI = Verbal Comprehension Index; POI = Perceptual Organization Index; PSI = Processing Speed Index; WMI = Working Memory Index.

References

American Psychiatric Association. (1994). *Diagnostic and statistical manual of mental disorders* (4th ed.). Washington, DC: Author.

Anastasi, A., & Urbina, S. (1997). *Psychological testing* (7th ed.). Upper Saddle River, NJ: Prentice-Hall.

Atkinson, L. (1992). Mental retardation and WAIS-R scatter analysis. *Journal of Intellectual Disability Research, 36,* 443–448.

Atkinson, L., & Cyr, J. J. (1988). Low IQ samples and WAIS-R factor structure. *American Journal on Mental Retardation, 93,* 278–282.

Bannatyne, A. (1974). Diagnosis: A note on recategorization of the WISC scaled scores. *Journal of Learning Disabilities, 7,* 272–274.

Barkley, R. A. (1996, January). *ADHD in children, adolescents, and adults.* Symposium presented at the University of California, Northridge.

Barkley, R. A. (1997). Behavioral inhibition, sustained attention, and executive functions: Constructing a unifying theory of ADHD. *Psychological Bulletin, 121,* 65–94.

Barron, J. H., & Russell, E. W. (1992). Fluidity theory and neuropsychological impairment in alcoholism. *Archives of Clinical Neuropsychology, 7,* 175–188.

Benton, A. L., Eslinger, P. J., & Demasio, A. R. (1981). Normative observations on neuropsychological test performances in old age. *Journal of Clinical Neuropsychology, 3,* 33–42.

Binet, A., & Simon, T. (1905). Méthodes nouvelles pour le diagnostic du niveau intéllectuel des anormaux. *L'Année Psychologique, 11,* 191–244.

Birren, J. E., & Morrison, D. F. (1961). Analysis of the WAIS subtests in relation to age and education. *Journal of Gerontology, 16,* 363–369.

Botwinick, J. (1977). Intellectual abilities. In J. E. Birren & K. W. Schaie (Eds.), *Handbook of the psychology of aging* (pp. 580–605). New York: Van Nostrand Reinhold.

Brinkman, S. D., & Braun, P. (1984). Classification of dementia patients by a WAIS profile related to central cholinergic deficiencies. *Journal of Clinical Neuropsychology, 6,* 393–400.

Cattell, R. B., & Horn, J. L. (1978). A check on the theory of fluid and crystallized intelligence with description of new subtest designs. *Journal of Educational Measurement, 15,* 139–164.

Cohen, J. (1952). A factor-analytically based rationale for the Wechsler-Bellevue. *Journal of Consulting Psychology, 16,* 272–277.

Costa, L. D. (1975). The relation of visuospatial dysfunction to digit span performance in patients with cerebral lesions. *Cortex, 11,* 31–36.

Daniel, M. H. (1997). Intelligence testing: Status and trends. *American Psychologist, 52,* 1038–1045.

Feagans, L. V., & McKinney, J. D. (1991). Subtypes of learning disabilities: A review. In L. V. Feagans, E. J. Short, & L. J. Meltzer (Eds.), *Subtypes of learning disabilities* (pp. 3–31). Hillsdale, NJ: Erlbaum.

Flanagan, D. P., Genshaft, J. L., & Harrison, P. L. (Eds.). (1997). *Contemporary intellectual assessment: Theories, tests, and issues.* New York: Guilford.

Flynn, J. R. (1987). Massive IQ gains in 14 nations: What IQ tests really measure. *Psychological Bulletin, 101,* 171–191.

Frauenheim, J. G., & Heckerl, J. R. (1983). A longitudinal study of psychological and achievement test performance in severe dyslexic adults. *Journal of Learning Disabilities, 16,* 339–347.

Fuld, P. A. (1984). Test profile of cholinergic dysfunction and of Alzheimer-type dementia. *Journal of Clinical Neuropsychology, 6,* 380–392.

Galton, F. (1833). *Inquiries into human faculty and its development.* London: Macmillan.

Galton, F. (1869). *Hereditary genius: An inquiry into its laws and consequences.* London: Macmillan.

Gittleman, R., Mannuzza, S., Shenker, R., & Bonagura, N. (1985). Hyperactive boys almost grown up. *Archives of General Psychiatry, 42,* 937–947.

Glasser, A. J., & Zimmerman, I. L. (1967). *Clinical interpretation of the WISC.* New York: Grune & Stratton.

Gold, J. M., Carpenter, C., Randolph, C., Goldberg, T. E., & Weinberger, D. R. (1997). Auditory working memory and Wisconsin Card Sorting test performance in schizophrenia. *Archives of General Psychiatry, 54,* 159–165.

Gregg, N., Hoy, C., & Gay, A. F. (1996). *Adults with learning disabilities: Theoretical and practical perspectives.* New York: Guilford.

Gregory, R. J. (1987). *Adult intellectual assessment.* Boston: Allyn & Bacon.

Guilford, J. P. (1967). *The nature of human intelligence.* New York: McGraw-Hill.

Guilford, J. P., & Fruchter, B. (1978). *Fundamental statistics in psychology and education* (6th ed.). New York: McGraw-Hill.

Harrison, P. L., Kaufman, A. S., Hickman, J. A., & Kaufman, N. L. (1988). A survey of tests used for adult assessment. *Journal of Psychoeducational Assessment, 6,* 188–198.

Heaton, R. K., Nelson, L. M., Thompson, D. S., Burks, J. S., & Franklin, G. M. (1985). Neuropsychological findings in relapsing-remitting and chronic-progressive multiple sclerosis. *Journal of Consulting and Clinical Psychology, 53,* 103–110.

Helms, J. E. (1997). The triple quandary of race, culture, and social class in standardized cognitive ability testing. In D. P. Flanagan, J. L. Genshaft, & P. L. Harrison (Eds.). *Contemporary intellectual assessment: Theories, tests, and issues.* New York: Guilford.

Horn, J. L. (1985). Remodeling old model in intelligence. In B. B. Wolman (Ed.), *Handbook of intelligence: Theories, measurements, and applications* (pp. 267–300). New York: Wiley.

Horn, J. L. (1989). Cognitive diversity: A framework of learning. In P. L. Ackerman, R. J. Sternberg, & R. Glaser (Eds.), *Learning and individual differences* (pp. 61–116). New York: Freeman.

Horn, J. L. (1991). Measurement of intellectual capabilities: A review of theory. In K. S. McGrew, J. K. Werder, & R. W. Woodcock (Eds.), *Woodcock-Johnson technical manual: A reference on theory and current research* (pp. 197–246). Allen, TX: DLM Teaching Resources.

Horn, J. L., & Cattell, R. B. (1966). Refinement and test of theory of fluid and crystallized intelligence. *Journal of Educational Psychology, 57,* 253–270.

Horn, J. L., & Cattell, R. B. (1967). Age differences in fluid and crystallized intelligence. *Acta Psychologica, 26,* 107–129.

Horn, J. L., & Hofer, S. M. (1992). Major abilities and development in the adult period. In R. J. Sternberg & C. A. Berg (Eds.), *Intellectual development* (pp. 44–99). Boston: Cambridge University Press.

Johnson, D. J., & Blalock, J. W. (1987). Summary of problems and needs. In D. J. Johnson & J. W. Blalock (Eds.), *Adults with learning disabilities: Clinical studies* (pp. 9–30). Orlando, FL: Grune & Stratton.

Kamphaus, R. W. (1993). *Clinical assessment of children's intelligence.* Boston: Allyn & Bacon.

Kaufman, A. S. (1983) Intelligence: Old concepts-new perspectives. In G. W. Hynd (Ed.), *The school psychologist: An introduction* (pp. 95–117). Syracuse, NY: Syracuse University Press.

Kaufman, A. S. (1990). *Assessing adolescent and adult intelligence.* Boston: Allyn & Bacon.

Kaufman, A. S. (1994). *Intelligent testing with the WISC-III.* New York: Wiley.

Kaufman, A. S. (1998, August). What happens to our WAIS-III scores as we age from 16 to 89 years and what do these changes mean for theory and clinical practice? Invited Division 16 award address presented at the meeting of the American Psychological Association, San Francisco.

Kaufman, A. S. (1999a). The effects of aging on WAIS-III IQs at ages 20 to 89 years. Unpublished manuscript.

Kaufman, A. S. (1999b). Seven questions about the clinical interpretation of WAIS-III IQs, factor indexes, and scaled scores. Unpublished manuscript.

Kaufman, A. S. (in press). Tests of Intelligence. In R. J. Sternberg (Ed.), *Handbook of intelligence.* New York: Cambridge University Press.

Kaufman, A. S., & Horn, J. L. (1996). Age changes on tests of fluid and crystallized intelligence for females and males on the Kaufman Adolescent and Adult Intelligence Test (KAIT) at ages 17 to 94 years. *Archives of Clinical Neuropsychology, 11,* 97–121.

Kaufman, A. S., & Kaufman, N. L. (1990). *Administration and scoring manual for Kaufman Brief Intelligence Test (K-BIT).* Circle Pines, MN: American Guidance Service.

Kaufman, A. S., & Kaufman, N. L. (1993). *Manual for Kaufman Adolescent and Adult Intelligence Test (KAIT).* Circle Pines, MN: American Guidance Service.

Kaufman, A. S, & Kaufman, N. L. (1994). *Kaufman Functional Academic Skills Test.* Circle Pines, MN: American Guidance Service.

Kaufman, A. S., Kaufman, J. C., Chen, T., & Kaufman, N. L. (1996). Differences on six Horn abilities for fourteen age groups between 15–16 and 75–94 years. *Psychological Assessment, 8,* 161–171.

Kaufman, A. S. & Lichtenberger, E. O. (1998). Intellectual assessment. In A. S. Bellack & M. Hersen (Series Eds.) & C. R. Reynolds (Vol. Ed.), *Comprehensive clinical psychology: Vol. 4. Assessment* (pp. 187–238). New York: Pergamon.

Kaufman, A. S., Reynolds, C. R., & McLean, J. E. (1989). Age and WAIS-R intelligence in a national sample of adults in the 20- to 74-year age range: A cross-sectional analysis with educational level controlled. *Intelligence, 13,* 235–253.

Kohs, S. C. (1923). *Intelligence measurement.* New York: Macmillan.

Leckliter, I. N., Matarazzo, J. D., & Silverstein, A. B. (1986). A literature review of factor analytic studies of the WAIS-R. *Journal of Clinical Psychology, 42,* 332–342.

Lezak, M. D. (1995). *Neuropsychological assessment* (3rd ed.). New York: Oxford University Press.

Lipsitz, J. D., Dworkin, R. H. & Erlenmeyer-Kimling, L. (1993). Wechsler Comprehension and Picture Arrangement subtests and social adjustment. *Psychological Assessment, 5,* 430–473.

Loro, B., & Woodward, J. A. (1976). Verbal and Performance IQ for discrimination among psychiatric diagnostic groups. *Journal of Clinical Psychology, 32,* 107–114.

Luria, A. R. (1966). *Human brain: An introduction to neuropsychology.* New York: Basic Books.

Mandes, E., Massimino, C., & Mantis, C. (1991). A comparison of borderline and mild mental retardates assessed on the Memory for Designs and the WAIS-R. *Journal of Clinical Psychology, 47,* 562–567.

Matarazzo, J. D. (1972). *Wechsler's measurement and appraisal of adult intelligence* (5th ed.). New York: Oxford.

Matarazzo, J. D. (1985). Review of Wechsler Adult Intelligence Scale-Revised. In J. V. Mitchell (Ed.), *The ninth mental measurements yearbook* (pp. 1703–1705). Lincoln: The Buros Institute of Mental Measurements, University of Nebraska.

Matarazzo, J. D., & Herman, D. O. (1984). Base rate data for the WAIS-R: Test-retest stability and VIQ-PIQ differences. *Journal of Clinical Neuropsychology, 6,* 351–366.

Mayman, M., Schafer, R., Rapaport, D. (1951). Interpretation of the WAIS in personality appraisal. In H. H. Anderson & G. L. Anderson (Eds.), *An introduction to projective techniques* (pp. 541–580). New York: Prentice-Hall.

McGrew, K. S., & Flanagan, D. P. (1998). *The intelligence test desk reference.* Boston: Allyn & Bacon.

Miller, G. A. (1956) The magical number seven, plus or minus two: Some limits on our capacity for processing information. *Psychological Review, 63,* 81–97.

Morgan, A. W., Sullivan, S. A., Darden, C., & Gregg, N. (1997). Measuring the intelligence of college students with learning disabilities: A comparison of results obtained on the WAIS-R and the KAIT. *Journal of Learning Disabilities, 30,* 560–565.

Murray, M. E., Waites, L., Veldman, D. J., & Heatly, M. D. (1973). Differences between WISC and WAIS scores in delinquent boys. *Journal of Experimental Education, 42,* 68–72.

Nair, N. P. V., Muller, H. F., Gutbrodt, E., Buffet, L., & Schwartz G. (1979). Neurotropic activity of lithium: Relationship to lithium levels in plasma and red blood cells. *Research Communications in Psychology, Psychiatry, and Behavior, 4,* 169–180.

Nixon, S. J. (1996). Alzheimer's disease. In R. L. Adams, O. A. Parsons, J. L. Culbertson, & S. J. Nixon (Eds.). *Neuropsychology for clinical practice: Etiology, assessment and treatment of common neurological disorders* (pp. 65–105). Washington, DC: American Psychological Association.

Oakland, T., & Zimmerman, S. (1986). The course on individual mental assessment: A national survey of course instructors. *Professional School Psychology, 1,* 51–59.

Parsons, O. A. (1996). Alcohol abuse and alcoholism. In R. L. Adams, O. A. Parsons, J. L. Culbertson, & S. J. Nixon (Eds.). *Neuropsychology for clinical practice: Etiology, assessment and treatment of common neurological disorders* (pp. 175–201). Washington, DC: American Psychological Association.

Pernicano, K. M. (1986). Score differences in WAIS-R scatter for schizophrenics, depressives and personality disorders: A preliminary analysis. *Psychological Reports, 59,* 539–543.

The Psychological Corporation. (1997). *WAIS-III and WMS-III technical manual.* San Antonio, TX: Author.

Rapaport, D., Gill, M. M., & Schafer, R. (1945–46). *Diagnostic psychological testing.* Chicago, IL: Year Book Publishers.

Raven, J. C. (1938). *Progressive matrices.* London: Lewis.

Reitan, R. M., & Wolfson, D. (1992). *Neuropsychological evaluation of older children.* South Tucson, AZ: Neuropsychology Press.

Sandoval, J., Sassenrath, J., & Penzloza, M. (1988). Similarity of WISC-R and WAIS-R scores at age 16. *Psychology in the Schools, 25,* 373–379.

Sattler, J. M. (1988). *Assessment of children* (3rd ed.). San Diego, CA: Author.

Sattler, J. M. (1992). *Assessment of children: WISC-III and WPPSI-R supplement.* San Diego, CA: Author.

Sattler, J. M., & Ryan, J. J. (1998). *Assessment of children: Revised and updated third edition WAIS-III supplement.* San Diego, CA: Author.

Schaie, K. W. (1983). The Seattle Longitudinal Study: A 21-year exploration of psychometric intelligence in adulthood. In K. W. Schaie (Ed.), *Longitudinal studies of adult psychological development* (pp. 64–135). New York: Guilford.

Schwean, V. L, & Saklofske, D. H. (1998). WISC-III assessment of children with Attention-Deficit/Hyperactivity Disorder. In A. Prifiteria & D. Saklofske (Eds.), *WISC-III clinical use and interpretation.* San Diego, CA: Academic Press.

Shiffrin, R. M., & Schneider, W. (1977). Controlled and automatic human information processing: II Perceptual learning, automatic attending, and a general theory. *Psychological Review, 84,* No. 2.

Siegel, L. S. (1990). IQ and learning disabilities: RIP. In H. L. Swanson & B. Keogh (Eds.), *Learning disabilities: Theoretical and research issues* (pp. 111–128). Hillsdale, NJ: Erlbaum.

Silver, L. B. (1993). Introduction and overview to the clinical concepts of learning disabilities. *Child and adolescent psychiatric clinics of North America: Learning disabilities, 2,* 181–192.

Sparrow, S. S., Balla, D. A., & Cicchetti, D. V. (1984). *Vineland Adaptive Behavior Scales.* Circle Pines, MN: American Guidance Service.

Spearman, C. E. (1927). *The abilities of man.* New York: Macmillan.

Sperry, R. W. (1968). Hemisphere deconnection and unity in conscious awareness. *American Psychologist, 23,* 723–733.

Spruill, J. S. (1984). Wechsler Adult Intelligence Scale—Revised. In D. J. Keyser & R. C. Sweetland (Eds.), *Test critiques* (Vol. 1, pp. 728–739). Kansas City, MO: Test Corporation of America.

Sternberg, R. J. (1985). *Beyond IQ: A triarchic theory of human intelligence.* New York: Cambridge University Press.

Sternberg, S. (1966). High-speed scanning in human memory. *Science, 153,* 652–654.

Tellegen, A., & Briggs, P. F. (1967). Old wine in new skins: Grouping Wechsler subtests into new scales. *Journal of Consulting Psychology, 31,* 499–506.

Terman, L. M. (1916). *The measurement of intelligence.* Boston: Houghton-Mifflin.

Terman, L. M., & Merrill, M. A. (1937). *Measuring intelligence.* Boston: Houghton-Mifflin.

Terman, L. M., & Merrill, M. A. (1960). *Stanford-Binet Intelligence Scale.* Boston: Houghton-Mifflin.

Wang, J., & Kaufman, A. S. (1993). Changes in fluid and crystallized intelligence across the 20- to 90-year age range on the K-BIT. *Journal of Psychoeducational Assessment, 11,* 29–37.

Wechsler, D. (1939). *Measurement of adult intelligence.* Baltimore: Williams & Wilkins.

Wechsler, D. (1944). *The measurement of adult intelligence* (3rd ed.). Baltimore: Williams & Wilkens.

Wechsler, D. (1955). *Manual for the Wechsler Adult Intelligence Scale (WAIS).* San Antonio, TX: The Psychological Corporation.

Wechsler, D. (1958). *Measurement and appraisal of adult intelligence* (4th ed.). Baltimore: Williams & Wilkins.

Wechsler, D. (1974). *Manual for the Wechsler Intelligence Scale for Children—Revised Edition (WISC-R).* San Antonio, TX: The Psychological Corporation.

Wechsler, D. (1981). *Manual for the Wechsler Adult Intelligence Scale—Revised (WAIS-R).* San Antonio, TX: The Psychological Corporation.

Wechsler, D. (1991). *Manual for the Wechsler Intelligence Scale for Children—Third Edition (WISC-III).* San Antonio, TX: The Psychological Corporation.

Wechsler, D. (1997). *WAIS-III administration and scoring manual.* San Antonio, TX: The Psychological Corporation.

Whitworth, R. H., & Gibbons, R. T. (1986). Cross-racial comparison of the WAIS and WAIS-R. *Educational and Psychological Measurement, 46,* 1041–1049.

Woodcock, R. W. (1990). Theoretical foundations of the WJ-R measures of cognitive ability. *Journal of Psychoeducational Assessment, 8,* 231–258.

Zimmerman, I. L., & Woo-Sam, J. M. (1973). *Clinical interpretation of the Wechsler Adult Intelligence Scale.* New York: Grune & Stratton.

Annotated Bibliography

Flynn, J. R. (1998). WAIS-III and WISC-III: US IQ gains 1972 to 1995. How to compensate for obsolete norms. *Perceptual and Motor Skills, 86,* 1231–1239.

Flynn compares the IQ gains from the WISC-R to WISC-III revision to those of the WAIS-R to WAIS-III revision. The important differences in samples are noted. The negligible differences between a sample tested on both the WISC-III and WAIS-III are also presented. The various explanations for the results are discussed.

Gregory, R. J. (1987). *Adult intellectual assessment.* Boston: Allyn & Bacon.

This book is a reference source for adult assessment, with particular focus on the Wechsler measures. Research on the WAIS and WAIS-R is examined and presented in a clinical context. The author presents an outline for a comprehensive intellectual assessment. Other topics covered include brain-behavior relationships, screening tests, and a guide to report writing.

Kaufman, A. S. (1990). *Assessing adolescent and adult intelligence.* Boston: Allyn & Bacon.

This book on the WAIS-R provides in-depth discussion of topics that pertain to adult assessment in general. The review of research studies conducted on the W-B, WAIS, and WAIS-R are especially relevant to the WAIS-III. Topics include relationship of IQs to background variables (occupation, race-ethnicity, education, gender), as well as studies of patients with unilateral brain damage, Alzheimer's disease, Huntington's chorea, dyslexia, alcoholism, mental retardation, multiple sclerosis, learning disabilities, and other disorders. A discussion of the scales from a theoretical perspective is presented, along with numerous hypothesized explanations for Verbal > Performance or Performance > Verbal profiles and the two small factors. The philosophy of the intelligent testing approach is woven throughout the text and is exemplified in several case studies. The history of the Wechsler scales is also presented.

Kaufman, A. S. (1994). *Intelligent testing with the WISC-III.* New York: Wiley.

This book on the WISC-III covers several topics relevant to the WAIS-III. The third and fourth factors (Freedom From Distractibility and Processing Speed on the WISC-III) are reviewed in-depth through multiple possible explanations and interpretations. A theoretical understanding of scales and tasks (especially from Horn's theory) is presented along with many hypothesized explanations for Verbal > Performance and Performance > Verbal profiles. Numerous case reports illustrate how to combine and present complex test data and how to utilize the philosophy of intelligent testing.

Kaufman, A. S., & Lichtenberger, E. O. (1998). Intellectual assessment. In A. S. Bellack & M. Hersen (Series Eds.) & C. R. Reynolds (Vol. Ed.), *Comprehensive clinical psychology: Vol. 4, Assessment* (pp. 187–238). New York: Pergamon.

This chapter reviews several measures of intelligence with a focus on the Wechsler scales. It provides an overview of the WAIS-III, its standardization properties, and the research available on the test. A brief guide to analysis of WAIS-III data is introduced. This chapter also discusses how clinicians may integrate various cognitive instruments with the Wechsler scales to provide a more comprehensive picture of client functioning.

McGrew, K. S., & Flanagan, D. P. (1998). *The intelligence test desk reference (ITDR): Gf-Gc cross-battery assessment.* Boston: Allyn & Bacon.

This book provides information about the fluid and crystallized (Gf-Gc) intelligence theory. It presents information on various tests of intelligence, including the WAIS-III. The authors detail an approach that spells out how practitioners can conduct assessments that tap a broader range of abilities than any single cognitive test alone can. Suggestions are made that help practitioners combine WAIS-III subtests with other battery's subtests to measure specific abilities from the Gf-Gc theory.

The Psychological Corporation (1997). *WAIS-III and WMS-III technical manual.* San Antonio, TX: The Psychological Corporation.

This manual comes as part of the WAIS-III kit. It provides introductory information on the WAIS-III and WMS-III. Development of the norms and the standardization procedures are detailed in the text. Reliability and validity studies are presented. The WAIS-III is compared to other measures of cognitive ability, memory functioning, language functioning, and motor speed. Studies on groups with neurological disorders such as Alzheimer's disease, Huntington's disease, Parkinson's disease, Traumatic Brain Injury, Multiple Sclerosis, and Temporal Lobe epilepsy are reviewed. In addition, studies of mental retardation, Attention-Deficit/Hyperactivity Disorder, learning disabilities and other disorders are addressed. Global information on interpretation is provided along with a plethora of statistical tables for clinicians and researchers.

Sattler, J. M., & Ryan, J. J. (1998). *Assessment of children: Revised and updated third edition WAIS-III supplement.* San Diego, CA: Author.

This supplement to Sattler's text provides information on the latest version of the WAIS. Basic technical information such as reliability and validity is reviewed, as well as statistical information such as intercorrelations between subtests and scales, and factor analyses. Values obtained on the WAIS-III are compared to those obtained from the WAIS-R. A checklist is provided for examiners to use to ensure proper administration of each of the subtests. Very brief information is provided on interpreting the WAIS-III. Strengths and weaknesses of the tests are reviewed. Supplementary tables are provided for calculating short form scores on the WAIS-III.

Tulsky, D. S., Zhu, J., & Prifiteria, A. (in press). Assessing adult intelligence with the WAIS-III. In G. Goldstein (Ed.)., *The Handbook of Psychological Assessment.* Boston: Allyn & Bacon.

This chapter reviews the development of the WAIS-III, from a history of the Wechsler scales to a description of the new facets of the WAIS-III, and offers a brief description of interpretive issues. The authors expound upon the goals in developing the WAIS-III and describe how and why new subtests were added to the test. New factor analytic data that were not presented in the WAIS-III manuals on different ethnic groups are presented in this chapter. In addition, discussion is provided on use of the Wechsler Individual Achievement Test (WIAT) and Wechsler Memory Scale—Third Edition (WMS-III) with the WAIS-III.

Wechsler, D. (1997). *Wechsler Adult Intelligence Scale—Third Edition, (WAIS-III) administration and scoring manual.* San Antonio, TX: The Psychological Corporation. *This manual comes as part of the WAIS-III kit. It provides a basic description of the WAIS-III scales and subtests. Revisions from the WAIS-R to the third edition are reviewed in a subtest-by-subtest manner. WAIS-III examiners can gather important information about administration from this manual. For each WAIS-III subtest, the starting, discontinue, and timing rules are articulated. Examiners are provided a basic script and detailed directions of how to administer each subtest in a standardized manner. Subtest norms are provided in Tables A.1 and A.2, IQ and Index Scores are provided in Tables A.3 through A.8. Supplementary data for determining the size of differences needed for significance are provided in Tables B.1 through B.7.*

Index